Lifelong Learning
in
Higher Education

Lifelong Learning
in
Higher Education

Third Edition

Christopher K Knapper and Arthur J Cropley

KOGAN
PAGE

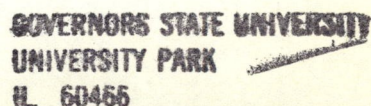

First published in 1985 by Croom Helm
Second edition published by Kogan Page in 1991
This third edition published in 2000

Kogan Page Limited
120 Pentonville Road
London N1 9JN

Stylus Publishing Inc
22883 Quicksilver Drive
Sterling, VA 21166, USA

British Library Cataloguing in Publication Data

A CIP record for this book is available from the British Library.

ISBN 0 7494 2794 9

Typeset by Kogan Page
Printed and bound in Great Britain by Clays Ltd, St Ives plc

Contents

List of figures

List of tables

Preface to the third edition

This book was first published in 1985 when the term 'lifelong learning' was less fashionable than it is today. At that time many educators assumed that the term was a sort of synonym for traditional continuing education involving courses offered by traditional educational establishments outside their normal credit programmes. Our intention was to correct that misreading, to explain the conceptual roots of lifelong learning and lifelong education, and explain how higher education institutions might better facilitate the development of lifelong learning skills and attitudes in their students – attitudes and skills that would serve them long after they left college and university and help them learn throughout their lives, in a wide range of situations, and from many different sources.

In the year 2000 the term 'lifelong learning' is widely used in higher education: it has become trendy, even perhaps a cliché. In 1995 this was the only book available on lifelong learning and higher education, but there are now many other publications which deal with similar issues. Yet many of the objectives we spelt out 15 years ago are as valid as ever. Nowadays, nearly all universities claim to espouse lifelong learning goals, but their educational programmes, teaching methods and organizational structures often discourage lifelong learning. This book examines why that is the case and what may be done about it.

Although the organizational structure in this third edition is very similar to that of its two predecessors, in fact the book has been very substantially revised and rewritten. The theoretical discussion at the beginning now reflects additional important contributions to the field that have appeared since the second edition, and examples and case studies throughout have been updated or, if necessary, replaced. We have added new sections where appropriate to reflect new developments that affect lifelong education, such as the growth of the Internet. References have been updated and comprise the most comprehensive collection of sources available anywhere on lifelong learning in higher education. Finally, we have added an important 'stock-taking' chapter that takes a hard look at the rhetoric of lifelong learning and compares it to the reality.

In our view the goals of lifelong learning are as valid as ever – so is the need. However, achieving those goals and fulfilling that need still require considerable resources and will to change.

Christopher Knapper and Arthur Cropley, July 1999

Preface to the second edition

Since the first edition of this book appeared in 1985 the world has seen some major political changes. Developments in Europe seem to hold out prospects for an end to the arms race and the possibility of a new era of international cooperation. However, the planet continues to face formidable problems, notably those of protecting the environment, controlling population growth and coping with severe human deprivation in many parts of the world. These are not just political issues, but also provide a formidable educational challenge.

Higher education institutions are still groping for an appropriate response to these profound political, economic and ecological developments. In this context the central theme of the present volume remains as valid as ever: to cope with the demands of a rapidly changing world we need an educated population, capable of taking the initiative for their own education, and motivated to continue learning throughout their lives and in many different situations. *Lifelong Learning in Higher Education* attempts to show how colleges and universities may respond to this pressing need, in particular through changes in organizational structures and teaching methods. This is the major goal of the 1991 edition of the book, just as it was for its predecessor. Naturally, we have tried to update the monograph to reflect important societal changes that have taken place in the last five years, and we have also included more recent examples of educational initiatives.

This book aims to balance theory and practice – the former because we wish to encourage academic staff to reflect more profoundly on the underlying goals of their teaching efforts, the latter because we wish to provide some useful advice on strategies for change. For this reason we have added a new final chapter to this edition which provides some concrete ideas for instructors to use in their own teaching as a way of encouraging student autonomy and lifelong learning. Critical reaction to the first edition was gratifyingly positive, which has encouraged us to believe that many academics share our views about the mission of higher education and our concerns about some of its shortcomings. However, many readers who accepted our arguments for the importance of lifelong learning asked for help in devising ways that they might work to stimulate change in their own institutions. We hope that this revised edition will provide some help in that direction.

Acknowledgements are due to a number of organizations and individuals who contributed to the preparation of the manuscript. The research that enabled us to develop our ideas was funded, in part, by the Social Sciences and Research Council of Canada. Bibliographic and word-processing assistance was provided by Marlene Bechtold, Verna Keller and Susan McKenzie of the University of Waterloo. Carl Hennig gave cheerful and invaluable advice on computing problems. Lastly, our appreciation to Maryellen Weimer, of Pennsylvania State University, for her constant encouragement to prepare a second edition of the book.

Christopher Knapper and Arthur Cropley, November 1990

Preface

The origins of this book go back several years, and reflect the authors' research interests and practical experience as teachers in higher education. We began our research collaboration over 20 years ago, and have continued working cooperatively in a variety of areas, although separated by a considerable physical distance. The present project stems from our mutual concern about the importance of university teaching and learning and how it may be improved. Arthur Cropley is Professor of Educational Psychology at the University of Hamburg, and was previously on the staff of the Unesco Institute for Education in that city. It was there that he developed many of the theoretical conceptualizations of lifelong education that are discussed in the first part of this book. Through his association with the Unesco Institute, Arthur Cropley was able to help plan and monitor implementations of lifelong education in many different parts of the world. While he has written widely on this topic, the major focus of his work has been on primary and secondary education, and it is only with the present book that the notion of lifelong education, developed by Faure and his colleagues, has been applied systematically to higher education.

Instructional methods in universities and colleges are the special interest of Christopher Knapper, who is a consultant on teaching and learning (as well as Professor of Psychology and Environmental Studies) at the University of Waterloo. A sabbatical leave in 1981–82 allowed him to work with Arthur Cropley in developing ideas about how lifelong learning skills could be promoted within higher education – ideas that shaped the outline of this book. During this leave Christopher Knapper was also fortunate enough to be able to travel widely and visit universities and colleges in many different parts of the world, ranging from Washington to Tonga. Examples from institutions he visited occur from time to time in the following pages. So, too, do the ideas derived from many of the hundreds of people with whom our ideas were discussed. We offer our apologies to those who may recognize in print an unattributed notion developed in the course of conversation, especially in those instances where what they said has been unwittingly misrepresented.

Although examples are cited from many types of institution in contrasting parts of the world, we cannot claim to transcend the limitations of our particular biases and experiences as students and teachers. Thus, the book leans heavily upon problems and issues within the developed English-speaking nations that have long-established systems and traditions of higher education. In particular, there is a focus upon those countries with which we are most familiar, specifically the UK, Canada and the USA and to a lesser extent Australasia.

Geography is not the only limitation of this book's scope. In giving instances of educational practice – especially those that seem to consist of valuable implementations of the principles of lifelong education – we have inevitably been restricted, not only by our own knowledge, but also by constraints of space imposed by the publishers. We attempt to introduce the concept of lifelong learning, tracing its implications for higher education, and developing a blueprint for the adoption of lifelong learning principles within colleges and universities.

Chapter 1 provides a brief history of the concept of lifelong education, as developed by Faure and others, and argues the case for why lifelong learning skills are needed in contemporary society. In Chapter 2 we describe the essential characteristics of a system of lifelong education and discuss differences between this approach and other systems with which it is often confused, for example adult or recurrent education. Chapter 3 focuses on the types of student who stand to benefit most from the acquisition of lifelong learning skills in higher education: what are their learning needs and how might these best be met? In Chapter 4 we turn to higher education institutions, in particular to examine how they might be transformed to reflect better the goals of lifelong education; a special concern here is with teaching methods and procedures for student assessment. Chapter 5 reviews existing approaches to teaching and learning that seem to us to have the potential for fostering lifelong learning skills in students, while Chapter 6 discusses mechanisms within post-secondary education institutions that may help transform them in directions that would place a major emphasis on the principles of lifelong education. In Chapter 7 we evaluate the teaching and learning strategies described in previous chapters in terms of the criteria discussed at the beginning of the book, in an attempt to pinpoint most promising areas for future emphasis. We also discuss barriers to implementation of new instructional approaches, as well as ways of trying to overcome such obstacles.

We do not advocate any single innovation, but instead draw together ideas from a wide variety of sources. As such, it describes a great deal of research. However, it is not intended primarily as a book for researchers, but for those university and college teachers – and we believe there are many – who are concerned to examine the goals of higher education, and may wish to consider alternative teaching and learning strategies that can better equip their students to become self-directed learners who can function successfully in a changing and increasingly complex world.

Christopher Knapper and Arthur Cropley, November 1983

1

Lifelong learning: basic concepts

The basic idea behind the term 'lifelong learning' is simple. It is that deliberate learning can and should occur throughout each person's lifetime. This view is by no means new. It is found in ancient writings, and was emphasized in the works of earlier European educational theorists such as Comenius and Matthew Arnold. The term 'lifelong education' appeared in English language writings about 75 years ago, and many of the main contemporary ideas about lifelong education were stated immediately after the Second World War (Jacks, 1946). Since about 1970 the idea has been the object of intense attention, resulting in a flood of conferences and publications, as well as calls for its implementation from politicians, industrialists and educators. These have occurred in waves, with peaks and troughs of attention alternating over the last 30 years. In both 1985 and 1991 – in the first and second editions of this book – we reviewed discussions of lifelong learning since the mid-1960s, and concluded that thinking had advanced sufficiently to define a new educational principle. Despite this, in 1991 we continued to refer to emphasis on lifelong learning as 'an emerging approach'. There was substantial theory and widespread discussion, but effects on practice were superficial.

Recently there has been a renewed peak of interest at the level of international policy-making bodies. The European Union (EU) designated 1996 'the year of lifelong learning'. The meeting of the education ministers of the Organization for Economic Co-operation and Development (OECD) in

January of the same year used the slogan 'Making lifelong learning a reality for all'. The 1996 report of the United Nations Educational, Scientific, and Cultural Organization's (Unesco's) International Commission on Education for the Twenty-first Century adopted 'learning throughout life' as its key concept. At their meeting in Cologne in June 1999 the members of the Group of Eight (G8) (the UK, Canada, France, Germany, Italy, Japan, Russia and the USA – essentially the world's greatest powers) agreed to promote mass education throughout the world, and named 'lifelong retraining' as a major priority.

In addition to being the subject of statements of political will, lifelong learning has also established itself as a topic of scholarly interest. There are numerous lifelong learning World Wide Web sites and several journals that include the term in their titles (eg *The International Journal of Lifelong Learning, The Journal of Continuing Engineering Education and Life-Long Learning*), and at least one Professor of Lifelong Learning (at Birkbeck College of the University of London). Thus, it is tempting to assume that lifelong learning has well and truly arrived. Indeed, Hasan (1996, p 33) came to the optimistic conclusion that 'lifelong learning has become a pivotal framework for educational reforms in a large number of countries'. However, while it is true that the idea is an ancient one that has received considerable attention in the last 75 years and has aroused renewed interest in the last few, our observation of higher education, especially in Western societies, suggests it is premature to draw overly optimistic conclusions.

The first step in answering the question of whether lifelong learning has now become the accepted norm in practice – as against rhetoric – involves examining the felt need for change in education that led to calls for the adoption of lifelong learning. An assessment of how well these needs are being met would help in judging the extent to which the implementation of lifelong learning has actually occurred. Unesco, the OECD and the EU all foresee widespread, if not worldwide, application of the principle. Thus, it is also interesting to ask whether it is possible to work out a concept of lifelong learning that transcends regional and cultural traditions, needs and interests.

The focus of this book

Focus on practice

About 25 years ago, Cropley (1977) published an early attempt to sort out the practical issues arising from the theory of lifelong learning. He dealt with psychological questions such as whether adults really are capable of or willing to learn throughout life, the differences between adults and children as learners and the effects of school learning on adult learning. He also developed 'action guidelines' for a school curriculum oriented towards fostering lifelong learning (see Chapter 3 for an example). These guidelines related to, among other things, learning materials, teacher activities, pupil activities and assessment methods. Subsequently, the present authors looked at the implications of adopting the principle of lifelong learning for schools (Cropley and Knapper, 1982), teacher training (Cropley, 1981) and higher education (Cropley and Knapper, 1983). The question we posed was: 'What would schools, teachers' colleges and universities be like within a system dedicated to lifelong learning?'

In this book, we do not ignore the conceptual, social and political debate about lifelong learning. Especially in the first three chapters, many such issues are reviewed, because they were at the heart of the surge of interest in modern times and cannot be regarded as trivial. However, here we go beyond theoretical discussions to consider what adoption of the idea of lifelong learning would mean for the practice of teaching and learning. This includes issues that are psychological, paedagogical and organizational. For example, do adults learn differently from children and, if so, what are the implications for a theory and definition of lifelong learning? Does technology facilitate lifelong learning, and in what ways? How should institutions of lifelong learning be coordinated with one another, who is to be given access to such institutions and how are they to be financed? The dominant orientation of this book is psychological, which is scarcely surprising in view of the fact that both authors are psychologists. However, other perspectives are by no means ignored, especially as they relate to issues of effective teaching and learning.

Focus on higher education

Higher education merits special study because of its particular importance in helping to develop and implement a system of lifelong education, and thus provide the necessary organizational framework for lifelong learning. This importance derives from the prestige and influence of universities and colleges within the educational systems of most countries and from their role in developing theory and conducting research. What universities teach, investigate and promote influences knowledge, attitudes, values and practices in many areas of society. Tertiary institutions educate the people who will later shape the development of society (see later discussions of change and lifelong learning).

They also play a major role in the training of teachers, where they provide not only knowledge, but also theoretical principles (such as belief in the importance of lifelong learning), and practical experience. In addition, university teachers can serve as important role models by employing teaching strategies that are oriented to learning throughout life. Higher education is what Williams (1977, p 17) referred to as the 'dominant force' in education, or the National Research Council (1996) called the 'spring-board' for entering the world of work. As a result, it seems plausible that learners' experiences in higher education will have ramifications for the practice of teaching and learning at all levels.

Focus on traditional learners in traditional institutions

More or less inevitably, a major thrust of this book is provision of higher education to new groups of learners, especially those who are often called 'mature-age' students – people beyond the conventional age for tertiary education. At present, taking a worldwide perspective, this group is still dominated by people who have already had a high level of contact with the formal educational system and are returning after a break during which they pursued a career or raised a family (van der Kamp and Scheeren, 1997). At the same time, the proportion of people who have never previously experienced tertiary education has risen in recent years.

However, our main focus here is not on these special learners or on special programmes and institutions to meet their needs. Rather, we are concerned principally with the implications of lifelong learning for conventional universities and traditional students. We see a role for universities not only as providers of lifelong learning opportunities but also as an important preparation for lifelong learning in other settings. In this sense, this study differs sharply from many other discussions of lifelong learning, which have been primarily interested in non-traditional learners and new institutions that may serve them better.

The educational crisis

According to Coombs (1982, p 145), education in general has been facing a crisis since the late 1960s. This has intensified, and has yielded 'critical educational challenges' that are making themselves felt not only in highly industrialized Western European and North American societies, but in virtually all nations. Since 1950, Coombs has documented the huge increases in the number of potential learners worldwide. He also drew attention to continuing social inequalities in access to higher education, and (p 145) called for 'a much more comprehensive, flexible and innovative educational strategy in the coming two decades'. Such a strategy would involve 'radical changes in conventional educational thinking, methods, organizations, structures and practices'. In other words, perceived shortcomings in existing education mean that a new approach is needed, touching upon virtually all aspects of systematic education.

The challenges observed by Coombs included:

- *changed learning needs* (more people wanting to learn different things);
- problems of *financing* (reduced funding, demands for more effective use of resources);
- increased concern about *democratization and fairness* (elimination of socioeconomic, gender and geographic inequities);
- a perceived need for closer *ties to day-to-day life* (harmonizing education and culture, relating education to work, linking education to peace and preservation of the ecosystem);
- a need for changed *teaching and learning strategies* (flexible and democratic educational planning, more self-direction in learning, team learning, problem-based learning, learning through case studies).

More recent challenges arise from:

- the emergence of *new forms of communication* other than written language;
- *new methods of educational delivery*, such as home-based learning or learning via the World Wide Web;
- *changing demands of work*, such as the need for periodic retraining as existing job skills become obsolete;
- *new career patterns*, such as women alternating work and child-raising;
- home-based work;
- *changing clientele for education*, in particular large increases in mature-age students resulting from both the work and career changes already mentioned and also from demographic trends.

Coombs demanded radical change within 20 years. This period is coming to its end, but the challenges remain. At the same time, Lynch (1982) applied the idea of an educational crisis directly to higher education. He spoke of a 'legitimation crisis' (p 8), and listed some of its dimensions, including:

- financial stringencies and related cutbacks in higher education;
- failure of higher education to accommodate later practical training needs of individuals or the needs of industry;

- a lack of response of post-school education to industrial and economic changes;
- inability of higher education to take account of rising unemployment and the educational needs which this gives rise to;
- the need for higher education to offer some kind of adaptive response to social unrest and growing alienation among the young.

Lynch argued that what is needed in higher education is not simply more of the same, albeit with a few minor modifications, but 'wider structural and systematic change' (p 12). Echoing this view, Mezirow (1990) endorsed the earlier call by Botkin, Elmandjra and Malitza (1979, p 10) for education '... that can bring change, renewal, restructuring ...'. More recently, the Wingspread Group on Higher Education (Johnson Foundation, 1993) called for 'a simultaneous renewal' of school and higher level education, and linked this to the organization of learning over time by arguing that the two should form 'one continuous learning system'. Resnick and Wirth (1996, p 1) also emphasized the importance of the temporal aspect, and identified the central ideal of recent educational theory as 'the idea of maximum access to education for all, of keeping options open for everyone *well into adulthood*' (our italics). Although their discussions focused on linking school and work, Resnick and Wirth, without mentioning it specifically, summarized clearly what the changes demanded by Lynch should lead to: lifelong learning. Unfortunately, they were forced to conclude that 'the dream has turned sour'. In other words, the task still lies before us. What is required are forms of education that will solve what Lynch called the crisis or, in the terms of Resnick and Wirth, will restore the dream.

Lifelong education: an alternative approach

Almost 30 years ago, Faure (1972) suggested that the concept of lifelong education offered a possible solution to the crisis described above, and indeed should be adopted as the guiding principle for reforming education at all levels and in all countries. Since then the notion of lifelong education has been the subject of considerable discussion, and has been spelt out in terms of its implications for schooling, teacher training and adult education. Its interest for the present discussion derives from the fact that lifelong education is a set of organizational, financial and didactic principles established with the aim of fostering lifelong learning. Lifelong education is the system and lifelong learning is the content, the goal and the result.

The meaning of lifelong education

Different writers use the term 'lifelong education' in various ways. In Europe, the concept has most frequently been associated with the linking of learning and work, especially through provision of paid educational leave, recurrent education or open learning – as exemplified by the British Open University. In the USA it was initially regarded as simply a new term for traditional adult education (as in the 1976 *Lifelong Learning Act*). However, more recent discussions in that country have also promoted lifelong education as a way of responding to changes in the workplace (Resnick and Wirth, 1996), and have suggested that education in schools and universities should 'proceed in tandem' with changes in the organization of work.

In a more conceptual vein, Rüegg (1974, p 7) referred to lifelong education as 'a utopian idea' whose main function is stimulating people to think critically about learning. As Long (1974) pointed out, the idea of lifelong education also reflects a belief in 'the mystique of education': since education is self-evidently good, lifelong education must be even better! At the same time the idea was criticized by Pucheu (1974, p 375) as an 'elastic concept' which means whatever the person using the term wants it to mean.

One way of looking at lifelong education is to regard it as a rationalization of a number of existing trends in contemporary educational theory and practice. These emerged in a variety of settings without necessarily any reference to the concept as defined by Faure and others. The trends include expansion of educational services beyond the conventional school ages (ie for adults and for preschool children), greater interest in education as an instrument for improving the quality of life, concern for the development of forms of education that are more closely linked with the needs of everyday life, participation in decisions about education by workers, parents, and members of the public, greater openness in goal setting, planning and administration, concern about the short-lived nature of academic qualifications, changing teaching and learning approaches, and the growing influence of computers on learning and work. Other prominent themes are democratization of education, elimination of inequality and achievement of higher levels of self-actualization. These issues are discussed separately in later sections.

In a sense, lifelong education can be seen as a reaction against certain features of existing educational practice. It includes a rejection of authoritarianism (but not necessarily authority), unwillingness to accept that school is the dominant institution in all learning and dissatisfaction with the view that all necessary qualifications can be acquired during a brief period of learning prior to commencement of the working life.

Finally, when viewed as a unifying principle linking existing trends and tendencies, lifelong education is a useful device for bringing together under a common heading a number of ideas and practices which, although possessing an inherent unity, would otherwise have continued to be treated as distinct from each other. The value of lifelong education as a concept is, therefore, that it makes it possible to discern the central and definitive elements of these practices and ideas. Links are seen between education and various social issues and trends that would otherwise not have been regarded as related to each other, or connected with education at all. Examples include problems arising from the increasing demand for education at a time of financial strictures, problems of obsolescence of job skills, problems of social change, and issues arising from the growth in both quantity and power of the mass media. Lifelong education has the advantage of placing all these, and many similar issues, in a single context, showing their connection with education, and suggesting ways in which educational practice needs to be changed.

Lifelong education as a paradigm

At least to some extent, lifelong education can also be thought of as encompassing a philosophy or model of education. In this sense, the term is used to refer to:

- a set of goals for education;
- a set of procedures for realizing these goals;
- a set of values.

It is the values that specify which goals should be given precedence, which procedures are desirable and which undesirable, whose needs education should serve, what kind of society people should live in and so on. As we discuss in more detail later, statements about goals, means and values are indeed to be found in the literature on lifelong education. Hence, regarding the concept as involving a 'philosophy' of education is helpful, even if many of the goals and values do not seem to arise directly out of the idea of 'lifelongness,' but have been grafted on, more or less in the 'elastic' way described by Pucheu.

Perhaps the term 'philosophy' is a little pretentious here. An alternative conceptualization was provided by Turchenko (1983) who pointed out that lifelong education is best viewed as a 'paradigm'. It entails 'a system of fundamental principles which serve as a basis for raising and tackling... problems'. What this means is that the implementation of lifelong education would not involve putting in place a special, separate system, complete in itself and intended to replace existing structures.

Rather, the lifelong education paradigm provides a way of looking at what already exists in order to perceive shortcomings or see ways in which improvements could be made. One consequence of this view is that different systems of education, apparently all seeking to implement lifelong education, could differ markedly from each other, for instance according to national policies, educational traditions, or degree of industrial development. It is also possible that quite different educational practices could be identified as examples of the implementation of lifelong education. All would have in common, nonetheless, acceptance of the same set of fundamental principles. The first step in a discussion of the implications of lifelong education for higher education thus involves sketching out these principles. Stated as a paradigm they are of necessity abstract and general. However, in later sections of this book, we will give concrete examples of how principles can be translated into practice in a variety of settings.

To anticipate Chapters 2 and 3 and risk oversimplification, the single crucial element in the notion of lifelong education is to be found in the word 'lifelong'. It embraces a set of guidelines for developing educational practice ('education') in order to foster learning throughout life ('lifelong learning'). Lifelong education thus defines a set of organizational, administrative, methodological and procedural measures that seek to promote lifelong learning. Practical discussions in later sections of this study are concerned with how to arrange educational experiences in higher education in a way that does this effectively.

Values in lifelong education

Despite what has just been said, many proponents of lifelong education – for example, Lengrand (1970) and Faure (1972) – argue that fostering lifelong learning would also lead to the achievement of a number of desirable educational goals that do not, in our view, arise directly out of the notion of lifelongness, but are part of any liberal-humanistic approach to education. In this sense, the ideas associated with lifelong education can be seen as a rationalization of a number of existing trends in educational thinking which, not infrequently, came into existence without any direct reference to lifelong learning or lifelong education. Among these reasons for adopting the principle of lifelong education are its potential for promoting equality of educational opportunity, its possible role in the democratization of education and its potential contribution to the achievement of higher levels of self-actualization. As Cropley (1979) pointed out, lifelong education cannot lay a unique claim to interest in promoting equality, democratization and self-actualization. Furthermore, it is possible to imagine lifelong approaches to education that did not have these as goals, even if most people would find such forms distasteful. Thus, these 'reasons' should really be seen as possible *products* of certain approaches to lifelong education, depending on the presence of an appropriate value system.

The question of values is thus of considerable importance in any discussion of lifelong education. Karpen (1980) dealt directly with this issue, pointing out that in principle a despotic, totalitarian regime could implement lifelong education without any intention of achieving equality or democratization. He argued that lifelong education is, therefore, only to be recommended if it is offered in a framework of liberal-democratic values. According to the report of a Unesco Meeting of Experts (Unesco, 1983), lifelong education is defined as education for 'liberation', 'self-realization' and 'self-fulfilment'. In declaring 1996 the European Year of Lifelong Learning, the EU (European Commission, 1996) called for the implementation of lifelong education in order to promote the 'personal fulfilment of every individual' and the achievement of equal opportunities (ie for women, the elderly and the disadvantaged). Mayo (1997), in a report encompassing case studies in Tanzania, Cuba, India and Nicaragua, concentrated on technologically less developed, less wealthy countries and concluded that learning in adulthood is essential for 'sustainable development for social justice'. Important in this context are, on the one hand, democracy, justice and equality; on the other, values such as respect for the environment and for the traditions of indigenous peoples.

Lawson (1982) went so far as to propose that the very term 'education' automatically implies humanistic, socially responsible, environmentally aware values of the kind just mentioned. Otherwise, it is a matter simply of training, and not education at all. This would mean that the values just discussed are not really part of the definition of lifelong education, but of education in general. Lifelong education is then seen to be essentially a policy for implementing 'education,' and not a new philosophy of education at all. Values of this kind have become so strongly associated with writings on lifelong education that they now form part of its definition, although they are not inherent in the notion of 'lifelong,' and not exclusively associated with lifelong education.

As we discuss in a later section, lifelong education may truly be a policy that offers special opportunities to achieve equality and self-actualization. For instance, the idea that personal development occurs throughout the entire life span is a point of view that has found increasing acceptance in psychological thinking (for an informative summary, see Mackeracher, 1996). Coupled with the notion that education is capable of making a contribution to such personal development, this implies that lifelong education would be uniquely placed to facilitate lifelong self-actualization. In a similar vein, it can be argued that extending state-subsidized learning beyond traditional school-leaving ages would promote the achievement of true educational equality, since this would enhance the possibility for learners who start later in life to equal or exceed the achievements of those who had had better opportunities as children. These possible outcomes of lifelong education may be mentioned as reasons for adopting the concept, despite the risk of teleological thinking that this entails.

Lifelong education and the Third World

Lifelong education may offer special prospects for technologically less developed nations. Such societies often have a pressing need for modernization in concrete areas such as health care, primary and secondary production, as well as in social philosophy and values such as democratization, human rights and the like. Many of these nations were subjected to exploitation by colonial powers, especially exploitation of natural resources. Some even seem to have inherited environmentally irresponsible attitudes and policies, as in the example of deforestation in Brazil. In others, there is no indigenous tradition of democracy or equality, with results such as the continuing practice of female circumcision in some societies. Some traditional lifestyles are contributing to destruction of the environment, such as the continuing desertification in parts of Africa.

It is obvious that a great deal of learning will be necessary for this process of modernization to occur. Unless those who are already beyond school age are to be discarded as dead wood, this will mean not only education of children but also education beyond school age – lifelong education. For the learning that takes place to lead to democracy, self-determination and environmental responsibility, it is essential that it is guided by principles such as concern for the general good, and not by narrow self-interest. Mayo's (1997) report is an example of the acceptance of the idea of lifelong education as a reform principle in Third World countries. Its title, 'Imagining tomorrow', gives an idea of the role foreseen for lifelong learning.

Lifelong learning

Lifelong education, as it has just been described, is a set of organizational and procedural guidelines for educational practice. Its goal (and also its method and its content) is lifelong learning – learning carried on throughout life. It is important to make clear at once that what is meant here by 'learning' is not the spontaneous, day-to-day learning of everyday life, such as when people learn to proffer the correct amount in payment after bus fares are increased. It is perfectly clear that such learning is lifelong, no doubt always has been, and will continue to be, regardless of the pronouncements of educational theorists. The kind of lifelong learning that is the object of lifelong education is what Tough (1971) called 'deliberate' learning. Such learning has the following four definitive characteristics:

1. It is intentional – learners are aware that they are learning.
2. It has specific goals, and it is not aimed at vague generalizations such as 'developing the mind'.
3. These goals are the reason why the learning is undertaken (ie it is not motivated simply by factors like boredom).
4. The learner intends to retain and use what has been learnt for a considerable period of time.

In a recent analysis based on Coombs and Ahmed's (1974) distinction between formal, non-formal and informal learning, Coletta (1996, p 22) identified four dimensions that are very useful in the present context: *deliberateness*, *structuredness*, kind of *content* and role of *certification*. Formal education, for instance, is deliberate, highly structured, emphasizes acquisition of predetermined knowledge, and leads to acquisition of a formal certificate or qualification. It is typified by traditional school and university learning as it occurs in technologically highly developed societies, and is dominated by models from North America and Western Europe. Informal education involves incidental learning in the sense that it is not deliberate, normally not structured, and learners and teachers may not see it as learning at all. This type of learning is usually uncertified and typically occurs when younger people 'pick up' ideas through contact with models, and these ideas are frequently attitudes, values or skills, rather than bodies of facts. Non-formal learning is deliberate but lies outside schools, and thus seldom leads to formal qualifications. The main emphasis is on acquisition of skills.

Lifelong learning has some of the properties of all three forms distinguished by Coletta. This distinction between deliberate learning and spontaneous, unplanned, incidental, even unconscious learning is important in the present context because it permits a differentiation between the lifelong learning that is a normal and natural part of everyday life and the systematic, purposeful, organized learning that lifelong education seeks to foster. Of course, the distinction is to some extent artificial. The same fundamental psychological processes are involved. Organized learning – such as that which takes place during a university class – obviously interacts with day-to-day learning, for instance in the sense that learning in the classroom can be facilitated or inhibited by learning in everyday life, and vice versa. Nonetheless, a distinction, albeit an artificial one, is essential for the purposes of this study. The whole question of the interrelationship of deliberate learning and day-to-day learning, and of the significance of this interaction for higher education, is discussed in more detail later.

Adults' participation in informal and non-formal learning

In the USA, even 30 years ago, the average adult spent some 500 hours a year engaging in 'learning projects' (Tough, 1971). However, this high level of activity occurs largely outside the formal education system. In Europe, for example Norway (Eide, 1980), well over half of all systematic learning takes place outside schools. In OECD countries nowadays (van der Kamp and Scheeren, 1997) between 22 and 63 per cent of employed adults aged up to 45 (according to the particular country) participate in adult education. Among people aged between 66 and 75 only 7–10 per cent participate, for instance through evening classes or universities of the third age. Here, the focus is largely on preparation for retirement, memory training and health education. In other words, the learning is concerned with adaptation to the immediate and acute concerns of everyday life for this age group.

Despite the relatively high levels of participation by adults, only about 20 per cent of their learning occurs within the framework of organized adult education, while a high proportion of adults never participate in such activities (van der Kamp and Scheeren, 1997). Furthermore, both in the USA and Western Europe, the best predictor of participation in higher education outside the traditional ages is level of traditional education (van der Kamp and Scheeren, 1997). Essentially, only the 'educational junkies' are being reached at present, while at least half the population can be classified as non-participants in traditional forms of provision for mature learners. Thus, promoting broader participation in college and university study will require more than mere administrative changes, since adults, despite being perfectly capable of learning, do not make use of the opportunities already available.

The need for lifelong learning

Early discussions of the necessity of lifelong learning emphasized the phenomenon of change (Cropley, 1977). As de Sanctis (1977) pointed out, such change is social, economic and cultural in nature and possesses an urgency that has not previously been experienced. Agoston (1975, p 6) referred to a 'scientific-technological revolution', while Stonier (1979) mentioned the 'two revolutions' of ordinary life: technological change and changes in the information domain. McClusky (1974, p 101) made the connection between change and lifelong learning in a particularly succinct way, pointing out that 'continuous change requires continuous learning'.

The importance of lifelong learning as a reaction to change has not lost its relevance in recent years. In an authoritative review, Neice and Murray (1997) identified change as the core educational issue, and called for a commitment to fostering lifelong learning as the 'pedagogical ethic' (p 186) made necessary by change. The EU's declaration of 1996 as the year of lifelong learning (European Commission, 1996) also took change as its key idea, especially scientific and technological change, identifying the need for 'advances in methods of knowledge acquisition' as a way of coping. These advances, encapsulated in the principles of lifelong learning would, according to the Commission, lead to a 'learning society' with two broad goals: *personal fulfilment* of every individual, and achievement of *equal opportunities* (for women, the elderly, migrants, the disadvantaged and similar groups). Personal fulfilment involves integration into working life and society, a sense of initiative, participation in decision making and the ability to adapt to change.

In a similar vein, the recent G8 statement already referred to concluded that change will be the central characteristic of the next century. The statement identified fostering 'civic values' and 'tolerance' as key goals of lifelong retraining. However, it also emphasized 'entrepreneurship', 'a culture of entrepreneurship' and the need to develop strong links between educational institutions and industry, goals that would not be endorsed by all theorists in this area. Ügeöz (1998), for instance, warned that coordinating education to the needs of employers runs the risk of focusing excessively on specialized knowledge, work skills and related factors such as motivation, at the expense of aspects such as tolerance, self-respect or consideration for the less fortunate (what he calls 'social solidarity'). Candy, Crebert and O'Leary (1994) would add to the endangered list contextual knowledge and generic knowledge and skills.

Obviously, change is not necessarily a bad thing in itself. As mentioned earlier, there may well be aspects of life and areas of the globe where more rapid change is desirable. However, the present cycle of change has two distinguishing features that are potentially destructive. The first is the rapidity with which changes are occurring. In the past, change has always been slow relative to the life expectancy of a single human being, so that people could adapt themselves to a set of conditions that remained more or less constant during their lifetimes (Knowles, 1975). The present set of changes, by contrast, is occurring so rapidly that the cycle may repeat itself several times within a single lifetime. The second feature of change in the modern world is that it is global. It transcends regional and national boundaries. The globalization of change has led to a globalization of education, a phenomenon that introduces new problems and dangers (see Ügeöz, 1998, for a recent critical analysis).

The crucial point for the present discussion is that people must be able to adjust to change that is at once both rapid and sweeping, both for their own well-being and for that of the societies in which they live. In earlier models of education, most deliberate learning was supposed to occur in childhood and youth, and most learning in the adult years was expected to be of the everyday kind. However, such models are based on the idea that adulthood is simply a time for reapplying old learning, an assumption that is no longer tenable.

Demographic change

A major aspect of the crisis referred to earlier derives from demographic changes, which have been evident for a considerable time and are now approaching the acute phase. Populations in Western European and North American societies are becoming older. In the OECD countries (OECD, 1994), by 2005 the group of people aged over 65 will be up to 27 per cent of the size of the group of 15–64-year-olds. In Germany, one-third of the population of Hamburg is already 60 years of age or over. In the USA, by the year 2030, the age 'pyramid' will instead be a rectangle, with about 6 per cent of the population in each five-year age cohort from birth to over 80 years of age. For the universities this raises the question of how they are to justify their existence and expand their clientele at a time of budgetary constraints when many politicians and members of the public are calling for increased access to higher education.

Apart from the need to find new students as sources of revenue, universities have an important role in helping societies cope with the effects of demographic change. It has already become apparent that there is no longer an inexhaustible supply of youngsters to enter trades as beginners. In Germany, for instance, it is difficult to recruit apprentice shoemakers or janitors. One result in some countries has been the opening up of apprenticeships to 30- and 40-year-olds. To cite a related example, some police forces in the UK now accept recruits in their forties. There is an urgent need for universities to find a role in these changing circumstances, for instance by playing their part in training adults to undertake tasks that have traditionally been the domain of the young. These aspects of increased participation of mature-age learners in university studies can be seen as part of the phenomenon of 'adultification' of higher education (Parjanen, 1993, p 7).

Changes in the clientele of higher education

One solution to the changes just outlined has been to attract more 'non-traditional' students; for example, older students and those within the conventional age group who are underrepresented in the university population by virtue of socioeconomic status, gender, race or ethnicity, or disability. This has indeed happened in some countries, such as

Canada and the USA, where extensive opportunities for part-time study have allowed greater participation of older students with family and work responsibilities.

In the USA about 45 per cent of all college students were already over 25 by the mid-1990s (OECD, 1996), and, according to Kegan (1994), this figure will now have exceeded 50 per cent. In South Australia half of all students in the post-secondary sector are mature-age learners and 53 per cent of applications for admission to university in 1999 came from people who had not completed matriculation at the end of 1998. Even in societies where there is no strong tradition of participation in traditional tertiary education by older learners, some countries have seen noticeable increases. In Finland, for instance, the proportion of students admitted to university for the first time at age 24 or older increased from 12 per cent to 17 per cent between 1985 and 1991 (Parjanen, 1993).

Despite these facts, in some systems (eg the UK) the proportion of older students has grown only slightly. In Germany, some states have made provision for admission of people without the *Abitur* who have at least five years of work experience. Some of these have clearly been of mature age, but typically this form of admission is limited to one or two candidates per year in particular disciplines such as sociology, theology or philosophy.

Social change

The increasing availability of information through the media means that children are exposed to many socializing influences from outside the family. Not infrequently, people and situations depicted in the media (particularly television) may compete with parents, offering conflicting or contradictory sets of standards or values. One result is a decrease in the importance of the family as a source of education. This is further affected by factors such as social dislocation resulting from rapid urbanization, the greatly increased leisure activity seen in some societies, unemployment or changes in the role of work and relationships between workers and supervisors, and rapidly changing gender roles. These changes occurred on a dramatic scale in Eastern Europe at the end of the 1980s, and are still in progress. They will continue to have immense impacts on people's lifestyles and value systems in that region for years to come.

The effects of socio-cultural change are potentially disastrous, since they bring with them the possibility of a 'collapse of values' (Aujaleu, 1973, p 25). If people are unable to develop new kinds of relationship with other people and accept altered social roles, changes of the kind just outlined constitute a threat to psychological well-being (Suchodolski, 1976). Change thus brings psychological dangers and difficulties in situations where people are unable to cope with it. Lifelong learning can be seen as a constructive response that may help to avert these dangers – a device for helping people find patterns of life that satisfy their social, emotional and aesthetic needs, even in a rapidly evolving society.

Changed concern about special groups

Lifelong education is regarded by many writers as a concept that is particularly promising for meeting the newly recognized educational needs of special groups in society who are placed at a disadvantage by traditional education. These include people of low socioeconomic status, migrant or transient workers, the disabled, rural people and women. Members of such groups often found it difficult to learn effectively in schools during childhood, for instance because they did not see the utility of school learning, lacked familiarity with the language of instruction, were barred from attending by physical factors such as distance, or who were prematurely forced out of the educational system by the need to work and help support a family. People with such disadvantages would benefit from a system in which even school-level learning tasks could be undertaken at many different ages. For example, in poorer countries seeking to achieve rapid social and technological change, adults may well wish to upgrade their skills and modernize their lifestyles in areas such as health, environmental protection or even values (democratization, equality). However, they cannot be expected to return to the traditional school to do so, and instead must be offered learning opportunities tailored to their special needs and circumstances.

Changing concepts of literacy

Nowadays, many workers must acquire new skills even though they have not experienced a lengthy absence from work. In Canada, to take one concrete example, the strongest growth in employment in recent years has been in the areas with the highest literacy requirements (Tuijnman, Kirsch and Wagner, 1997), such as information services, personal counselling and advising, and financial services. These require writing letters and reports, explaining and clarifying, settling misunderstandings, mediating and the like. This change in the requirements for work means that many people, both those already at work and those about to enter the workplace, will find themselves employed in the 'knowledge economy' (Neice and Murray, 1997, p 156). Fundamentally, this means working with information technology, of which the personal computer will probably be the simplest form. The result is that 'information literacy' is of vital importance.

According to Kirsch and Jungeblut (1986), in the past schools worked reasonably well as promoters of information literacy (they are still not completely ineffectual), but by 1985 it was becoming apparent that a bifurcation was occurring between the information literate and the information illiterate. Today, it is commonplace for employers to complain that new employees arriving from school possess neither the 'foundation' (Neice and Murray, 1997, p 166) or 'basic' (Tuijnman, Kirsch and Wagner, 1997) skills of information literacy nor the ability to adapt to changes in this form of literacy. (For a discussion of the psychological dimensions of the ability to adapt, see Chapter 3.)

In the USA, an extraordinary situation has developed where, alone among industrially highly developed countries (at least at present), the highest literacy level is not found among the young aged 16–35, but among those aged 36–45 (Neice and Murray, 1997, p 166). In Canada, the pattern is moving in this direction, with the literacy level approximately equal in all age groups up to age 55. This is despite the fact that changing employment patterns mean that most youngsters will spend their working lives in the information economy and hence the level of information literacy should be at its highest in this group. Some firms have responded to this situation by establishing their own schools, essentially moving towards private provision of rudimentary forms of lifelong education. Universities are faced with the dual problem of working with entering students who lack the basic skills of information literacy, but having to prepare graduates who possess these skills and are capable of adapting as the demands of the knowledge economy change.

Change in work

Resnick and Wirth (1996, p 5) summarized the crucial change in the world of work: it is experiencing a conversion from a low-wage, low-performance system to a high-wage, high-performance system. Candy, Crebert and O'Leary (1994, p 39) listed four main factors in work that are making change and adaptation necessary:

1. internationalization;
2. reduction of critical lead times;
3. implementation of total quality management;
4. workplace restructuring.

Both groups of authors made a direct link between change in work and consequences for learning and teaching. A special example of the change phenomenon in work is to be seen in career patterns of women. It is becoming increasingly common for younger women to alternate periods of work with child-bearing and child-raising, or for older women to return to the workplace after a long absence. Not infrequently, they find it necessary to improve or update qualifications as career demands change during periods of absence from the workforce.

The changes outlined earlier, centring on technological progress, development of manufacturing techniques, emergence of new products, and increases in knowledge, are combining to produce a situation in which some jobs are simply ceasing to exist. In the case of others, the basic skills are changing so extensively and rapidly that it is no longer possible to acquire them once and for all during an initial education and then spend the rest of one's life applying them. Dubin (1974) showed that, even 25 years ago, the 'half life' of an average engineering class taught in a US university (the period of time during which half of its content becomes obsolete) was diminishing. What is being learnt today may be irrelevant in only a few years.

For example, technological advances are rapidly transforming diagnostic procedures in medicine, while chemotherapy is constantly altered by new discoveries. This is true not only of professions, but also of manual skills and trades. The whole printing industry, for instance, has been transformed by the disappearance of traditional typesetting methods and their replacement by word processing, while layout and graphics are now in the domain of desktop publishing. Changes of this kind mean that it may well be necessary, even for workers at fairly humble levels, to renew, upgrade or even change basic job qualifications at least once during a normal lifetime.

More and more commonly, professional bodies are demanding that their members undertake regular upgrading, refreshing and retraining on a recurring basis, often through short courses, residential programmes or self-directed learning such as reading educational material. Universities are major players in this type of continuing professional education. They provide much of it through their own staff and programmes, they specify its contents (even where they do not offer the instruction), they determine its format and they prepare students for it – or at least they should.

Resnick and Wirth (1996, p 5) emphasized that the process of change in work must be accompanied by change in education. They pointed out that the educational reaction to change needs to go beyond simply adding new knowledge or new skills. Newly emerging work conditions require people who are able to analyse, make reasoned judgments, use complex tools, procedures and technologies, and communicate. (We discuss new concepts of learning and knowledge in Chapter 3.) In addition, work increasingly requires high levels of performance that will demand great effort from workers, leading Resnick and Wirth to call for 'standards-driven education' or an 'effort-oriented system'. In the area of evaluation, for example, this will necessitate agreement between employers and institutions of higher education on the capabilities they value in graduates, and recognition of the effort students make to obtain them. Some of the chapters in the Resnick and Wirth book stated this view very plainly and called for genuinely intellectually demanding coursework and evaluation methods. The authors questioned some popular positions on teaching and learning suggesting, for instance, that calls for teachers to be mentors, guides and co-learners may well work against acquisition of a 'healthy respect for effort' by students.

The imperatives of lifelong learning

Hasan (1996, p 35) focused on three 'imperatives' for education systems. He argued that satisfaction of these essentials would provide the necessary solutions to the problems and challenges outlined earlier, and saw implementation of the principles of lifelong learning as a necessary step for doing this. The three imperatives are:

1. fostering individual development;
2. fostering social development;
3. mastering the computerized world.

Fostering individual development involves factors such as emancipating people from the limitations imposed by socioeconomic constraints (poor education, low-paid work, poverty), promoting motivation and self-image for learning throughout life, improving the quality of out-of-work time, and making the long period of retirement that is now common in Western developed societies productive and enjoyable. Fostering social development includes promoting innovation, productivity and economic competitiveness, achieving social advances (democratic values, social cohesion, solidarity, etc), and distributing productivity/economic activity beyond the 'shrinking middle'.

The imperative of mastering the computerized world arises from the emergence of the 'information society'. Highly technologically advanced industrialized societies are already increasingly dependent upon the creation and manipulation of information. In addition to creating whole new industries, the computer is also the basis of most of the growth in new patterns of work, such as those evident in the growth of the home office. Not only is it imperative that societies adapt to rapid technological change, but there is a danger that individuals who cannot cope will be excluded. A substantial proportion of the present workforce is faced with this danger, so that their needs cannot be dealt with in traditional schools.

In summary, it is increasingly being argued that both highly and less developed countries are faced with a crisis that demands radical rethinking of how education is to take place. In particular, lifelong learning is seen as the key, and forms of education are required that are capable of fostering such learning. These forms, referred to here as defining a system of 'lifelong education', involve not only administrative and organizational elements of education, but also instructional content and materials, teaching and learning strategies, and evaluation. The balance of this book is concerned with outlining what the promotion of lifelong learning implies in these areas, and showing what this means for the practice of higher education.

2

Lifelong education as a system

Systematic support of lifelong learning

Learning is a normal and natural psychological process that occurs at all ages and in all kinds of settings (Mackeracher, 1996). Education is a set of circumstances that facilitate learning. Formal education, as it is found worldwide, is deliberately organized to foster learning. It involves various elements that together define an educational system: physical structures, most notably schools; organizational arrangements; experts who guide and direct other people's learning; goals and a philosophy defining what should be learnt and how; and provision for financing the whole process. The basic issues considered in this chapter are:

- the characteristics this system needs to facilitate lifelong learning;
- whether present arrangements display these characteristics;
- how existing systems would have to be changed in order to make them more supportive of lifelong learning.

Education as schooling

There was a time when the young learnt work and life skills by watching adults performing them, and when it would have been incomprehensible to have talked about education in any other terms. Learners served masters of a craft or trade, watched them at work, helped with manual tasks, participated in the simpler aspects of the job, practised the necessary skills, and in this way slowly acquired appropriate knowledge and techniques, as well as associated attitudes, values and self-image.

Learning in this way has by no means ceased to exist. Indeed, it is still very important, and may contribute as much as formal learning in technologically less-developed nations. Nonetheless, with the rise of technology, this kind of 'non-formal' learning (Coombs and Ahmed, 1974) has begun to be seen as less and less efficient. As a result, the idea has gained strength that education is something that precedes real life, should provide the young in advance with the skills they will need in the future and requires a specialized learning environment watched over by experts. The child has begun to be seen as a receptacle that has to be filled with knowledge via a set of stages and means that together define a system of formal education, usually centred on schools. The latter are regarded as essential for learning and, indeed, many parents place high value on their children attending 'good' schools, a term that usually implies they are dominated by the 'high' culture of the society in question.

Thus, not only has education come to be equated with schools, but schooling has come to be seen as something that precedes real life, or even constitutes a kind of qualification or precondition for entering adulthood. The function of schooling is regarded as communicating to the young knowledge and skills that will prove valuable in their future adult life, even if they are of minimal relevance to the immediate, day-to-day experiences of the children. Because of their role in preparing students for citizenship, schools have consequently begun to be regarded as primarily concerned with the transmission of useful information and skills that can eventually be applied more or less directly in life. In other words, schooling is seen as a way of collecting ready-made answers.

Weaknesses of existing education systems

Hubermann (1979) pointed out that justifying lifelong education by criticizing existing institutions has become almost a cliché and is to be found in almost all discussions of the topic. Despite this, a review of the decisive weaknesses is important for our purposes here. In the USA, the most damning review of conventional schooling in modern times was contained in the report of the National Commission on Excellence in Education (1983). The report's title, *A nation at risk,* summarizes the gravity of the perceived problem. Since the report appeared, various remedial measures have been introduced. For example, in 1994 President Clinton signed two bills into law: *Goals 2000: The Educate America Act* and the *School-to-Work Opportunity Act.* Although these acts are concerned with linking school and work, their emphasis on linking academic learning to real-world settings is of great relevance to the present discussions. Nonetheless, a good 12 years after the National Commission's identification of a high level of risk, Braun (1996) was forced to pessimistic conclusions about the difficulties associated with achieving change.

Conventional education systems often impede development of skills and attitudes necessary for lifelong learning (Cropley, 1999a). They perpetuate the idea that there is always a single best solution to every problem, and that this can readily be ascertained by correct application of set techniques and conventional logic. It is believed that teachers possess this solution and it is their duty to pass it on to their students, thus saving learners the effort involved in seeking answers for themselves.

Formal education can also be criticized for promoting the development of intelligence in a one-sided way. According to Gardner (1993) there are seven 'intelligences':

- linguistic;
- musical;
- logical-mathematical;
- spatial;
- bodily-kinaesthetic;
- intuitive;
- personal.

When excessive emphasis is placed on some 'intelligences' to the neglect of others, development is one-sided. For example, it can be argued that traditional education favours linguistic and logical-mathematical intelligence, but neglects what Gardner calls 'intuitive' intelligence.

Existing formal systems for supporting learning are also one-sided in another sense: they stress some forms of learning, but not others. For example, most schools emphasize other-directed, face-to-face learning, while neglecting self-directed and independent learning (Cropley and Kahl, 1986). These weaknesses limit the abilities, values, attitudes and self-image that learners develop, and thus have unfavourable consequences that are particularly problematic for lifelong learning.

In this context, a remark made to the press by the President of the Students' Association of the Flinders University of South Australia in 1998 is very enlightening. The occasion was the announcement of the introduction of a special academic unit to teach 'tertiary study skills'. The student leader greeted the new programme enthusiastically, and complained that at school students learn to work mainly in small groups under the close guidance of a teacher. In fact, learning in groups offers considerable advantages by:

- demonstrating a model of learning behaviour;

- providing a scaffold for learning (ie some members of the group may already possess partial information that helps to facilitate further learning);
- fostering motivation (ie through competition and by offering a social system in which effective learning may lead to rewards and status).

Despite these favourable effects, the student leader concluded that high school graduates come to university seriously lacking in *independent learning skills*, and that this causes them substantial problems, especially when they find themselves in situations where they have to learn without the nurturing influence of a group. Thus, aspects of conventional education may be inimical to lifelong learning. Nonetheless, neither the presence of an organized learning system nor awareness that learning is taking place necessarily impede lifelong learning. On the contrary, it is perfectly possible to imagine education systems that foster lifelong learning, and we do not wish to deny their value. What is important here is to ask how systems of education can be reorganized so that they do so.

Institutionalized and non-institutionalized learning

Cropley (1980) has provided a schematic conceptualization of educational development in Figure 2.1. Non-institutionalized influences act in conjunction with systematic, planned education to mould a given individual, who is thus the product of both kinds of factor. Influences in the area designated 'A' take effect with or without conscious awareness on the part of learners and 'teachers'. Even when such factors are to some extent conscious and deliberate, they are not formalized or institutionalized. Area B consists of activities deliberately planned to promote learning. Lifelong education stresses that Area B should become more open to the influence of Area A. In other words, formal or institutionalized learning settings and procedures should:

- be recognized as comprising only a portion of the total spectrum of educational influences;
- acknowledge the importance of learning occurring outside the formal education system;
- be more open to interaction with everyday learning influences.

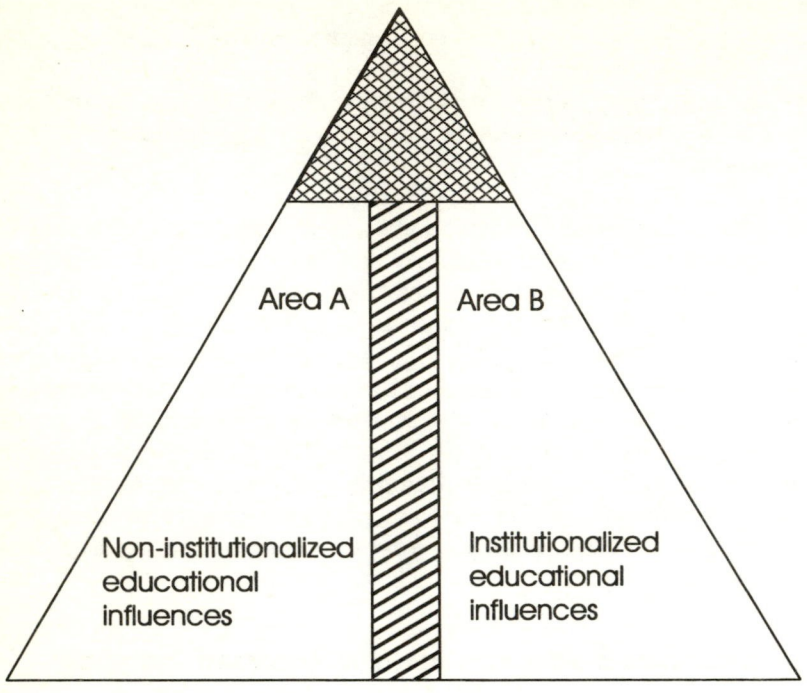

Figure 2.1 Educational influences on the individual

The learning continuum

Strictly speaking, these different kinds of influence comprise not two separate domains as Figure 2.1 may seem to imply, but a continuum. This ranges from the most unorganized and uninstitutionalized kinds of learning activity, which take place in the course of day-to-day life, to the most highly organized kinds characteristic of formal education. Figure 2.2 provides a diagrammatic representation of this continuum. The settings listed along the horizontal axis are merely examples of kinds of learning having different degrees of systematization, not definite labels for the regions in question. Relative distances between examples are merely schematic, and have no significance.

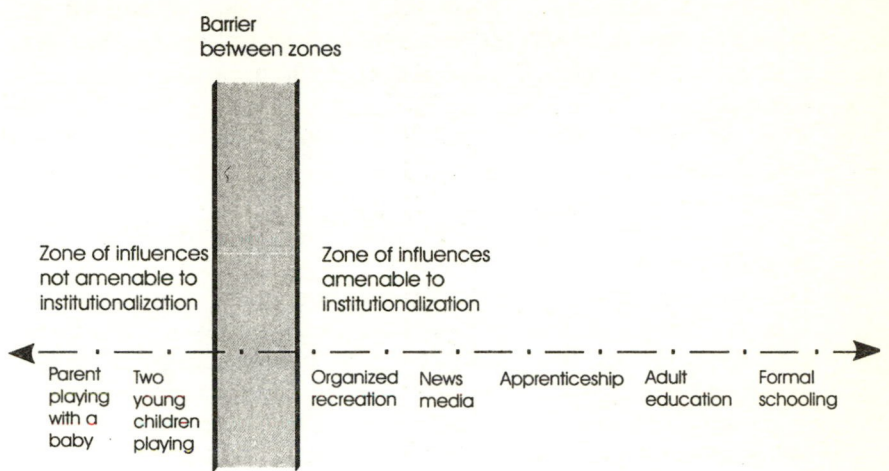

Figure 2.2 The continuum of influences on learning

All learners engage in activities from different parts of the spectrum, although the proportion of time spent on activities of a particular kind may differ markedly from person to person. Generally, it is recognized (Karpen, 1980) that not all learning settings can be subjected to organization and systematization – some aspects of life are sacrosanct. This means that there is a barrier separating those learning settings that organization could, in principle, 'improve' from those that must always remain private and personal, although the position of this barrier may well be dependent upon the values of a particular society. The placing of the barrier could be seen as defining the degree of what Karpen called 'educational imperialism'. For instance, in some societies television is regarded primarily as an educational tool, while in others it is used almost exclusively as a means of entertainment. The implementation of lifelong education would simply mean increased recognition of activities at the left-hand side of Figure 2.2.

It is important to emphasize that this shifting of the barrier would not necessarily mean making the less formal learning experiences more like school. In a discussion of distance education, Cropley and Kahl (1986) gave several examples of organizational aspects of distance learning that are often viewed as shortcomings, but can, in fact, have beneficial consequences for learning:

- Learners at home do not have their time on task organized and supervised by an expert (a teacher). As a result, they must take at least partial responsibility for planning and organizing their own learning.
- They do not receive regular and immediate feedback during a learning task. As a result, they must themselves evaluate their learning.
- They do not learn in a group. As a result, they must develop skill in learning alone.
- Learning outside settings specifically designed to foster it requires *special learning skills* such as planning and organization of learning, and evaluation by learners of their own progress. It also involves *special psychological components*, of which motivation is possibly the most obvious. In particular, learners outside the traditional system must be largely self- or intrinsically motivated.

The value of such psychological properties is, of course, not confined to distance learning. The ability to plan, organize and evaluate one's own learning, for instance, is sensible, even desirable, in school-based learning. Cropley and Kahl (1986) emphasized this point by arguing that, rather than trying to make learning in out-of-school settings more closely resemble learning in schools, many elements that lead to effective learning outside schools should be incorporated into teaching and learning in the classroom.

It is necessary at this point to stress that lifelong learning is not confined to adulthood, otherwise it would not be lifelong. Nonetheless, while most societies already make extensive provision for intensive learning experiences for children, most people spend far more of their lives as adults. Thus, it is inevitable that a system of lifelong education will have a major impact on learning in the adult years. Furthermore, since this book is concerned with the contribution of higher education to lifelong learning, our principal interest is, by definition, in adult learners and learning processes. By 'adult' we mean here simply anyone beyond the age limit defining childhood as it is understood in the society in question.

A system of lifelong education

Lifelong education as an organizing principle has a number of characteristics that derive not so much from criticism of traditional practice as from the various goals and values spelt out in Chapter 1. Dave (1973) developed a list of 'concept characteristics' which have been restated by Cropley (1980, p 3) as a set of definitive principles for a system of lifelong education. In such a system, education would:

- last the whole life of each individual;
- lead to the systematic acquisition, renewal and upgrading of knowledge, skills and attitudes, as this became necessary in response to the constantly changing conditions of modern life, with the ultimate goal of promoting self-fulfilment of each individual;
- be dependent on people's increasing ability and motivation to engage in self-directed learning activities;
- acknowledge the contribution of all available educational influences, including formal, non-formal and informal.

The characteristics just listed define an educational system that would start prior to the normal school age, and would continue beyond the end of formal schooling. It would encompass many learning settings including the home, the community, the place of work, clubs and societies, and would involve many different learning and teaching strategies. This study assumes that traditional institutions such as schools, universities and colleges would continue to have an important role, although in their present form they encompass only a narrow range of learning settings and approaches. Proponents of lifelong education emphasize, among other things, two important principles that are of relevance here. On the one hand, traditional educational institutions do not enjoy a monopoly on educating people; on the other, it is highly undesirable that they continue to function in a kind of splendid isolation from other learning settings.

Differences from adult education

It is quite obvious that a system of lifelong education would deal predominantly with adult clients, simply because in the normal course of events most people spend far more of their life as adults than as children or adolescents. Thus, the principle of lifelong education has important consequences for adult education. This does not, however, mean that the term 'lifelong education' is simply another way of saying 'adult education'. While proponents of lifelong education obviously have much to learn from people already working in the field of adult education, the reverse is also true.

Discussions at a European conference on adult education in the late 1980s made it plain that the overwhelming majority of the practitioners in attendance found it difficult to accept adult learning as part of the same system as learning during the conventional school years. They dismissed as absurd the idea that, in principle, *all* adults, as an integral part of their life histories, should engage in lifelong learning and pointed out that this would be simply too expensive. A major conceptual problem was that these specialists accepted a front-end model of teaching and learning processes. They regarded expansion of adult education as something that would involve larger numbers of people engaging in traditional learning activities, rather than as a radical re-evaluation of the role of learning in the adult years that calls for different educational content and a major reorganization of the educational system. For example, many in the group found absurd the idea that schools are largely there to prepare children for participation in learning *as adults*.

Despite this, adult educators commonly recognize that teaching and learning methods in adult education need to break away from the traditional face-to-face methods of conventional schools. This is necessary, among other things, to avoid 'sleeper effects' from clients' school-days. Such effects include negative attitudes to schooling and learning, low value placed on formal learning, or unfavourable self-image resulting from lack of success at school. However, as we argue in subsequent sections, the solution is not simply to reduce formality or be less stringent and demanding. Two areas where theorists and practitioners on adult education think differently from proponents of lifelong education are their understanding, on the one hand, of motivation and, on the other, of the relationship between schooling, age and learning.

Motivation

Research on motivation for participation in adult education (Knoll, 1985) is dominated by two kinds of study. In the first, adults are asked about their preferences for different content areas, and in the second they are asked what they hope to get out of participation. Results frequently indicate that people say they want to learn, for instance, foreign languages, or the basics of information technology. Their stated motivation may also be to get more enjoyment out of holidays abroad, meet new people, keep up with new ideas or – of great importance – to keep up with the latest advances so that they can cope better with demands at work. None of these goals is stupid or undesirable, but surveys of this kind reduce the whole idea of motivation for learning in adults to the status of a hit parade of expected benefits, rather than probing more deeply into underlying psychological reasons for engaging in learning. Furthermore, these goals are largely, although not exclusively, connected with recreation and leisure. High dropout rates indicate that this approach to studying motivation frequently leads only to sporadic and short-lived activation of the urge to learn.

Barbuto (1993) examined drop-out behaviour in 12 parallel introductory Italian courses in a large German *Volkshochschule*. He showed that there were dramatic differences in the goals and preferred teaching activities of the various instructors. Some wanted their students to have fun, pick up some elements of the Italian language and speak these freely, if with strange pronunciation and only approximate grammar. By contrast, others wanted their students to concentrate and work hard, and to have a perfect mastery of the basics of Italian grammar by the end of the semester, even if they could scarcely speak the language. Most instructors lay somewhere along the continuum defined by these two extremes. The variability in instructors' goals was matched by the variability of the students' goals. At one extreme, some students wanted to have fun trying out a new language or to prepare for a holiday in Italy. At the other extreme, however, were some who wanted to develop a high level of mastery of Italian vocabulary, grammar and syntax.

At the end of the semester, the usual overall drop-out rate of about 50 per cent was recorded. Of interest, however, was the observation that the students who did not drop out were mainly those whose own goals matched those of their instructor. Unfortunately, the simple measure of matching students and instructors according to goals, which was suggested for the next semester, was rejected by the administration. It was seen as regimentation of what should be an essentially recreational experience. Particularly strongly rejected was the thought of 'élite' courses involving demanding instructors with high standards teaching students who wanted to reach a high level of mastery of formal Italian. This suggests to us that some institutions and instructors engaged in traditional adult education underestimate both themselves and at least some of their students.

Organization of learning over time

Parjanen's (1993, p 7) diagram showing the temporal relationship between school-level education and adult education can be used here with minor modifications to depict the traditional relationship of school and out-of-school learning (see Figure 2.3). Traditionally, school initially offers a broad education in general cultural skills such as the three Rs. Passage through the school system is accompanied by the narrowing of content focus as students get older and by the emergence of specialization for later life in the world of work. By the end of formal schooling, this specialization is very advanced, so that the relationship between school learning and time resembles a triangle, broad at the base in the early years, but reaching a narrow point towards the end.

Traditionally, adult education commences at the point of maximum narrowness, where young adults have just left school and are absorbed with work, and makes it possible for them to broaden the contents of their learning once again. The relationship of learning in out-of-school settings (especially adult education) and time is thus also represented as a triangle, but this time one standing on its summit (the upper half of Figure 2.3). This organizational model implies an approach to adult learning that emphasizes broadening and generalizing after school has been completed.

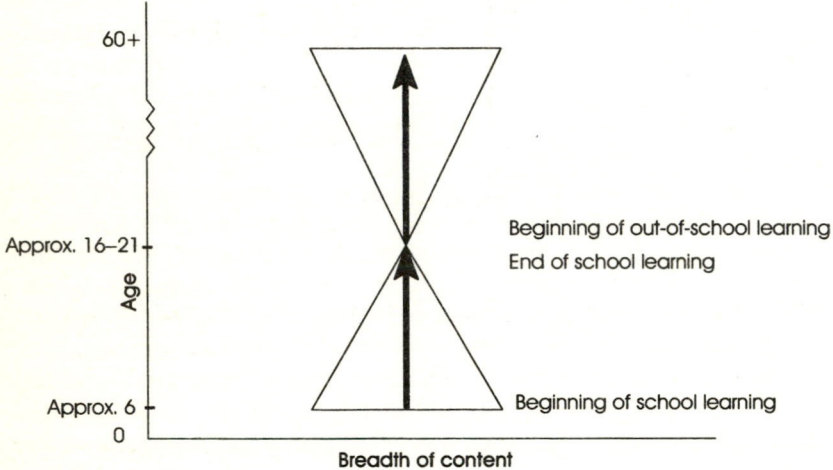

Figure 2.3 Traditional model of school learning, out-of-school learning and time

By contrast, as visualized by proponents of lifelong learning, the integration of learning in childhood and learning as an adult would lead to the situation shown in Figure 2.4 (Parjanen, 1993, p 8). In this model, learning would be broad at all ages, and would incorporate learning both in and out of school at all levels. However, the share of learning carried out in schools and school-like institutions (including universities) would diminish with the passage of time, and in non-school settings would increase proportionately. The distinction between the two forms of learning would become increasingly blurred and 'adult education' would, in a certain sense, cease to exist as a separate element, although in another sense, of course, it would become far more important.

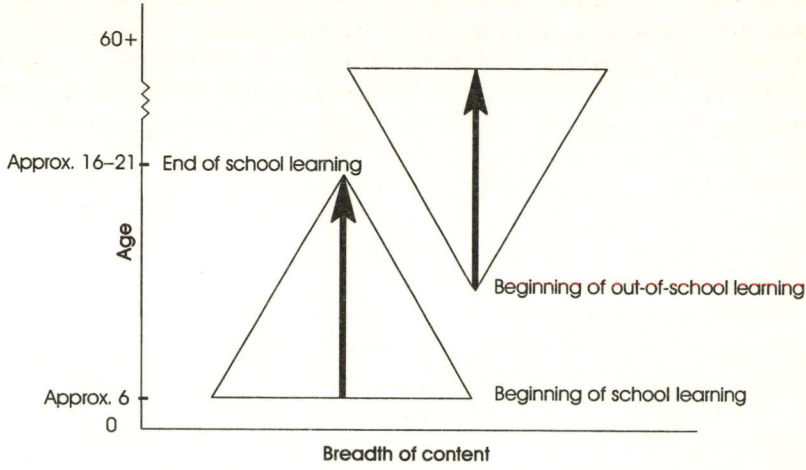

Figure 2.4 New model of school learning, out-of-school learning and time

The problems discussed above are part of an identity crisis in which adult education has found itself for some time (Kegan, 1994). Its traditional guiding philosophy has been 'disinterested learning' aimed at 'liberation of the mind' and 'self-growth' (p 273). This has led to a situation in which there has been a lack of clarity about what its goals and purposes really are. There has been no coherent, practical theory of adult education. What is it for? Who should it serve? How stringent should it be? What should it lead to? According to Kegan, a new goal is now emerging. Practitioners are beginning to accept a goal that stresses helping participants to become *self-directed learners*, people capable of critical thinking and individual initiative.

While this goal is perfectly consistent with the values that have become part of the ideology of lifelong education, it is global, abstract, philosophical and idealistic. As we have already pointed out (and will emphasize even more in Chapter 3), adults, even those of relatively advanced age, commonly have a quite practical orientation when they make decisions about engaging in learning activities. Thus, the goal of helping people to become self-directed learners, while extremely admirable and even noble, is not sufficient as the basis of a system designed to deal with the educational, personal and economic needs outlined in Chapter 1.

In summary, despite the emphasis on the importance of learning in adulthood, lifelong education goes far beyond conventional adult education. A system of lifelong education envisages a drastic change in the relationship of school-level learning, post-school learning and work, in the purpose and status of systematic learning at various ages, in the worth of different kinds of learning, and in the educational methods and procedures to be used at different age levels. Adoption of lifelong education would greatly enhance the importance of adult education, but it would also require adult educators to make considerable changes in, for example, their roles, responsibilities, relationships with other post-school agencies, teaching and learning methods, and evaluation procedures.

While our line of argument here perhaps represents an extreme position, it is certainly true that a full-fledged acceptance of the promotion of lifelong learning as the guiding principle for educational systems would involve a very strong shift in thinking about adult education. Finally, we should recognize that a variety of terms are used in the educational literature, and by practitioners, to refer to a wide range of learning experiences available to adults. In this section, we have talked of 'adult education'. Other familiar expressions include 'continuing education', 'extramural studies', 'extension teaching', 'recurrent education' and 'further education'. No attempt is made here to distinguish these different terms. More importantly, some aspects of all these educational approaches are consistent with the principles of lifelong learning (eg study tours, factory-based courses, joint programmes with local museums and libraries), while other aspects are less so (eg a traditional lecture course offered in the evening). Use of an educational slogan is no guarantee of a matching educational philosophy.

Organization of lifelong education

The discussion in this section needs to deal firstly with a possible misunderstanding. This is the notion that a system of lifelong education would extend the values and methods of traditional institutions to all aspects of each person's entire lifetime. If lifelong education were to mean, in effect, lifelong schooling, it would become the 'trap' about which Illich and Verne (1975, p 11) warned, condemning people, to use Dauber and Verne's (1976) metaphor, to school 'for the term of their natural life'. Lifelong education as a set of principles for organizing systematic provision of learning opportunities is thus not a form of 'educational imperialism' (Karpen, 1980, p 32) but an alternative approach to the provision of learning experiences. In this chapter we discuss further what this means for the educational system, while its implications for educational institutions will be spelt out in Chapter 4. In Chapter 3, the relationship of lifelong education to learners and learning will be discussed in greater detail. The organization of lifelong education is presented here in terms of two perspectives on the one hand, the temporal dimension (when will learning occur?), and on the other, the spatial (where will it take place?). These were referred to by Dave (1973) as 'vertical' and 'horizontal' integration.

Vertical integration

The representation of the relationship between learning and age given by Parjanen (1993) depicts the two variables on a graph, with time defining the vertical axis (see Figures 2.3 and 2.4). Lower positions on this axis indicate earlier times in a person's life (younger ages), and higher positions later times (higher ages). This metaphor will be continued in discussions in this section. Childhood and youth are conceptualized as lying at the lower end of a vertical continuum; adulthood and ultimately old age at the upper end. The temporally separate elements of the education system, such as preschool, elementary schooling, secondary schooling, initial post-school education, further education and the like, are seen as occurring at progressively higher positions on the vertical continuum.

The first and the most obvious organizational principle of lifelong education is that it must facilitate learning from the bottom to the top of this continuum (ie throughout the entire life span). Critics of conventional models of education argue that the various levels along the vertical dimension of age are at present poorly linked to each other. At most, phases lower on the continuum are seen as preparation for higher phases. Not uncommonly, however, learning at one level may actually hinder learning at a higher level, as in the example of the incompatibility of school and university learning given above. The principles of lifelong learning mean that these various levels would all need to be coordinated (or integrated) with each other.

Parjanen (1993, p 15) translated this view into economic terms, again providing a graphical representation of the traditional way of seeing schooling and work, on the one hand, and of the lifelong education approach on the other (see Figure 2.5). The traditional approach is the *exchange value model*, which sees learning as occurring in school and leading to a qualification that can later be exchanged for a job. At this point learning is over, except for 'catch-up' learning in response to changing skill requirements (eg to cope with new technology), 'disinterested' learning for self-development and self-direction (see above), or 'recreational' learning (preparing for holidays, advancing hobbies, etc).

The lifelong learning approach involves the *use value model*. Here learning and work can occur at the same time. Work experiences could enhance later school learning or school learning could make later learning at work more effective. The concept of vertical integration is not confined to school learning and work. It can be generalized to all aspects of education that are traditionally separated vertically – in other words that traditionally occur at different ages, such as school and higher education, work training and university education, or postgraduate education and work experience.

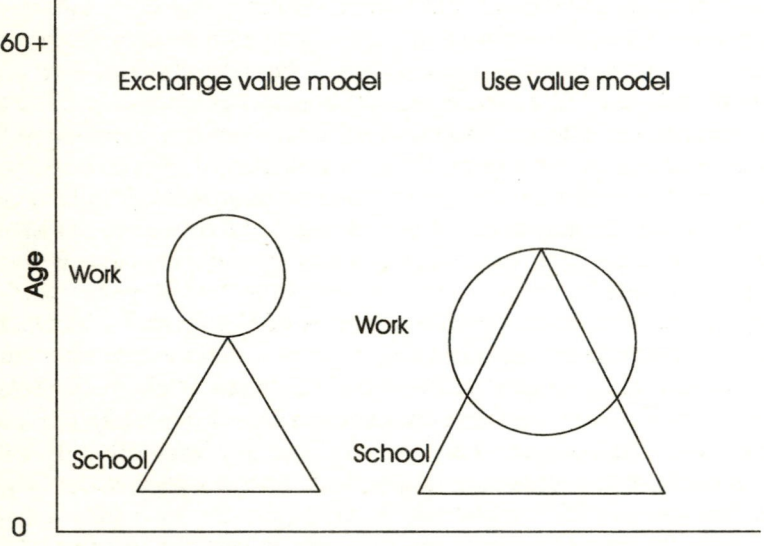

Figure 2.5 Integration of school learning and work

It may well be argued that these types of link already exist, especially as it is usually necessary to obtain some kind of lower qualification before proceeding to a higher stage. However, coordination of this kind is one-way in nature, with lower levels of education having a preparatory, even gatekeeper function in regulating passage to higher levels. What is meant by proponents of lifelong learning when they speak of vertical integration is considerably more than regulation of the speed and direction of movement through the system. For instance, it would be necessary for education to be organized in such a way that a particular learner could move backwards or forwards. It should also be possible for different people to enter the same level of the system (eg tertiary education) at different ages. Vertical integration would require that movement within the system be based not only on a decision about whether the necessary basic knowledge had been mastered. Equally important would be whether learners had developed appropriate attitudes towards both learning and themselves, skills for continuing to learn after formal education had ceased, and understanding of the relationship between learning at differing age levels.

Horizontal integration

We have already pointed out that lifelong education would not mean lifelong schooling. First, it would be absurd to imagine adults continually returning to school throughout their lives. The prospect of being subjected to lifelong control by conventional teachers is also an unpleasant one that many people would reject out of hand. Thus, especially in the case of learning occurring beyond the conventional school ages, it is apparent that the majority of learning experiences will take place outside the present formal system of education. Indeed, there is evidence that this is what happens to a large extent already. For example, Eide (1980) reported that in Norway in the early 1970s only 40 per cent of all learning was carried on under the auspices of the formal educational system, and he estimated that the proportion was falling. The remaining learning, although systematic and purposeful in the sense of the Tough definition already referred to, went on at work, in the family, in the course of leisure activities and so on. The coupling of learning in traditional institutions to learning in settings such as those just mentioned constitutes *horizontal integration*.

Cropley (1981) discussed in greater detail the educational role of the workplace, zoos, museums, libraries, clubs, churches, political parties and similar organizations. Even recreational activities such as playing a sport, going to the cinema, perhaps even drinking with friends in a pub can be seen as having a significant educational value. One element in systematic lifelong education would be acknowledgement of the worth of learning in such settings, the strengthening of it, and even incorporation of some of its major features into learning within institutions.

An interesting discussion of the need to link learning with real life was offered by Brown, Collins and Duguid (1989), although they did not use the term 'lifelong learning' in their paper. The authors distinguished between 'decontextualized' and 'situated' learning (p 32). The former occurs in formal educational institutions and rests on an assumption that knowledge exists independently of the contexts in which it is applied. In contrast,

situated learning occurs in everyday settings and is one of the normal products of life. Brown *et al* gave the example of learning a native language,
where in daily life it is estimated that children acquire new words at a rate
of 5,000 per year from the age of about 12 months, and are able to use these
words both appropriately and correctly. In contrast, in the classroom, students are able to learn no more than 100–200 words per year, and this
vocabulary is often used incorrectly, since it is acquired by means of
abstract definitions and frequently learnt out of context. Much the same
can be said of other content areas, with the result that children can pass
exams in a discipline, but may be unable to apply such knowledge in
real-world situations.

Brown *et al* went on to argue that learning should occur through participation in 'authentic' activities, which they defined as 'the ordinary practices of the culture'. At present, someone who wishes to learn a new skill
has two alternative, more or less competing, options. The first involves
carrying out the activity in question in a real-life setting with the help of
someone who knows how to do it (eg by means of an apprenticeship). The
second is to learn it in an 'academic' way by going to school. Unfortunately, however, the way in which, for instance, mathematics is taught in
school often bears little resemblance to what practitioners of mathematics
actually do. The same is true for other skills.

Brown *et al* suggested that the concept of apprenticeship should be
extended to areas such as language, mathematics and history. Students
would learn better by means of participation in authentic activity in normal situations, which should include the social and cultural interactions
that are part of such settings. They called this learning/teaching
approach 'cognitive apprenticeship' (p 39), and gave examples from the
teaching of mathematics of how this kind of learning could be promoted.
In one instance, students bring examples of mathematical problems
encountered in real life to school, and attempt to find solutions with the
help of the teacher and other class members. In another, students make
up stories in which mathematical principles are demonstrated in action –
for instance, the multiplication of 12 by 4 is learnt by means of a story
involving 12 jars each containing four butterflies. Brown *et al* argue that
it is possible, through cognitive apprenticeship, to go beyond learning
simple practical examples to achieve a level of abstraction, generalization and articulation (in the sense of communication), comparable to
what is possible by means of decontextualized learning. At the same
time, students acquire the additional context knowledge associated with
situated learning.

To return to our earlier theme of educational imperialism, it is important to emphasize once again that lifelong education would not mean the
imposing of values of the formal educational system on all elements of
life, despite the importance of recognizing the worth of learning in

non-school settings. In this context, it is useful to think in terms of two kinds of educational influence. The first consists of institutionalized factors such as the school and similar agencies, while the second comprises non-institutionalized educational influences, of which a number of examples have just been given (see also Figures 2.1 and 2.2). Although, in principle, learning in all settings would be of interest in the context of lifelong education, there must be areas of experience that remain strictly private. A small child playing with a grandparent may well be learning, but it would somehow be repugnant to try and systematize this process.

Indeed, Walker (1980) made the point that achievement of systematic horizontal integration runs the risk of trying to organize the unorganizable. It seems arrogant or repulsive for formal education to turn its attention to these newly discovered learning arenas. Thus, the achievement of horizontal integration, in which learning in all settings is seen to be interrelated, must tread a narrow path between educational imperialism and worthwhile reform. One guiding principle that may help to achieve horizontal integration while avoiding imperialism involves ensuring that the flow of influence between educational domains is reasonably balanced. In other words, the influence of the non-formal domain on events in the formal system should be at least as strong as the influence in the other direction.

A broader definition of education

The two principles just outlined, especially when taken in combination with learning principles to be discussed in detail in Chapter 3, lead to an altered notion of what is meant by 'education'. Instead of being regarded as fixed or static, 'an asset to be received' or 'a legacy to be acquired' during childhood and youth, as is presently the case (Pineau, 1980), education would take place at all ages and in many different settings. The implementation of vertical and horizontal integration would have implications for all aspects of an educational system, including its goals and content, the institutions upon which it is based, the structure of responsibility and authority, forms and methods of financing, its legislative basis, as well as the nature of credentials and the procedures through which they are acquired.

For example, the relationship between different learning settings and providers such as businesses, professional associations, colleges and universities would alter in such a way that boundaries between them would become 'porous' – learners would be able to transfer backwards and forwards between providers, or select various mixtures of settings. The idea of the 'normal' age of entry into a particular institution would be radically altered, as would the notion of the 'drop-out', since different people would leave and enter various educational settings at different times during their lives, or would remain in particular settings for differing periods of time. Many institutions not normally regarded as having a substantial educational role, such as museums or zoos, libraries, radio stations, churches, voluntary agencies, and so on, would have their contribution to purposeful learning acknowledged and emphasized. These changes would be both quantitative and qualitative. In other words, it is not simply a matter of increasing the number of settings that are regarded as important in post-school education, but of changing the nature of the relationships among them and of the things that go on within them.

The notion that learning in institutions should be closely linked with educational experiences in life itself is more than simply a trite association with the word 'life' that occurs in the expression 'lifelong education'. Education is always related to the society in which it occurs. However, an education that continues throughout each person's lifetime will need to be particularly closely linked with fundamental social, economic and even political issues in the society concerned. Otherwise, it would move in the direction of lifelong schooling, a conceptualization that we have already rejected. One of the major justifications of a system of lifelong education, as discussed in Chapter 1, is the phenomenon of change in everyday life. Thus, lifelong education would be closely bound to the transformations taking place in day-to-day life. This link would include not only scientific and technical aspects of a society, but also cultural, economic and even religious elements.

Liberal education and the core curriculum

In the field of higher education, what might be thought of as an early blueprint for lifelong education was provided by Cardinal Newman, who articulated the principles of 'liberal' education (Newman, 1973 [1852]). Newman's writing had a major influence on post-secondary education, especially in the USA, and provided a philosophical basis for many college curricula and degree programmes in the 'liberal arts'. Like Faure, Newman was concerned with the type of person moulded by experience with formal education. Ideally, for Newman, this would be a type of 'renaissance man' (in Newman's day the notion of a renaissance woman had less currency) who could use the knowledge, skills and attitudes learnt in university to guide him through the rest of life.

In its North American manifestation, the planning of a liberal arts programme primarily involved decisions about curriculum. Many institutions adopted the notion of a 'core' of courses that would supposedly provide students with an introduction to basic areas of knowledge and inquiry. A typical liberal arts core curriculum, for example, may include a course in English, a foreign language, a laboratory science, plus mathematics or perhaps symbolic logic or the history of science. (Other approaches include the University of Chicago's 'great books' syllabus and Keele University's foundation year.) During the 1970s, the North American liberal arts curriculum lost some ground to specialized, professionally oriented programmes. However, the idea of a common core of courses is far from dead, and still provokes an ongoing debate in the educational literature (Gose, 1999; Healy, 1999; Schneider, 1999).

Professional and vocational education

Although the term 'liberal education' has a somewhat grandiose ring to it, and is one that is often contrasted with professional, technical or vocational education, Newman was quite clear that universities should prepare their graduates for working life. This is hardly surprising since the early students at Oxford and Cambridge were in a sense preparing for jobs in the church, in teaching, at the court and within the legal system. In the USA, Harvard was established in the 17th century to prepare men for the professions (medicine, law, etc). The issue of course is not whether universities should prepare their students for life and work, but rather what form that preparation should take – a general education, as in the liberal arts curriculum, or more specialized training, as found in the professional schools.

Universities have never forsaken vocational education, but it is interesting to note that many nations have established alternative institutions with a specific mandate to serve vocational training needs that the universities, presumably, were not meeting satisfactorily. Thus, for example, the *Grandes Ecoles* in France and the German *Technische Hochschulen* were established to provide a cadre of highly trained professionals and technicians. More recently, the British polytechnics, set up for the most part during the mid-1960s and now largely transformed into universities, were created with similar aims in mind and in the hope that they would provide a much needed stimulus to industrial revival.

Despite the special provisions made for educating professionals, both in technical institutions and traditional universities, there is by no means universal agreement about what constitutes appropriate professional education, either in terms of aims, content areas, or – especially – instructional methods. In many instances, the members of the profession itself, through their licensing associations, have had a major, if indirect, say in university curricula leading to professional qualification. However, even where such professional associations are strong, the profession prestigious and of long standing, there can be disagreements about appropriate training, often producing new initiatives in educational programmes and teaching methods. A notable example (which we discuss further in later chapters) is the field of medicine, where certain universities have developed radical alternatives to the traditional curriculum and have introduced novel approaches to learning that are, we argue, highly consistent with our criteria for lifelong education.

3

The nature of lifelong learning

The meaning of 'learning'

Focus on intentional learning

The importance of distinguishing between everyday learning and intentional or deliberate learning has already been mentioned in Chapter 1. Nonetheless, this distinction is sufficiently important to warrant further discussion here. As Lawson (1982, p 98) pointed out, without a tighter definition of learning the whole notion of lifelong learning would become trivial. He contrasted simple exposure to the 'general mass of formative influences,' which results in 'general learning which any intelligent being undergoes in adapting to circumstances', with 'planned, intentional preparation', that is not simply a reaction to day-to-day happenings but 'a way of short-circuiting personal experience by drawing upon the accumulated experience of others'. It is the second kind of learning that is the primary object of systematic lifelong education, not the first. However, this does not mean that learning in ordinary life settings is ignored. On the contrary, such learning is important both in its own right and also because it enriches institutionalized learning. As has already been argued in Chapter 2, it involves special skills, attitudes and learning conditions that favour lifelong learning and could profitably be given more emphasis in formal settings.

The concept of knowledge in lifelong learning

The most obvious result of learning is acquisition of *knowledge*, and this provides an appropriate starting point for the present discussion of the special characteristics of lifelong learning. Anderson's (1993) definition of knowledge is helpful here. He emphasized not possession of discrete pieces of information (factual knowledge), but (a) generalized schema or master plans for making sense out of new events, and (b) effective tactics for dealing with these events. Candy, Crebert and O'Leary (1994) stressed the importance of not only domain-specific information, but also 'generic knowledge', and knowledge about the interconnectedness of fields. These, in turn, lead to what they labelled 'helicopter vision' (p 43). Frederiksen and Collins (1996, p 195) referred to 'flexible knowledge': not just facts that can be applied profitably to new variants of familiar situations, but also knowledge that allows people to respond effectively when exposed to novelty and change. Botkin, Elmandjra and Malitza (1979) had much the same idea in mind when they wrote about the importance of 'anticipatory learning', or the ability to solve novel problems that have not been seen before by either learners or their teachers. Anticipatory knowledge is precisely what is needed in responding to change.

In the USA, the Secretary of Labor's Commission on Achieving Necessary Skills (SCANS, 1991, p 147) laid down a 'foundation body of skill and knowledge that prepares [students] for change'. Although the Commission was addressing the question of what students need in order to leave school equipped to adapt to the demands of the workplace, its recommendations are highly relevant to the present discussion. Indeed, one of the 'necessary skills' identified by the Commission refers directly to lifelong learning, despite the fact that the term was not employed in the SCANS report – namely skill and knowledge leading to readiness for *learning (and teaching) on demand*. For the present purposes, it is the cornerstone of the whole list. The body of skills and knowledge recommended by the Commission includes:

- collecting, analysing and organizing information;
- communicating ideas and information;
- planning and organizing resources;
- understanding and designing systems;
- solving problems;
- using technology;
- using mathematical ideas and techniques;
- working with others.

Several writers have discussed such key competencies in a somewhat more psychological way. Tuijnman, Kirsch and Wagner (1997) focused on *skills*:

- skill in dealing with information presented in abstract, symbolic form, both verbal and numerical;
- analytical skills;
- problem-solving skills;
- adaptation skills: for example, the ability to work with the unfamiliar;
- technical skills, especially those associated with information technology.

In a discussion of adult education that is relevant here, Kegan (1994, p 274) listed the skills characterizing the 'self-directed' learner. These include time management, project management, goal setting, evaluation, information gathering and use of resources. Changing the emphasis slightly, Dohmen (1997) focused on *abilities*, especially the ability to think autonomously, which includes independent thinking, decision making and acceptance of responsibility. Other important factors were ability to think in broad concepts such as 'the common good', ability to process information constructively, ability to cope with the unexpected, and ability in problem-solving and creativity.

Resnick (1987, p 3) focused on thinking, especially higher-order thinking, which she considers has the following characteristics:

- it is non-algorithmic (the pathway to the required solution is not specified in advance);
- it is complex;
- it often yields multiple solutions;
- it requires 'nuanced judgement' from the learner (there are choice points where the learners must take the next step on the basis of experience, or even intuition);
- it involves multiple criteria;
- it entails uncertainty;
- it requires self-regulation;
- it demands that the learner impose meaning on apparent disorder, rather than discover a pre-existing meaning;
- it requires effort.

These characteristics can be contrasted with those that focus on acquisition of 'set knowledge' at one time, followed by reapplication of this knowledge in the future, which we are arguing here is inadequate to cope with a rapidly changing world. Higher-order thinking, by contrast, makes the learner capable of new learning in the future, as the need arises.

Resnick also emphasized the 'executive processes' (p 17) necessary for higher-order thinking. These encompass what are often called meta-cognitive aspects of learning: the ability to reflect on one's own learning processes and change them as necessary. They include:

- keeping track of one's own understanding of the issue under consideration;
- organizing one's attention;
- organizing the available resources;
- reviewing one's own progress with the learning task.

To these can be added (Frederiksen and Collins, 1996) effective strategies for representing and solving problems, strategies for choosing more promising approaches, insight into how systems work and skills for applying this understanding. The ability of students to articulate their own meta-cognitions is of considerable importance here. Articulation permits conscious self-reflection, highly specific feedback (correction) by teachers, and communication with other learners to compare methods, identify different approaches and make improvements.

Non-cognitive aspects of lifelong learning

The discussion so far has concentrated on cognition: especially knowledge, skills, abilities and thinking processes. These define the *ability* to learn. However, promotion of lifelong learning goes beyond the cognitive aspects to include motivation, attitudes, values, self-image and similar non-cognitive factors. These define *willingness* or *readiness* to learn.

In his discussion of adult education, Kegan (1994) put this issue in a more philosophical way, contrasting teaching aimed at fostering necessary knowledge and skills with efforts to promote the development of 'order of consciousness' (p 274). As Kegan argued, it is not so much a matter of teaching people the difference between what they value and what they ought to value (ie focusing on content), but of creating a level of consciousness where they really are able to perceive a difference. For the purpose of the present discussion, this includes a positive attitude to learning, confidence in oneself as capable of learning, willingness to question received wisdom, or ability to cope with anxiety arising from questioning the traditional and well known. Taken together with knowledge and skills, these factors define *readiness for lifelong learning*.

The 'lifelong learner'

Taken together, the ability and readiness outlined above define an idealized lifelong learner. Adapting the list developed by Cropley (1981, p 59), this individual:

- is strongly aware of the relationship between learning and real life;
- is aware of the need for lifelong learning;
- is highly motivated to undertake lifelong learning;
- possesses a self-concept conducive to lifelong learning;
- has the necessary skills for lifelong learning.

These skills include the following:

- capacity to set personal objectives in a realistic way;
- effectiveness in applying knowledge already possessed;
- efficiency in evaluating one's own learning;
- skill at locating information;
- effectiveness in using different learning strategies and in learning in different settings;
- skill in using learning aids such as libraries or the media;
- ability to use and interpret materials from different subject areas.

Candy, Crebert and O'Leary (1994, p 43) summed up the characteristics of the person well qualified for lifelong learning in a somewhat different way. According to them, such people have:

- an inquiring mind characterized by a love of learning, curiosity, a critical spirit and self-monitoring of their own learning;
- 'helicopter' vision involving mastery of a particular field paired with broad vision and a sense of the interconnectedness of different fields;
- information literacy, including skill in locating, retrieving, decoding (from different sources, such as words, charts or diagrams), evaluating, managing and using information;
- learning skills focused on 'deep' learning: deduction of general principles underlying specific knowledge that can be applied in novel situations, not just ones identical to the situation in which the learning occurred; deep learning is to be contrasted with 'surface' learning, that consists essentially of acquisition of facts;
- a sense of 'personal urgency' deriving from a favourable self-concept, self-organizing skills and a positive attitude to learning.

Learning to learn

Many authors such as Neice and Murray (1997) emphasize that the necessary abilities and skills, especially essential executive processes (meta-cognition), are not innate. The same is true of the non-cognitive factors just described (favourable attitude to learning, positive self-concept as a learner). Such psychological factors not only constitute processes and mechanisms through which learning occurs, but are themselves acquired via learning. This process of acquisition of the skills and abilities, attitudes, values and self-image required for lifelong learning involves what we understand by the term 'learning to learn'. Neice and Murray emphasized the role of school in this process (acquisition of the cognitive and non-cognitive properties discussed above), and thus demonstrated the importance of school in helping people learn in adulthood. Our concern in this study is with the possible contribution of higher education to learning to learn.

The influence of school on lifelong learning

By the time higher education begins, many major learning experiences have already taken place in the home or in school. In fact, the influence of school is often negative. As von Bernem (1981) pointed out, many adults are actively inhibited from taking part in lifelong learning activities by unhappy experiences in the classroom. However, the inhibiting effects of schools are not confined to unpleasant memories. Even a person who as a child experienced unbroken success in school may well have acquired habits and attitudes that are not conducive to lifelong learning. Among these are the idea that learning only occurs under the supervision of an authority figure, that success or failure is always externally defined, that the speed of learning or appropriate learning tactics are always specified by others, or that all worthwhile knowledge is found in books. In other words, even successful learners may acquire habits of passivity, or a one-sided view of what activities constitute worthwhile learning. Not uncommonly, they fail to acquire the knowledge and skills needed for lifelong learning, and thus do not learn to learn.

This implies that the school curriculum must be changed in order to promote growth of the personal prerequisites just listed. In an earlier paper, Cropley (1979) emphasized that schools have a major role in fostering development of the ability and willingness to engage in lifelong learning. The 'action guidelines' that were spelt out there were designed with school curricula in mind, but many of them can be modified as guidelines for higher education. For this reason, a number of the objectives of instruction in the context of lifelong education are presented in a slightly modified form in Table 3.1.

Table 3.1 Objectives of instruction in the context of lifelong education

Objectives related to	
Vertical Integration	**Horizontal Integration**
Students acquire self-image as lifelong learners	Student regard learning in life as relevant to formal learning
Change produces positive motivation for further learning	Students are able to learn in a variety of settings
Students regard learning as an ongoing process	Students regard other learners as a valuable source of knowledge
Students gain experience in planning learning	Students are able to integrate material from different areas to solve problems
Students evaluate their own learning and identify necessary further steps	Students evaluate their progress in terms of broader societal criteria

Clearly, few existing systems of higher education would achieve all the objectives for vertical and horizontal integration listed in the table, but the goals cited here can serve as a set of criteria for lifelong education against which many of the innovative learning approaches described in later chapters may be judged. These criteria are considered again at various points throughout this study.

Adults as learners

The whole topic of adult learning has been the subject of a lively debate in recent years, characterized among other things by the assertion that the commonly accepted notion of declining learning ability in the adult years is a myth, and counter-claims that this assertion is itself a myth (ie that ability really does decline with age). It is clear that there are real differences in performance on learning tasks between adults and children, and also between older and younger adults. However, these differences do not derive from differences between age groups in global learning ability. Rather, they imply differences in the kinds of thing that are most readily or least readily learnt, the circumstances most favourable for promoting learning, and the speed or efficiency with which certain kinds of learning are carried out. Even then, however, it is not clear whether these variations reflect purely or mainly changes in learning ability, or whether they are better regarded as reflecting differences in interests, motivation, self-image and similar factors. In other words, it seems probable that discrepancies in learning performance between people of different ages reflect special characteristics of learners and learning situations rather than, for instance, the onset of a fundamental inability to learn beyond certain age levels.

Learning differences between adults and children

A number of early studies examined the ways in which adult learners differ from children (Boshier, 1977; Cross, 1981; Knox, 1974; Wiens, 1977). Knowles (1970, p 43) introduced the term 'andragogy' (paedagogical principles for fostering learning in adults), which he contrasted with 'paedagogy' (principles for teaching children). Knowles initially emphasized differences between children and adults in self-concept, experience, readiness to learn and time perspective. For example, in the case of self-concept, children are more dependent, whereas adults are more independent and self-directed. Adults naturally have a greater body of collected experience, which increases with age, and their readiness to learn is motivated by factors from their immediate social environment rather than being externally imposed. Finally, adults are more likely to expect that new learning will be immediately applicable, while children have to hope that applicability will become apparent in the future.

More recently, Zmeyov (1998, p 107) summarized the special characteristics of adult learners as follows:

- They already possess considerable practical, social and occupational experience.
- They are conscious of their own life goals and of the relevance to these goals of knowledge and skills to be acquired by lifelong learning.
- They usually already possess a certain degree of background knowledge in the areas in which they want to learn more.
- They often feel the need to achieve new learning as quickly as possible.

According to Mezirow (1990), learning is a 'process of making a new or revised interpretation of an experience' (p 1). Adults already possess 'habits of perceiving, thinking, remembering, problem-solving' (p xiv) that have been acquired during a lifetime, and that are in the normal course of events far more highly developed than those of children. These habits provide frames of reference that make it possible to categorize and interpret new events. Although such habits or frames make it easy to interpret experience, they also 'constrain' meaning, because they lead to interpretations, evaluations, and decisions on action that stick to the tried and trusted from the past. They thus limit, among other things, creativity and self-development. Mezirow called for provision of learning experiences in adult education that emancipate adults from their limitations in dealing with the present – and indirectly the future – only in terms of the past. He called the necessary emancipatory approach 'transformative learning' (1990, p. xv). This concept will be referred to again in later sections of this study.

Adopting a more psychological position, learning can be defined as involving two phases. In the first, new experiences are rendered meaningful by being compared with an existing mental map of the external world. When a new experience is seen to possess at least the key defining characteristics of certain earlier experiences, 'pattern recognition' occurs, and the new experience is treated as a further example of the earlier experience. In other words, a new experience is assigned to an existing category of events. This process is referred to as 'coding'. In the second step, the new experience is assumed to possess at least the general properties of the category to which it has been assigned, even if these properties are not all directly observable in the present situation. These two steps make it possible to go beyond the bare bones of a specific new situation and flesh it out on the basis of past experience.

It is important to keep three principles in mind. First, the categories into which new events are coded are built up during the course of earlier learning. Second, this learning includes value judgements and attitudes. Third, the key features of a new event that are decisive in assigning it to a category are also largely learnt. For example, most people would probably code a large white grub into a category like 'wildlife', and evaluate it as wriggly and disgusting. By contrast, a person with different but appropriate previous learning experience may code it as 'food' and evaluate it as juicy and delicious. The consequences of this difference in what is more colloquially referred to as 'perception' could be life-threatening if the two people were lost and starving in the Australian bush.

The effect of past experience on perception has been well documented in psychological research. The coding of new experiences depends upon what is already known; for example, the capacity of a wine buff to distinguish different vintages by grape type and origin, or ability of the Inuit to perceive at least 9 or 10 different kinds of snow. However, people also learn strategies or tactics for simplifying the coding of new stimuli (eg scanning versus focusing, levelling versus sharpening), while they also employ special cognitive strategies to make it easy to fit new stimuli into existing categories (eg selective perception, dissonance reduction). Perception is also affected by factors such as anxiety and motivation: a frightened person is likely to code a new stimulus as threatening; a hungry one to perceive it as food.

The crucial element for this discussion is that, by means of the mechanisms just outlined, past learning to a considerable degree guides or even controls present learning. It is here that the essence of the difference between adults and children as learners can be seen most clearly. The greater the past learning, the stronger its effect on new learning. Adults are, in principle, capable of making novel codings, but their learning is greatly influenced by the process of fitting in new experience with what already exists. This requires *modifying, transforming and reintegrating knowledge and skills* (Mackeracher, 1996, p 29). Children, by contrast, do not possess the elaborated system of categories that adults possess, with the result that their learning largely involves *forming and accumulating new categories*.

Adopting Mezirow's terminology, the 'frames of reference' possessed by adults include:

- a model of reality based on experience;
- learnt tactics for perceiving and encoding new material;
- a self-image that encompasses factors such as social roles and self-esteem (which can be positively or negatively influenced by learning experiences);
- a history of success or failure in learning;
- articulated goals for life and work;
- experience in dealing with both learning frustration and disappointment, as well as with success.

As a result, new learning requires much more psychological 'work' for adults than for children. Because of the human tendency, both physiological and psychological, to try and maintain a state of equilibrium, changing what already exists – and may be working well – demands a greater cognitive effort from adults than it would take for children to learn something new. Sticking with the tried and trusted is also encouraged by non-cognitive factors such as complacency, fear of failure, unwillingness to accept the social status of a beginner, or even the beginnings of burnout. Personal history, too, can inhibit willingness to change; for instance negative experiences with new material at school, at work or in social settings. These individual differences are much greater from adult to adult than from child to child, because of the longer and more diverse life histories of adults, so that they account for more of the variance of adult learning. In teaching children, differences from child to child in ability and level of motivation are of paramount importance, whereas in the case of adults what often matters more is the kind of motivation, the self-image, the social role acquired over many years, or the degree of fear of the novel that mature learners bring to the situation.

Fostering adult learning

A major practical issue for educational institutions is how to respond to the special characteristics of adults as learners. To use an expression formulated by Knox (1974) about 25 years ago but still highly relevant, adults are seldom interested in learning answers for which they do not already know the questions. Zmeyov (1998, p 104) stated the issue bluntly by condemning '...the low efficiency of using in adult learning the paedagogical principles that were developed in the framework of children's education'. He saw the ' ...issue of developing and introducing into educational practice an efficient technology of [adult] learning...' as one of the most important tasks facing proponents of lifelong learning.

The issues outlined in the previous section mean that for adults, by comparison with children, learning requires more *effort*, more *time*, more *critical reflection* on what they already know, more *opportunity to test new learning* in safety from feeling foolish, incompetent or helpless, clearer *pointers to the essential core* of what is to be learnt and more help in *recognizing the personal factors within themselves that may inhibit learning*, such as anxiety, rigidity, negative attitudes to learning or fear of social consequences. Zmeyov (1998, p 106) translated these principles into more practical guidelines by enunciating special properties of learning itself, rather than of learners. According to him, teaching of adults should emphasize:

- self-directed learning;
- experiential learning (the adults' own lives are a rich resource);
- contextual learning (goals of learning derive from the learner's own life, and learning activities must fit in – both in time and space – with the everyday context, including work, family and social life);
- actualized learning (immediate application of the results of learning to the individual's situation);
- systemic learning (coordination of goals, content, methods and evaluation of learning in the light of the four characteristics listed above).

Candy, Crebert and O'Leary (1994, p ix) also suggested special forms of learning that are particularly important for adults, and it is apparent that there are some overlaps with Zmeyov's ideas. Their list includes:

- peer-assisted learning;
- experiential learning;
- problem-based learning;

- resource-based learning;
- open learning;
- learning based on promoting critical self-awareness and reflection on learnt material.

To these may be added transformative learning (Mezirow, 1990). While these kinds of learning are also appropriate for children, in the adult phase of lifelong learning, they are vital.

Adult learning problems

From a psychological point of view, it is possible to identify a number of areas in which adults experience special difficulties in learning. These involve the cognitive domain (thinking, learning, memory), the affective (attitudes and values, motives and self-image) and the social (societal roles, social stereotypes). In the case of cognition, to oversimplify, memory becomes problematic. Search and recall tactics seem to become less effective. The ability to work at high speed may be greatly reduced. Strategies for storing information may also become less efficient as older people try to make new information fit into established categories. In principle, this is a good thing, but it can impede learning in situations where the new ideas demand formation of new frameworks. The well-known 'inflexibility' of mature adults is largely a result of such factors.

Since mature adults already have well-developed cognitive structures and behavioural tactics for dealing with a wide range of events, they naturally seek to reapply these frameworks. Unfortunately, however, what they already know can easily interfere with their learning of new material. Thus, older learners need more help than younger adults in structuring new information and avoiding inappropriate attempts to deal with genuinely new constructs in terms of pre-existing structures. They can also be assisted to cope with other cognitive difficulties by slowing down the pace at which new information is presented.

Turning to non-cognitive factors, it is apparent that in many Western European and North American societies there is a stereotype that older adults are largely incapable of learning ('You can't teach an old dog new tricks.'). In the course of socialization, people learn the various roles appropriate to the society in question, so it is not surprising that many adults, especially older ones, regard themselves as incompetent. This goes with the idea that schooling is something for children, and that no longer going to school is a sign of being adult. Indeed, many of those who fail to complete formal education are motivated by a desire to enter the 'real world' as soon as possible. It is as if this is a place where learning will no longer be required – like the student who discards his or her texts after leaving school with the comment, 'Thank goodness I won't need books any more'. Although this is often hard to grasp for teachers and academics who, by definition, fared well as students, many adults have a negative attitude to formal learning, and look back on their school years with distaste, even anxiety. School was for them a place where they were made to feel incompetent and where the instruction had little to do with the outside world of work and leisure.

Those adults who do pursue further formal learning opportunities study for a wide variety of reasons; for self-development, to make social contacts, to escape boredom and even to please others. However, the most common motivation for learning is frequently external – to obtain the skills or knowledge needed for some special purpose, such as a job (Houle, 1961). Studies in both the UK (Stock, 1979) and the USA (Loring, 1978) showed that about half of all adult learning was carried out for the sort of external reasons our discussion to date has emphasized – the need for new skills and knowledge in the light of changing circumstances.

Thus, a substantial proportion of adult learners in a sense 'have to' learn. Allied with the factors outlined above (changed cognitive abilities, negative attitudes to learning and problems with self-concept as a learner), this means that many adults enter learning situations with a good deal of anxiety. Anxiety, in turn, has known effects on cognition, including selective attention, narrowing of interpretation of events, repetition of 'old' solutions and an inability to break out of a stereotyped interpretation of a situation. There are also effects on emotions, such as feelings of humiliation, self-doubt, anger or projection of negative feelings on to the teacher or the subject matter. These phenomena further increase anxiety, so that a vicious circle can develop; anxiety negatively affecting cognition and emotion and thus heightening the anxiety, and so on. Thus, adult students may face psychological difficulties in learning new skills that differ from the problems of 18–21-year-olds, and teachers need to take such factors into account when planning and delivering instructional programmes. On the other hand, many adults also have powerful internal motivations to study, an ability to link what they learn to their own experiences and learning expectations that are far more realistic than those of their younger counterparts. As many instructors of mature students will testify, teaching older learners can be an especially rewarding experience.

Implications for higher education

As we have just pointed out, the implementation of lifelong learning as a norm in a given society would require particular kinds of knowledge, skills, attitudes and values on the part of learners. Despite the foregoing comments, it would be a mistake to think that the best prescription for lifelong higher education is solely a matter of catering to mature students through special adult programmes, increased budgets for continuing education departments, more part-time learning opportunities etc. Indeed, these are worthy initiatives, but they ignore the fact that a major clientele for higher education will continue to be the traditional full-time student entering college or university directly from secondary school. Laying the basis for lifelong learning among these individuals will thus be a major task for higher education, and one that will have important implications not only for *how* people will learn, but also for *what* they will learn.

Institutions have an important part to play in promoting the development of the personal prerequisites and competencies for lifelong learning. This could be done partly by training people in lifelong learning competencies, and partly by providing them with opportunities to exercise skills they had already acquired. The major purpose would be to equip people in such a way that they wanted to continue learning and believed they could do so. Achieving these goals would require teaching and learning activities that depart from the norms of conventional classrooms.

Adapting course content for traditional students

According to Candy, Crebert and O'Leary (1994, p 66), content of courses aimed at enhancing students' capacity for lifelong learning would have five characteristics:

1. It would provide a systematic introduction to a particular field (ie domain-relevant content).
2. It would put this content into a general context (ie *general* content – see also the earlier references to 'deep' learning).
3. It would emphasize 'generic' knowledge.
4. It would be flexible (eg offer choice and self-direction for students).
5. It would promote self-directed learning.

In a rapidly changing world, content is often ephemeral whereas learning skills themselves are applicable in a wide variety of situations that students may encounter after they have ended their formal university education (Lockwood, 1982). Nonetheless, as we have already argued, certain types of knowledge and skills are probably essential foundations for later learning. Indeed, the recent 'back-to-basics' movement in the USA attracted considerable publicity, and was perhaps an element in support of the renewed worldwide interest in core curricula stressing mother tongue (for US back-to-basics proponents this means English) and numerical skills. Clearly, very few people would argue against the proposition that a student in higher education must be able to process verbal information (and in many instances mathematical information) in order to be a successful lifelong learner. However, if the idea of the basic curriculum is expanded to include a wide variety of other disciplines and content areas, then – depending on the teaching methods employed – there is a sense in which the whole endeavour may be counterproductive from the point of view of lifelong learning. This is because of the danger that students may regard the curriculum as fixed and finite, and may lose the initiative to guide their own learning by selecting for themselves the relevant subject matter and appropriate skills most suited to their needs in later life.

In equipping students with the necessary abilities and motivation to tackle real-life problems, there are at least two broad viewpoints within higher education. The traditional approach of universities is to have students master a certain body of information, as defined by a teacher or textbook, ultimately learn to extract what is relevant, and apply their knowledge to help solve real-world problems. A contrasting approach is to begin with a problem and have students try to solve it, working 'backwards' to acquire the necessary information and skills. We return to this subject in Chapter 5 in the discussion of project work and independent learning methods.

Little (1983) pointed out the close parallels between Newman's definition of liberal education and the more contemporary goals of education spelt out in many university calendars and mission statements. When Newman's thoughts are translated into statements about course content, he can be seen as advocating that students acquire communication skills, ability in critical thinking, understanding of the local culture and differences between cultures, interpersonal skills (including empathy and tolerance), integrity and an ability to make informed and responsible value judgements, as well as knowledge and skills necessary for working life and the ability to learn how to learn.

Cropley and Dave (1978) discussed various specific attempts to develop courses with lifelong learning itself as subject matter. In general, however, the practical experiences they reported indicate that such courses are not particularly valuable, because they do not foster the desired skills, habits, attitudes, motives and values. It seems far more likely that lifelong learning would be facilitated by changes in the orientation or organization of existing content. As an example, they cited a college course in mathematics in which the contributions of various mathematicians were presented in a conventional manner, but were also related to life experiences of the scholars in question, societal trends of their time and so on.

Aalbeck-Nielson (1973) enunciated several principles for selecting content which, although intended for school curricula, are interesting in the present context. He concluded that the content of courses should be oriented towards themes such as *time*, *space* and *change*. He did not suggest the introduction of special courses on these topics, however, but rather that they should be used as organizing principles for the presentation of traditional content in conventional disciplines. He gave a striking example of how to teach history with this perspective, and it seems probable that university teachers could successfully adapt many courses along the lines he suggested, even in strongly fact-oriented disciplines. A study by the Unesco Institute for Education in Hamburg (Lengrand, 1986) identified a number of areas thought to define the minimum content necessary in a system of education devoted to lifelong learning. These include knowledge of communication, science and technology, the fine arts, ethics and citizenship, time and space, and how to care for one's own body.

In response to increasing concerns about degradation of the environment through pollution, global warming, disappearance of forests and extinction of plant and wildlife species, environmental education has been given great attention as one possible means of changing relevant attitudes and behaviour. For example, the Canadian government introduced a 'Green Plan' that proposed more information about the environment and better environmental education 'to translate environmental awareness into action', with the object of 'creating an environmentally educated population' (Environment Canada, 1990, p 9). In keeping with the principles of lifelong learning, the plan called for education 'formally, through the school system, and informally, in the community, the workplace, and elsewhere' (p 9). The Canadian government also proposed a Framework for Health Promotion in which education was seen as a major means of developing a new vision of health, in order to involve individuals and communities in the task of defining what health means to them and recognizing that health is 'an essential dimension of the quality of our lives' (Health and Welfare Canada, 1986, p 3).

It is not being suggested here that specific courses on the environment, health, ethics and so on should become compulsory for all students, but rather that the themes in question should run through all courses and programmes, to the maximum extent possible. The idea that the principles and practices of effective learning have to be embedded in a broader curriculum and cannot be taught as isolated skills is a theme we return to later when discussing study skills and learning to learn.

Despite increasing specialization within many disciplines, there appears to be a growing recognition on the part of many academics that, as the information available to students in any particular field grows exponentially, the ability to integrate and maintain an overall perspective becomes critically important – perhaps even more important than mastery of specialized technical expertise. Engineering is one example. Almost 20 years ago, Beuret and Webb (1982) accused engineering education in the UK of preparing students poorly in all but the most narrowly technical sense. They interviewed 250 graduate mechanical and electrical engineers and a further 200 of their colleagues working in a variety of organizations and industries. There was agreement that working engineers had little understanding of business practice, management skills or company policy. Furthermore, the engineers were reportedly inept at communicating what they did understand to others in the organization. The perceptions of colleagues were of special interest, and revealed a wide gap between what they would have liked the engineers to do and their actual capabilities. A major shortcoming was seen to be the engineers' inability to construe their work in a broad organizational context, to describe engineering problems clearly to non-experts, and so on.

The researchers came to the damning conclusion that, overall, engineers tend to be 'intellectually and culturally isolated, partly because they find it difficult to see, or at least to treat seriously, any other perspective than their own'. The blame for this state of affairs was laid squarely on the shoulders of higher education. In particular, engineering departments were accused of placing far too much emphasis on technical subject matter in science and mathematics, and too little on practical experience of a broad range of problems – both engineering problems and management decisions. Some of the respondents admitted that they had ignored more broadly based courses in order to concentrate on what they conceived as 'real engineering'. It came as a shock to them to find how little correspondence there turned out to be between the skills they had learnt at university and those that were demanded of them in the work situation. It is interesting to speculate whether research of a similar nature in other professions would reveal comparable discrepancies between what is taught in university and the skills and attitudes necessary for work and for life.

Many engineering departments have responded to criticism of this kind. For example, engineering students at Salford University take a course in which teams of students must identify the need for, design, build, develop and propose a marketing campaign for a commercial product. Despite such welcome moves, criticism has not abated in recent years. There have been repeated calls for engineers to become major contributors to innovation, which is seen as essential for the survival of firms and the career advancement of individuals. However, the response of engineering curricula in institutions of higher education is seen as less than satisfactory (Steiner, 1998).

The difficulty of breaking out of the straightjacket imposed by traditional skills, attitudes, values and self-image associated with engineering can be seen in an interdisciplinary project involving a psychology professor and an engineering instructor at the University of South Australia (Cropley and Cropley, 1998). They introduced a class on engineering innovation in an electronic engineering degree programme. Second-year students received lectures on creativity, emphasizing its importance for engineering practice and developing a practical definition (introduction of effective novelty). This material was made concrete with the help of case studies of famous innovations. As part of their assessment, students were required to design and build a wheeled vehicle powered by the energy stored in a mousetrap. Although a passing grade was guaranteed if the vehicle proved to be capable of moving under its own power, assessment emphasized the importance of novelty, elegance and germinality (all of which had been explained to the students) for obtaining a high mark. In addition, students were required to submit individual reports analysing the way their own thinking, motivation and personality characteristics, as well as social factors, influenced their approach to the task.

Almost all participants succeeded in constructing a vehicle that met the minimum formal requirements (it had wheels and was capable of moving itself). Several of the resulting models were elegantly designed and well finished. However, most students assumed that the vehicle had to be four-wheeled and had to run on the ground like a car or truck. In addition, most focused on the energy stored in the trap's spring as the source of power, as well as consciously opting for a vehicle that was *effective* in the sense that it could cover well over a metre, and was *socially acceptable* in that it looked like existing vehicles. Only a few were able to break away from conventional thinking: one group, for instance, constructed an aeroplane launched by a catapult powered by the mousetrap's spring (the plane had wheels and easily covered a metre); another built a large hollow wheel set rolling by a weight mounted in its interior and wound into position by the trap's spring, thus expanding the meaning of the term 'wheeled'.

Even more novel was the model built by a group that set fire to the mousetrap and used the heat generated by the flames to fire up the boiler of a steam locomotive, thus using the chemical energy stored in the wood. Finally, one group offered the most radical solution: a wheeled cart attached to the mousetrap by a string. When the mousetrap was thrown off the table on which the vehicle stood, its weight pulled the cart along as the trap fell to the floor, thus using the gravitational force acting on the mousetrap's mass as the source of energy. The only limit on the distance this method could propel the vehicle was the height of the surface from which the mousetrap was thrown.

Comparisons of the trained students with a control group suggested that the cross-disciplinary (psychological) content had had some positive effects, although it was apparent that a single class was not sufficient to achieve real change in adoption of lifelong learning approaches. The students' logs of their own thinking while designing their vehicles showed that many of them consciously opted for a 'safe' solution, despite the fact that they knew creativity was necessary for a high grade. These students elected to build a model of a conventional car or truck that they were certain would run a metre and would not strike others as odd or 'way out', preferring this to trying to be original, because of the risk of building a vehicle that did not work. (An example is a group whose members thought of using the mousetrap's spring to compress a set of bellows that would inflate a balloon, which would then deflate violently and drive the vehicle by its jet action. They abandoned this highly creative approach as too risky, since it might not have worked!) A few students, by contrast, indicated that they went all out for creativity, accepting the risk of a fiasco. The protocols suggested that risk takers were highly motivated by the task, whereas it intimidated risk avoiders.

4

Lifelong learning and higher education institutions

Transforming existing institutions

As mentioned in Chapter 2, lifelong education is sometimes understood as a synonym for a number of other terms, all of which have in common the notion of periodic renewal or refreshing of knowledge, for instance, 'recurrent education', *'éducation permanente'*, 'further education', 'adult education'. Earlier we criticized this tendency and attempted to show that lifelong education has far more comprehensive implications than the 'synonyms' just listed. This is not simply a matter of words or labels. Equating lifelong education with recurrent or continuing education can easily lead to the conclusion that it consists simply of the sum total of all institutions engaged in such activities. On the contrary, a system of lifelong education would encompass not only learning in such settings, but also in *all* settings, formal and informal, highly institutionalized and non-institutionalized. At the same time, there is no question that implementation of lifelong education has important implications for traditional educational institutions, and these are the subject of this chapter.

It is unlikely that any society will simply scrap existing institutions and start again from the beginning, regardless of the degree of enthusiasm with which lifelong education is embraced. This means that its adoption would involve a transformation of existing institutions rather than the sudden imposition of something completely new. The nature of this conversion would be derived, naturally, from the principles of lifelong education that have already been outlined. It is impossible here to give a single universal blueprint for these transformations, just as it is also not feasible to list all desirable changes that could occur in higher education. However, general principles can be outlined, along with the questions, problems and dangers that then become apparent.

Kulich (1982, p 136) summarized these seven practical questions as follows:

1. Where and when is instruction to be offered?
2. How are resources to be allocated?
3. What content will be necessary?
4. On what basis will certificates or credentials be issued?
5. What teaching and learning methods will be appropriate?
6. How will learners be financially supported?
7. What new or altered support services will be needed?

To these may be added the issue of who should be admitted and how clientele would be selected. This question touches on five basic issues:

1. Who will be the students in universities based on a system of lifelong education?
2. How will they learn?
3. How will their learning be evaluated?
4. How will institutions be coordinated?
5. How will the system be financed?

A number of these themes will be discussed in more detail in later sections. The intention is to provide a framework for presenting and discussing the various concrete steps that would need to be taken in existing higher education institutions in order to implement the principles of lifelong learning. These steps will be discussed in a more concrete way in subsequent chapters.

The students

The image of learning and learners outlined earlier deviates from the profile of the university student that is traditionally accepted. In nearly all cultures, higher education has until recently been restricted to a narrow spectrum of the population – restricted in terms of age, social class, ethnic origin and often gender. Thus, in many societies higher education has been confined to an élite group who have gone on to take leadership roles in government, business and the arts. Attempts have been made in a number of nations, however, to change this, for instance by such mechanisms as open admission policies.

Indeed, the types and numbers of students entering colleges and universities have changed dramatically in the past four decades. The number of students receiving higher education has grown enormously in most technologically highly developed (and many less highly developed) nations, and this has led to the establishment of new universities and colleges, and to a huge expansion in the size of existing institutions. Additional student numbers were, in part, provided by the results of the 'baby boom' after the Second World War and partly by changes in admission policies. The great expansion of higher education from the late 1950s to the mid-1970s has more recently given way to a period of retrenchment in many parts of the world. In Germany, for instance, there was a reduction of almost 10 per cent from 1992 to 1995, and after a brief 'recovery' there was renewed shrinkage of about 2 per cent in the winter semester 1998/99. New building has ceased, and university operating budgets have generally increased at a rate less than inflation. However, as the sons and daughters of the baby boom reach university age in the early part of the next millenium (the so-called 'baby boom echo'), it is likely that student numbers will again increase. For example, the Council of Ontario Universities forecasts that institutions in that province will need to accommodate at least 53,000 additional students by the year 2004/05, an increase of almost 25 per cent (Giberson, 1999). If the proportion of school-leavers opting to enter university also rises, as is predicted, that number could rise to over 90,000 additional students in the system.

In a discussion of university education that views several measures advocated here in a positive light (eg emphasis on liberal arts, cross-disciplinary studies), Newman (1998) documented rising student numbers, stable faculty size and decreasing funding in most institutions in the USA. Taken together, these trends have resulted not simply in increased numbers of students in traditional age groups and taking conventional courses, but in different kinds of student, sometimes learning in unconventional ways and settings.

Part-time students

During the late 1970s and early 1980s, higher education witnessed a marked change in the nature of the student body, although the trends we describe below have been far more prominent in some nations than others. The traditional time for higher education has been the years immediately after secondary school. Since study was generally full-time and often relatively costly, emphasis on the education of the young adult inevitably excluded other groups from participation in higher education.

Of course, there were always exceptions to this generalization. The tradition of university extension work goes back at least to the last century in many countries, with its aims of providing education to the surrounding community, often related to very specific vocational needs – for example, the needs of local farmers. Departments of extension or continuing education were generally distinctive entities, with their own administrative structures, programmes and staff, although regular university faculty were often called upon to take part in teaching courses. Typically, programmes offered through extension were not for academic credit and were perceived – accurately – as quite different from the mainstream teaching activities of the institution. Indeed, Marriott (1982) pointed out that the extension movement, as conceived in Victorian England, was directed towards the moral improvement of the working class, without any intention of elevating working people in social rank. Hence, the rejection of diplomas and certificates and the stress upon 'disinterested' study; two aspects that survive to this day.

While this impetus may in some ways be commendable (eg it gets around the problem of possible confusion between working for a qualification and learning something intrinsically worth while), traditional extension programmes have not been without their critics. For example, Hoggart, Stephens, Taylor and Smethurst (1982) argued that, in the UK, there is a latent demand for continuing education that is not being met by traditional mechanisms. They echoed the point made in Chapter 1 that rapid technological change has produced an urgent need for lifelong education, in contrast to the 'front-end loaded' model favoured by the higher education establishment (meaning provision of full-time courses for 18–24-year-olds). Hoggart *et al* made a further criticism that university extension departments suffer as a result of their status as separate units outside the regular academic programmes, and called for the integration of continuing education with the routine work of teaching departments, where it would become the responsibility of all staff. The continuing relevance of this issue is shown by the emergence of the development of self-directed learners as the main goal of modern adult education (Kegan, 1994).

One way of increasing access to higher education is to offer opportunities for part-time study, whereby individuals may, for example, take courses while still holding a job. This apparently simple expedient is, surprisingly, extremely difficult in some university systems, for example, in traditional British universities (Hubert, 1989). In German universities, the proportion of students in some disciplines who are actually *de facto* part-time students is as high as 75 per cent. Nonetheless, the official system usually ignores this, most universities insisting, for instance, that students take all final exams within a single exam period of three months, even if they are working full time.

In systems where programmes of study are compartmentalized into smaller course units, each awarding academic credit and evaluated separately, it is perhaps easier to accommodate students who wish to take only part of a programme. Hence, part-time students have been relatively common for many years in North America and indeed it has been quite usual to offer special courses to meet their needs – at night or in off-campus locations, frequently arranged under the auspices of the extension department. More recently, there has been a growth of programmes and even institutions that cater specifically for part-time study, for example, distance education programmes and open learning institutions, which will be discussed further in Chapter 5.

Mature students

Part-time students are not merely different in terms of their patterns of attendance at college and university. Not surprisingly, such students have many other characteristics that distinguish them from traditional full-time undergraduates. For example, they are frequently older, are more likely to hold full-time jobs, and are more likely to be married and have children (Maslen, 1982). As mentioned above, so-called 'mature' students (usually implying in North America people who have passed their mid-20s and have discontinued formal education after secondary schooling) are not a new phenomenon in higher education. Many North American institutions have had special programmes for such students for many years, often involving the waiving of normal admission criteria (perhaps with some type of aptitude test serving as a substitute). However, the great majority of such programmes typically have had the goal of assimilating older students into regular university degree courses. If any special provisions were made for mature students, they were likely to be in the nature of a modest counselling service that might give advice on choice of classes, help with study skills and so on.

In the past few years, however, older students have been courted with increasing fervency by some US colleges and universities, which have seen this group as a heaven-sent solution to the problem of declining enrolments among traditional-age students. The US population is aging and the median age is now over 34, and by 2000 will be over 37, compared with a median of only 27 in 1970 (Ostar, 1981). In 1972, 29 per cent of students in US higher education were over 24 years of age. Six years later this figure had risen to 35 per cent and currently is 50 per cent, with about 70 per cent of those enrolled part time. On the other hand, the population of 18–24-year-olds peaked in 1981 (it is now on the rise again), and it is for this reason that in the past two decades mature students were seen as a potential 'new market' for higher education.

Often overlooked is the fact that this new student population may, as has already been pointed out, have substantially different learning needs from the traditional undergraduate. To cite just a few obvious examples, there is a need for much greater flexibility in the times and locations at which instruction is offered. Adult students may drop in and out of courses in a manner that is incompatible with an orderly, concentrated, and lock-step curriculum. Perhaps more important, the mature student may approach the learning process itself in a markedly different manner. Ostar (1981) commented that adult learners appear to be concerned about aspects of their lives that have not typically been regarded as 'academic' – emotional, interpersonal, spiritual and social factors – although it is possible that mature students are simply focusing new attention on aspects of learning that are important for *all*, but have traditionally been overlooked.

In Germany, it is commonplace for students in certain disciplines to be much older than their Anglo-American counterparts, and many students (perhaps 25 percent) in more highly sought-after programmes are aged in their thirties and forties. This is partly an unintended side-effect of admission policies. Since there is heavy competition for places in these programmes, admission is administered centrally by a national admissions office, and is based essentially on marks in the matriculation examination (*Abitur*). However, *Wartezeit* – the number of semesters since obtaining the *Abitur* – is also taken into account. The older you are, the better your chances of being admitted, even with a lower *Abitur* grade. Coupled with this is the fact that many people working in life- and social-science areas – such as mental health assistants, community care workers or nurses – become aware of the desire for a more theoretical and scientific underpinning of their practical work only after several years in work settings. In the case of psychology, for example, because of the absence until 1998 of legislation governing the practice of the profession, many people may have worked for a number of years as counsellors or therapists, and may regard themselves as 'real' psychologists. This desire to obtain a scientific underpinning for practical experience is a common motivation for mature-age students seeking admission without the *Abitur* such as psychiatric nurses (see below).

There are also numbers of people who, having raised several children, become interested in areas such as child development, and now wish to study in more depth. In other words, without any deliberate intention, German universities have implemented through the back door a method of selecting students for some disciplines in which relevant life experience or work in an area precedes university training, rather than following it as in the front-end model. However, this fact is largely ignored by the institutions and politicians. Not only is no credit given for life or professional experience, but there is constant concern about the very high average age of German students.

Admission policies and procedures

Numerous attempts have been made in various countries to broaden the range of students attending college and university, using a variety of different mechanisms – financial, political and social. It is important to bear in mind that general consensus about the importance of equality of opportunity to enter post-secondary institutions can mask fundamental disagreements about who in society – and how many – can benefit from higher education. Hence there are very wide discrepancies between different countries in the proportion of school-leavers entering university: In North America, for example, the ratio is about double that of most Western European nations. However, simply allowing more students into higher education does not in itself guarantee true equality of opportunity. Even in Canada, where almost half of eligible school-leavers go on to college or university, this group is by no means representative of the general population, but rather is drawn disproportionately from upper socio-economic groups (Anisef, Okihiro and James, 1982).

The mechanisms for controlling who enters university vary from one system to another. Many European nations have public examinations, such as the A level in the UK, the French *baccalauréat* or the German *Abitur.* In North America, entrance requirements usually require successful completion of specified subjects in high school, depending upon the programme of study. Since high school marks are usually awarded by individual teachers, there are wide differences between schools, and some North American universities have their own clandestine systems for adjusting marks, based upon previous experience with undergraduates from the schools concerned. The Scholastic Aptitude Test (SAT) is also used widely in the USA as an important additional screening device for university admission, although it has been challenged in recent years on the grounds that it discriminates against certain minority groups.

Despite these differences in methods of student selection, many educational systems have in recent years been moving towards more open admission policies, in an attempt to recruit larger numbers and obtain a wider cross-section of students. There are at least three reasons for this trend. The first is philosophical, and is based on the egalitarian principle that all individuals in society should have the opportunity to enter higher education (even if they subsequently drop out). This is the spirit that guided the open admission experiment at the City University of New York, and the current open admission policies of many community colleges, such as the huge Miami-Dade Community College in Florida. The second reason, more pragmatic, is to increase the numbers and range of student intake in order to produce a more educated population and work-force that can cope with the demands of an increasingly complex society. Both of these ideas are consistent with the basic principles of lifelong education. A final reason, also pragmatic and perhaps a little crass, is to accommodate – or reduce – excess capacity in institutions of higher education. For example, the report of the 1983 Leverhulme study of British higher education pointed out that British colleges and universities would have to adapt to the needs of new types of student if they were to avoid substantial excess capacity (Leverhulme, 1983).

A combination of these reasons provided the impetus for changing admission standards, and helped stimulate the great expansion of higher education during the 1960s and 1970s. In the UK, for example, the Robbins report of 1963 proposed that the provision of places in higher education should be determined by the demand for qualified school leavers who were willing to enter degree-level courses. This rationale was accepted by subsequent national governments, and was the direct cause of the huge growth in British higher education, including the establishment of many new universities and polytechnics (most of which have now become universities).

Twenty years later, the Leverhulme Foundation sponsored the far-reaching study of higher education that has been referred to above. The final report (Leverhulme, 1983) addressed the question of access to higher education. While the authors welcomed the expansion of part-time and non-degree courses outside universities, they commented that the marked differences in participation rates between various social and economic groups, mentioned two decades earlier by Robbins, still remained. Indeed, they pointed out that in some ways the problem of equal opportunity had been exacerbated since the Robbins report. For example, the UK had become more ethnically diverse, and many minorities were poorly represented in higher education; the proportion of women students had risen but was still not equal to the rate of participation by men; disparities persisted in participation rates between different regions of the country and so on.

To quote another European example, in the late 1960s Sweden embarked upon a radical and far-reaching reform of its educational system. Important components of the reorganization were a policy of open admissions, abolition of tuition fees (indeed generous provisions for additional economic support where necessary), and implementation of a system of recurrent education that was intended to provide opportunities for higher education at various intervals throughout an individual's life. The Swedish National Board of Colleges and Universities (Universitets- och Högskoleämbetet) has been carrying out a comprehensive evaluation of the reform since it was initiated, but it is still not known how successful the changes have been in achieving the goal of democratizing higher education and improving learning skills across the Swedish population. Certainly, there is controversy among teaching staff in Swedish colleges and universities concerning the success of the reform, although it is not clear how much this is based upon objective evidence as opposed to a wistful desire to return to the halcyon days of the 1950s and early 1960s.

Several German states have introduced provision for admission without the *Abitur* of mature students who have a vocational qualification such as nursing or carpentry and five years' work experience. In general, such candidates must take a special admission examination that aims at establishing whether they possess the thinking skills and abilities, and the personal characteristics regarded as necessary for successful tertiary study (eg command of the German language, goal-directed motivation, ability to construct a logical argument). However, mature-age applicants do not have to demonstrate specific knowledge of the discipline they wish to study. People with an advanced vocational qualification may be exempted from the examination altogether, and merely be required to show that university study constitutes a logical extension of the non-university qualification they already possess. An example of a successful candidate in this latter category at the University of Hamburg is a master butcher (a man who had completed an apprenticeship, obtained a tradesperson's certificate, studied further and completed the qualification of master tradesman). He developed an interest in the relationship between meat consumption and social class over the past 2,000 years, and applied successfully for admission to the Department of Sociology, graduating in the minimum time with a high grade-point average.

Interest in admission to higher education based on something other than formal examinations at the end of 12 or 13 years of secondary schooling is not confined to Europe. In Australia, although there is a unified national system of tertiary education, there is still room for considerable local variation in admission procedures. In 1998, the Flinders University of South Australia announced that it was reviewing its method of selecting new students, previously based on academic achievement and, in particular, on a formal examination at the end of the twelfth year of school. The intention is to take account of other criteria such as work portfolios. This review reflected the widespread feeling that grades in the senior matriculation exam do not necessarily identify the students with the highest potential for benefiting from tertiary education.

The situation in the USA is highly diverse, with a wide range of types of higher education, sizes of institution and financing arrangements. It is not surprising, therefore, that the move to more open admission standards has been piecemeal. Some radical experiments have taken place and indeed are still continuing, as mentioned above. On the other hand, other trials with open admission have been abandoned, including the one at the City University of New York. To oversimplify, the sudden change to a policy of admitting all-comers threatened to overwhelm the system both organizationally and financially.

There are yet other difficulties with open admission policies. For example, certain specialized degree programmes, such as medicine, dentistry or architecture, are very much in demand, and are also extremely expensive. For this reason – and because most societies can employ only limited numbers of doctors, dentists and architects – it is common to find limitations on entry to professional programmes, even where the general institutional policy may call for open admissions.

In the USA, in order to provide more equal opportunities for different ethnic groups, affirmative action policies were introduced. This involved taking fixed quotas of minorities into certain programmes, despite the fact that they might have lower academic entry qualifications, at least according to traditional measures of achievement. For example, Title IX of the Education Amendment, 1972, bars sex bias in federally assisted programmes and activities (Fields, 1983). Affirmative action has always been controversial, especially among some students who feel they have been excluded from higher education by such policies. A well-known example was provided by the 'Bakke case' in which a student brought a successful action against the University of California at Davis on the grounds that he had been excluded from medical school when his academic qualifications were superior to those of other accepted students. The institution was compelled to admit Bakke to the medical programme (and in fact he graduated in 1982).

Another example of controversy surrounding changes in admission policies involved the reforms to higher education proposed by the French government, which were intended to allow initial entry to university for all students with a completed high school *baccalauréat*, while at the same time providing more rigid selection procedures at the end of the second year of study. The stated aim here was to introduce greater democracy into French higher education and to reduce class barriers, as well as to produce a larger number of skilled professional and technical workers. The reform generated violent opposition (including street riots) during the spring and summer of 1983 from both left- and right-wing student organizations. Students from the right protested that increasing access to fields such as law and economics would dilute the quality of education and lower the status of their degrees, while students from the left protested on exactly opposite grounds – that their choices of programme would be more strictly limited by the selection procedures proposed after the second year (Dickson, 1983).

Very recently in South Australia, the release of information on admissions to medical school for the 1999 university year led to considerable debate. As a rule, students in Australia enter medical school directly from high school, and the number of applicants far exceeds the number of places available. As in all but one other Australian university, the University of Adelaide no longer selects medical students solely on the basis of school grades, but since 1996 has made use of a combination of academic standing, an aptitude test (the Undergraduate Medicine and Health Sciences Admission Test) and interviews. The latter two procedures attempt to identify an applicant's personal qualities such as compassion, empathy or dedication, as well as problem-solving ability, communication skills and ability to work in teams. It is argued that these and not sheer academic brilliance are crucial for success in the real-life practice of medicine, although candidates must still achieve grades in the top 10 per cent. The policy has led to a substantial increase in the representation of certain groups among medical students (eg high school graduates from remote rural settings), and academic staff are reported to have observed no drop in academic performance of students.

Teaching and learning activities

Many changes of a kind regarded here as desirable have already occurred in contemporary institutions of higher education. Yet many traditional elements of teaching and learning activities still predominate, often with negative effects for the implementation of the principles of lifelong education.

The predominance of the lecture

The rich variety of instructional methods in higher education that seem to be particularly appropriate for the encouragement of lifelong learning skills will be reviewed in Chapter 5. These innovations should be seen, however, in the context of prevailing approaches to university and college teaching, which depend very heavily upon the lecture and, to a lesser extent, on the tutorial and formal laboratory. As Kozma, Belle and Williams (1978) noted in their comprehensive review of instructional techniques in higher education, 'For good or ill, the lecture hall remains the chief and usual meeting place for teachers and students' (p 145). In a similar vein, Eble (1972) concluded, on the basis of his study of 70 colleges and universities in the USA, that teaching in higher education primarily involves a single faculty member giving lectures to fairly large groups of students. Almost 30 years later, the lecture still predominates. Bligh (1998) stated that 'Lecturing is still the most common method when teaching adults. In spite of educational research and changing technology, surveys over the decades show remarkably little change' (p 6).

The lecture is one of the oldest types of teaching, and was used in higher education long before the development of the printed book. Indeed, in talking about the possible impact of information technology on higher education, some cynical observers have commented that the university may take the leap from oral to electronic transmission of information, having virtually ignored the use of print as a primary means for teaching. Clearly, this is an exaggeration and it is important to recognize that the lecture is only one component of a teaching method that involves the use of textbooks, library resources and so on. Nonetheless, a great amount of time is spent by students listening to lectures, which in many institutions are regarded as the most important means of communicating information. The very title 'lecturer', which has widespread currency for university teachers all over the world, is perhaps an indication of what type of teaching is expected, and for many academics and students 'lecture' is synonymous with 'class' and 'teaching'.

The ubiquitous nature of lecturing appears to be so much taken for granted that there is a paucity of empirical evidence on the actual teaching methods used in higher education. One of the few studies that attempted to gather hard evidence about teaching approaches reported the results of a survey at a large metropolitan university in the USA with a population of 13,000 students and 400 faculty (Evans and Leppman, 1968). Classroom lectures were ranked as the most used and most preferred teaching method by instructors, and ranked in second place by the students. More recently Knapper (1990) found the lecture method was used by over 90 per cent of faculty he surveyed in two large universities in Canada and Australia. Evans and Leppmann conducted informal interviews at nine further campuses and were able to confirm their original results. They commented (pp 56–7) that their results 'indicate a preference by professors for those methods which cast the university teacher in his traditional role: standing before the class, giving a lecture, using the blackboard, assigning some outside homework, and occasionally giving a classroom demonstration ... the students pretty much agreed with their professors about these methods'.

Despite this apparent satisfaction with traditional methods, criticism of the lecture technique has existed since the Middle Ages (Kozma, Belle and Williams, 1978). Arguments against the lecture are that it involves a passive approach to learning, and is largely out of the control of the student (see Cropley and Kahl's, 1983, recommendation that certain aspects of distance learning be adopted in face-to-face settings). Such criticisms have some support from empirical literature about the effectiveness of the lecture in comparison with other teaching methods. Bligh (1998) summarized the results of a large number of studies on the effectiveness of lectures for several different goals, including the acquisition of information, promotion of thought and changes in attitude. On the basis of his comprehensive analysis, he concluded that the lecture can be about as effective as other methods (eg classroom discussions) for transmitting information, but that for achieving higher-level conceptual skills most lectures are not as effective as active learning approaches. In addition, lectures are relatively ineffective for changing attitudes or fostering personal or social adjustment in students.

From the point of view of our interest in promoting lifelong learning skills, Bligh's findings on what he calls 'the promotion of thought' are of particular significance. He comments (p 15) that:

> if students are to learn to think, they must be placed in situations where they have to do so... The best way to learn to solve problems is to be given problems that have to be solved... If this thesis seems obvious common sense, it should be remembered that some people place faith in their lectures to stimulate thought and expect thinking skills to be absorbed, like some mystical vapours, from an academic atmosphere... Learning to think is not an absorption process.

Bligh even took issue with the conclusion of Evans and Leppmann, reported above, that the lecture is a popular teaching method for students. Citing evidence from several British studies, he concluded that on the whole lectures are less popular with students than other more active approaches. Lindquist (1978) supported this contention, and went further by pointing out that the very size, impersonality and traditionalism of many universities in the USA has led to student disenchantment with their teaching. Lindquist carried out surveys of students on a number of campuses and found that many of them believed their teaching to be 'too uniformly didactic', their learning 'too passive' and their teachers often too 'soporific'.

Despite this indictment, Bligh and Kozma, Belle and Williams were forced to admit that getting faculty to change from the lecture method (either by adapting it to allow for more student interaction or by replacing it with other, more active teaching methods) often meets with considerable resistance. It is often argued that the lecture is inexpensive, since it rarely involves equipment costs and allows a single teacher to address large numbers of students simultaneously. The lecture also makes fewer demands on the instructor's time, both in terms of interacting with students and in preparation for teaching, compared to, say, project-based learning (as discussed in Chapter 5). It seems likely, however, that the lecture has retained its prominence simply because it is the method that university teachers were themselves exposed to as students. Since the great majority of university lecturers receive no instruction in methods of teaching and learning, it is hardly surprising that they use the only role models available to them from their own higher education.

Laboratory instruction

While most concern about traditional teaching methods in higher education has focused upon the lecture, the formal laboratory is also not without its critics. Elton (1983), for example, discussed the high costs involved
in teaching practical work in laboratories, and also summarized the dissatisfaction with the method that has been expressed on both sides of the
Atlantic. A major concern here is that student work in the laboratory frequently gives a false impression of how science is carried out, how problems are solved and discoveries made. This is thought to be because of the
artificial constraints within the laboratory – the need for students to work
on set exercises within limited time periods. All too often, undue emphasis
is placed upon the importance of getting the correct result, as opposed to
the process of investigation, and the impression is given that science is a
neat, cut-and-dried means of arriving at elegant solutions.

Pickering (1980), in a provocative article in the *Chronicle of Higher
Education*, asked whether lab courses were a waste of time, and this provoked a lengthy and sometimes vituperative correspondence in the
Chronicle's subsequent issues. One correspondent, in an ironic defence
of the formal laboratory, justified the method as part of a long-standing
religious ritual in science teaching. McConnell, in his 1980 presidential
address to the Division on Teaching Psychology of the American Psychological Association, presented a wry but disturbing account of his experiences as a distinguished professor who returned to the classroom to
study medicine at the University of Michigan, and encountered at first
hand the problems of coping with the weekly lab. Among the many problems revealed by McConnell's account was the frequent failure of lecturers to be aware of the real learning processes at work in the laboratory,
and the discrepancy between the learning that took place and the
instructional aims for practical classes. This situation is often exacerbated by the lack of frequent and careful liaison between the course
instructor and the laboratory demonstrators who run the labs and are
frequently drawn from the ranks of graduate students (McConnell,
1980).

Hazel and Baillie (1998) summarized the problems with traditional
labs, especially as they relate to learning goals and outcomes:

- Learning goals for the lab are often not made explicit to students
  and are sometimes not even clear to the teacher.
- Goals are often too diffuse, while some goals are not exclusive to
  labs and could be attained more efficiently elsewhere.
- Labs and the way they are assessed often emphasize low-level
  learning and discourage understanding of links between methods
  and theory.

- Assessment of labs often fails to test whether goals have been attained (and some students do well without even attending the lab!).
- Students often find cookbook labs tedious and do not take them seriously.

To this may be added the criticism that feedback to students on effective performance in labs is often lacking, and hence there is little chance for reflection and improvement in the problem-solving skills that laboratory work is supposed to encourage.

Hazel and Baillie went on to offer suggestions for improving the quality of learning in laboratories, many of which are consistent with the principles of lifelong learning; for example by introducing projects that require students to work more autonomously and in collaborative teams, use of peer assessment, learning portfolios and reflective journals. Other writers who have offered ideas for reform of labs to enhance higher-level learning objectives include Boud, Dunn and Hegarty-Hazel (1986) and Gibbs and Jacques (1990).

The special problem of professional education

The efficiency of traditional teaching methods has been a particular concern within professional higher education, where the defects resulting from inadequate preparation appear quite quickly and distinctly once graduates embark upon their careers. For example, dissatisfaction has been expressed with medical education, especially its emphasis on scientific and medical detail (taught primarily through lectures) as opposed to clinical skills learnt through practical experience.

Criticism of medical education goes back almost 70 years, when the Association of American Medical Colleges (AAMC) published its first report on the training of physicians in the USA (Rappleye, 1932). Half a century later Wallis (1983) reported that not much had changed; medical school deans and faculty were increasingly expressing disquiet about producing narrow-minded graduates who had little perspective on the facts they had memorized – facts that threatened to overwhelm the learner, despite the fact that they contributed little to successful medical practice. Around the same time comparable criticisms were made about medical education in West Germany, where a great deal of learning was said to consist of 'piecemeal acquisition of unrelated, detailed, factual subject matter' (Kloss, 1982). Kloss regretted that the vast number of medical students in Germany had made more active types of learning (eg in small tutorial groups) virtually non-existent, and he claimed that many students had never had the opportunity to examine a patient.

In 1984, the AAMC issued its report on 'Physicians for the twenty-first century' that contained sweeping recommendations for reform of curriculum and teaching methods to place much greater emphasis on real-world diagnostic and communication skills (AAMC, 1984). However, although substantial changes have taken place in medical education worldwide in the past two decades, especially the introduction of problem-based learning (see Chapter 5), in 1992 the Association was still dissatisfied with progress being made (AAMC, 1992). Its report on change in medical education described what it calls the 'disturbing reality' that 'over the last 60 years, most medical schools have done little to correct the major shortcomings in the way they educate their students' (p xi). The Association was equally concerned with the way most colleges evaluate student achievement and urged that assessment procedures move away from methods 'that stress recognition or memorization of facts to those that assess the behaviors and skills important for physicians' (p 29). They recommended a new attempt to foster self-directed and lifelong learning skills, including information management, pointing out that much of what medical students are taught in their first year of study is already out of date by the time they graduate. While the report recognized that many medical schools had adopted problem-based learning approaches, further progress was inhibited by reluctance of faculty to move away from a role of information provider to one of learning facilitator.

The 1993 World Summit on Medical Education also made a series of recommendations on future directions for the training of physicians, and that same year the General Medical Council did the same for medical education in Britain. The GMC recognized that 'a significant proportion of traditional medical education is overloaded with factual material which is frequently taught out of context and in large didactic lectures' (Exley and Dennick, 1996, p 6). Such a system was seen as discouraging higher-order cognitive functions, such as evaluation, synthesis and problem-solving, and engendering an attitude of passivity. Exley and Dennick (1996, p 6) recommended a move towards lifelong learning principles and 'an attitude of reflective practice... With rapid changes taking place in medical sciences doctors of the future need to be able to educate themselves to deal with new conceptual discoveries as well as new clinical skills, treatments and technologies'.

Turning to a different type of professional education, Broderick (1983) surveyed 300 Honeywell managers in an attempt to gain insights into the type of education and training they had received and its relevance to their current management tasks. He found that only a small fraction of an individual's management techniques had been learnt in the classroom, and he estimated that perhaps 80 per cent of real learning came from contact with other people and on-the-job experience. Somewhat similar conclusions were reached by Howard (1986) in a longitudinal study of the relationship between college experiences and managerial performance at AT&T.

Recent discussions of engineering education have emphasized the importance of the kind of skills and abilities described in Chapter 3 (eg ability to think autonomously, to solve problems, to cope with the unexpected). These are seen as crucial for innovation and regarded as a key but neglected element of engineering curricula (Steiner, 1998). The importance of training in innovative thinking is underlined by the fact that corporations, especially in the USA, are now spending billions of dollars on providing such training outside engineering schools, in effect introducing their own variant of lifelong education. Steiner saw failure to introduce such training into engineering education as depriving students of vital qualifications needed for career enrichment and advancement.

Specialization and integration: interdisciplinary studies

A different aspect of university and college teaching that relates to the goals of lifelong education is the question of specialization and fragmentation of content, as opposed to integrating insights from a variety of disciplines. This is a concern within individual disciplines (Solomon *et al*, 1982), within broader areas (such as the humanities, natural sciences etc) and across the entire curriculum.

Candy, Crebert and O'Leary (1994, p 43) gave great weight to the importance of 'deep' learning, especially the acquisition of transferable knowledge and skills. Nonetheless, they saw this as resting upon a foundation of domain-specific knowledge. Thus, they did not reject out of hand the idea of individual disciplines, as some earlier protagonists of interdisciplinary studies had done. Their model (p 66) of the undergraduate curriculum defined a hierarchical relationship between four elements:

1. domain-specific knowledge and skills;
2. 'contextual' elements;
3. generic or transferable knowledge and skills;
4. lifelong learning knowledge and skills.

They saw no difficulty with domain-specific knowledge, but rather in the hierarchical organization of knowledge. At present, teaching and learning is often preoccupied almost exclusively with discipline-specific content, while generic and lifelong learning knowledge and skills are merely a hoped-for, more or less incidental outcome derived from the process of acquiring the material of the discipline (in those cases where they are given any conscious attention at all). By contrast, Candy *et al* called for forms of teaching and learning in which lifelong learning knowledge and skills define the *core content* of university classes, generic elements the next level, with disciplinary content and contextual studies lying at the surface.

Some institutions have attempted to break down the disciplinary structures by employing organizational systems that are not based upon traditional departments. For example, both the authors of this book were once on the staff of a Canadian university established in the mid-1960s with a curriculum and organizational structure that was intended to foster integration. Originally all courses were offered within a single Faculty of Arts and Science; there were no departments as such, but 'divisions', including social science, fine arts and so on. An attempt was made to recruit staff who could transcend disciplinary boundaries in their teaching and who believed in the set of goals spelt out for the institution. Within a few years, however, the university had reverted to an almost entirely traditional system of discipline-based departments, each with its own 'major' and distinctive curriculum. The divisions were abandoned, and even the Faculty of Arts and Science split into its two component parts. The reasons appear to be those mentioned above, stimulated by the infusion of increasing numbers of teaching staff with traditional values during the university's rapid expansion in the late 1960s.

This is not to say that interdisciplinary integration is impossible, or that all attempts to foster it are doomed to failure. Notable examples remain, including the Faculty of Medicine at McMaster University, Ontario, Roskilde University in Denmark and Evergreen College in Washington State. Many of the successful experiments include a curriculum that involves students in tackling problems rather than mastering traditional bodies of subject matter from particular disciplines. Some of these experiments and the factors determining their success will be examined in Chapter 5.

Other approaches of a more limited nature include a requirement that students take part in an interdisciplinary course or courses (often at the beginning of their programme of study) but within the context of an otherwise traditional institution and discipline-based programme. One example of this type was the University of Keele's foundation year (just abandoned after 49 years), in which first-year students worked on a set of issues or problems that, by their nature, transcended disciplinary boundaries. A similar approach is exemplified by the University Foundation Units offered at Murdoch University in Western Australia, required for all beginning students, and intended to ensure all undergraduates have an experience of interdisciplinary study. The units explore themes of topical significance (examples include 'Age of Information', 'Evolution, Revolution and Choice') that are generally new to the students who take them. Tutors for the foundation units take part in a five-year induction programme to help ensure that the learning environment is truly interdisciplinary.

In view of the dissatisfaction with a good deal of professional education mentioned above, it comes as no surprise that there have been calls to move away from specialization. This was one of the recommendations of the Leverhulme Study (1983), whose authors talked of the need to reduce over-specialization, both in the secondary school system and in the early years of higher education. They pointed to the advantage of integrated degree courses in which students could be exposed to the methods and concepts of different disciplines. They also argued that the ability to integrate different ideas was justified not simply on philosophical grounds, but also had practical advantages, since jobs in future decades would require individuals who have the broad, general aptitudes that interdisciplinarity and integration imply.

The Leverhulme proposal to deal with this situation involved replacing the traditional British three- or four-year honours (specialized) degree programmes with a basic initial course of two years, or the part-time equivalent. They argued that a short initial and general course – providing there were possibilities for credit transfer between institutions, and entry requirements for subsequent courses were fairly open – would allow students the flexibility of tailoring higher education to meet their own particular needs and interests. Presumably, too, students would not be locked into a premature choice of discipline, and perhaps career, as often happens in the traditional British degree system.

The idea of a two-year initial course at a general level, which could subsequently lead to specialized training at a higher level, is comparable to the system prevailing in many parts of North America. Students enrol in a two-year programme, sometimes in a community college, and then go on to take an undergraduate degree at university. The Leverhulme proposal was criticized in the UK, on the grounds that the two-year qualification would have low status and might be 'relegated' to certain institutions, leaving the more prestigious universities to continue offering traditional discipline-based education. Thirty years later, the idea of a widely available two-year degree has been largely forgotten, although universities have moved towards more flexible programmes of study with increased possibilities for credit transfer and part-time attendance.

Of more importance for this study is the criticism that the Leverhulme recommendation spoke primarily to the question of content and organization, rather than educational process. It seems rather naïve to expect that the mere provision of a general programme would necessarily ensure the integration the study group valued so highly. This would require changes in approaches to teaching and learning to achieve this which, in turn, would have to be based upon increased knowledge about the process of learning as well as flexible attitudes on the part of instructional staff. In fact, such concerns were voiced in some of the individual reports commissioned by the Leverhulme organization (Bligh, 1982), but the ideas raised here with regard to methods of teaching and assessment were not given the prominence they deserved in the final Leverhulme report.

The role of instructors

Achieving radical changes in teaching and learning activities would depend to a considerable degree upon acceptance of an altered role for instructors in colleges and universities. For example, in a system of lifelong education, teachers would be seen more as guides or helpers than as authoritative sources of all knowledge. Staff are thus important not only because they specify content and teaching and learning strategies, as well as assessing students' work, but also because, on the one hand, they establish what Candy, Crebert and O'Leary (1994, p 39) called the 'climate', and on the other hand, they act as models. This means, among other things, that it is important that they show curiosity and passion, and are themselves obviously lifelong learners. It might be expected that they would try to involve practitioners or experts, especially people from real-life settings where the knowledge and skills being transmitted find their application. Another possibility is that instructors and students could work together in areas where neither are expert. This was the basis of Keele's Foundation Year, mentioned above, in which small groups of staff and students explored topics that lay outside the teacher's own expertise. This approach has been adopted in other British universities, as well as in universities elsewhere in the Commonwealth, such as Zambia. Equally important, if university teachers are to function effectively as lifelong educators, they themselves would have to engage in a process of lifelong learning. In fact, most university teachers already do this in their role as scholars and researchers, where updating knowledge and skills is an essential part of remaining current in the field. In the case of teaching, however, there is often little ongoing professional development, although with the growth of instructional development centres in many universities (see Chapter 6) this situation may be slowly changing.

Adopting teaching approaches consistent with lifelong learning may clash with some of the more traditional functions of universities. Although the early universities were primarily teaching institutions, the members of the community of scholars were, by definition, experts in their subject areas, and hence the academy was a custodian and repository, as well as a purveyor, of knowledge. Thus, research in the sense of reflective inquiry has always been a characteristic of higher education, even though the tradition of scientific empirical research developed rather later – notably in the German universities of the mid-19th century. Most universities in the developed Western nations (plus many more outside this geographical region) are active in research – both reflective and empirical – and teaching. A faculty member's duties at the University of Toronto, Hamburg or Harvard will normally involve some teaching and some research, plus the expectation of administrative service to the institution and possibly some type of service to the wider community. In many of the technical institutions much greater emphasis is placed upon teaching, in some cases to the exclusion of empirical research.

Concern with lifelong education and the promotion of lifelong learning skills in students, implies the need for considerable faculty emphasis upon teaching methods and the organization of instruction, yet in many institutions this requirement may conflict with the need for faculty to devote large amounts of time to research. This is a particular concern in an academic environment where the greatest professional rewards are accorded to accomplishments in scholarship and publication, as opposed to teaching and curriculum development (Knapper, 1997). The situation is compounded further by the fact that in the great majority of universities the faculty have no preparatory training in methods of teaching and learning. It is sometimes argued that the research activities of faculty are beneficial to their teaching, in the sense that active researchers are more up to date and involved. Unfortunately, the empirical evidence suggests that this is by no means always the case (Friedrich and Michalak, 1983; Linsky and Straus, 1975; Task Force on Resource Allocation, 1994). It is not our purpose here to deny the value of university research or to argue against the involvement of university teachers in active scholarship. We merely wish to draw attention to university roles and functions that place constraints on the time and attention that can be devoted to the encouragement of lifelong learning. This question will be returned to in Chapter 6 when the role of educational development activities in the promotion of lifelong learning will be discussed.

One reaction to the preoccupation of many North American academics with research and publication was the highly influential attempt by the Carnegie Foundation to redefine scholarship to include a 'scholarship of teaching'. The intention was to encourage teachers to reflect on and document their practice so as to continually improve the quality of student learning, in particular to 'encourage students to be critical, creative thinkers, with the capacity to go on learning after their college days are over' (Boyer, 1990, p 24). A key question here is whether faculty will be prepared to give up their traditional role as experts and instead become facilitators and mentors, helping students to take a more active role in directing their own learning. Heerman, Enders and Wine (1980, p 9) commented that 'at the heart of the matter is the question of whether the traditional roles of the classroom teacher and the campus will change in response to an emerging generation of learners and learning needs which are neither sequential, predictable, nor orderly in the manner to which educators have become accustomed'.

Some 15 years, later Barr and Tagg (1995) called for a paradigm shift away from a focus on *instruction* (eg through teaching that is largely based on lectures conveying traditional content) to a *learning paradigm*. Here the purpose of a university 'is not to transfer knowledge but to create environments and experiences that bring students to discover and construct knowledge for themselves, to make students members of communities of learners that make discoveries and solve problems' (p 15). Many of the characteristics of the learning paradigm defined by Barr and Tagg are consistent with the principles of lifelong learning we set out in Chapter 3. For example, they call for learning that is holistic, values any learning method that works (whatever the source of instruction), is responsive to societal needs, is available at times convenient to the learner not the institution, involves collaboration with other learners, recognizes individual student differences, is empowering and so on. Barr and Tagg's paper has provoked considerable debate in North American higher education, and the authors admit that there are formidable institutional and attitudinal barriers to change in the direction they recommend. We offer some strategies for such change in subsequent chapters.

Evaluation and certification

If only to facilitate student transfer from one institution or department to another, it seems inevitable that a system of lifelong education will have to make appropriate provision for examination and certification of student achievement. Indeed, Pineau (1980) made the point that certificates, even of a relatively traditional kind, would continue to be important in a system of lifelong education. This is because a mechanism to certify that certain learning has occurred makes the knowledge 'portable'. Without such certification, the danger exists that new knowledge and skills acquired in the course of lifelong learning would be negotiable only in the precise setting where the learning took place. A concrete example of the problem of certification is the difficulty being experienced by open entry programmes in assigning credit for learning taking place outside traditional institutions.

It is also important to note that formal qualifications in the form of certificates, credits and so on are not only important for the purposes of educational institutions, but that learners themselves are usually eager to obtain some kind of paper qualification. This is because they are aware that a certificate or similar tangible result of some learning activity can lead to job advancement or other material advantages. As Cropley and Dave (1984) pointed out in a summary of several studies on in-service training of teachers, potential clients are keenly interested in the question of whether or not a particular learning activity culminates in some kind of examination or other formal evaluation, because they have learnt in the past that 'serious' learning activities are usually concluded in this way. Students usually want to take part in learning activities that are academically respectable, and they equate respectability with a formal evaluation. Activities that yield a certificate or diploma based on measurable achievement (such as an exam) are thus regarded as especially worth while.

The tradition in higher education

The credentialling function is a familiar one in institutions of higher education. While teaching is perhaps their major activity, an equally important, related task involves the certification that learning has taken place. The role of colleges and universities in granting appropriate credentials to graduates has a very long tradition in higher education and operates through the award of degrees, diplomas, certificates and so on. In North America, most institutions go further by awarding credits for each component (course) that makes up a programme, and in many instances these credits have a 'value' and may be transferred to another institution. The credentials awarded by universities in some instances constitute quite specific licences to enter and practise a profession – as in the case of architecture, medicine, engineering and so on. Other qualifications are less closely tied to particular professions or careers, and yet in practice may be used by employers as indicators of general competence and possession of minimum requirements for positions within an organization. The credentialling role of higher education is thus of major importance for society at large, since it serves as a screening mechanism for a very wide variety of occupations. Indeed, the great importance attached to this activity is indicated by the fact that in the USA, for example, there exists a complex mechanism for accrediting the various institutions that provide credentials – the accreditation agencies that ensure the bona fides of colleges and universities within each state. Non-traditional and commercial institutions often lobby hard to achieve accredited status, and their attempts are generally fiercely resisted by the conventional higher education establishment. For example, when the University of Phoenix, an Arizona-based for-profit institution, recently attempted to obtain a licence to offer courses in New Jersey, neighbouring universities and colleges petitioned the state's Commission on Higher Education to deny the application (Selingo, 1998).

In effect, it is assessment methods, rather than stated course objectives, that drive learning; students study what they need to pass tests, and if this requires rote learning, then this will take priority over more lofty lifelong learning goals. This is an example of what Snyder (1971) described as the 'hidden curriculum', which may have little resemblance to the formal course requirements as laid out in course outlines and departmental calendars. Students are often extremely adept at pinpointing what is *really* required to do well in a course, based upon subtle cues from the instructors when they talk about assessment procedures, from inspection of previously used tests, conversations with former students and so on (Becker, Geer and Hughes, 1968; Kuh, 1981; Snyder, 1971).

Students' success at disentangling the hidden curriculum may be reflected in high marks, but these grades may be a poor reflection of the higher-level problem-solving and critical thinking skills that are generally associated with effective lifelong learning. Hence, it is not surprising that, as mentioned earlier, academic grades are poor predictors of success and satisfaction in many careers. Indeed, Heath (1977) showed that college grades and even receipt of college honours were not found to predict measures of adult maturity and competence – if anything, the reverse held true. This seems to raise serious questions about customary methods of teaching and assessing student performance in higher education. Dissatisfaction with assessment practices has continued to the present, and the past 10 years has seen increasing calls for 'alternative assessment' approaches that include performance-based assessment, portfolio assessment and 'authentic' assessment. Indeed, 'alternative assessment' has taken on the trappings of an educational movement (Anderson, 1998) with a focus on dissatisfaction with overuse of lectures and objective tests, the need to cater to more diverse student population and development of constructivist learning theory. The latter emphasizes concrete experience, collaborative discourse and reflection – all characteristics of lifelong learning (Brooks and Brooks, 1993).

Although grading and the award of formal qualifications could not simply be rejected out of hand in a system of lifelong education, for reasons stated earlier in this chapter, it is imperative that they take on different forms from those that predominate at present. The question of certification was discussed from the point of view of lifelong education by Pflüger (1979). He argued that certificates should describe not what level in a system has been reached or what formal examinations have been successfully negotiated, but rather what knowledge and skills have been obtained. For instance, the certificate might refer to a catalogue, in which the things the student has actually learnt to do were listed, rather than simply giving the title of an exam which had been passed. Assessment might also be seen as 'formative' rather than 'summative'. In other words, certificates and academic transcripts may provide a profile of strengths and weaknesses that could be used to plan further learning activities, rather than offering a statement that a particular number of points had been obtained. These assessments could well incorporate both peer- and self-assessment (Candy, Crebert and O'Leary, 1994). Other strategies for improving assessment and its effects on learning are to be found in Knight (1995) and Walvoord and Anderson (1998). These include making better links between learning goals and assessment methods, involving students in discussion of assessment criteria and standards (including through learning contracts), broadening the range of assessment methods (eg through learning portfolios) to include tasks that are more closely related to real-life competency ('authentic assessment'), and providing students with fuller and more timely feedback that might lead to change, reflection and improved learning.

Achieving coordination within and among institutions

A crucial idea in lifelong education is that valid educational opportunities exist outside traditional institutions. One major issue for existing formal institutions of post-school education would thus be how to achieve coordination with the complex array of educational opportunities existing 'outside'. This problem is not simply one of organization (eg ensuring that timetables do not conflict) but is, to a considerable degree, a social-psychological matter, since it would touch upon issues such as status and power, as well as decision making. There is also the need for greater coordination within institutions. Simple examples given by Candy, Crebert and O'Leary (1994) are the need for equal status of the library, study skills units, or learning centres with more traditional learning and teaching units of the university. In general, a much higher level of coordination and cooperation is needed than at present exists between universities and schools (and other providers), government and the community.

One possible administrative/management strategy that might be adopted to foster cooperation among colleges and universities is the exchange of teaching and administrative staff between institutions. For instance, a professor of mechanical engineering might spend a period working with future Industrial Arts teachers. Another possible mechanism for facilitating inter-institutional cooperation involves what Walker (1980) called 'adhocracies'. For example, personnel from industry and commerce could work on a short-term basis with university or college staff to develop a particular programme. A recent Canadian example is the collaboration between Dalhousie University and a large private business to jointly develop and offer a new degree, the Master of Information Technology Education, taught jointly by staff from the university and the private sector. Not to be forgotten in this process are members of the communities in which the institutions concerned are located. Indeed, involvement in decision making of learners themselves as well as members of the community at large is an important principle in lifelong education, and one that seems capable not only of facilitating coordination between different kinds of institution, but also of helping to strengthen links between institutions and the citizens they serve. Of course, many activities along this line already exist. Adoption of lifelong education would not necessarily involve implementation of previously unheard of measures, but rather a strengthening, expansion and improvement of existing procedures.

Administrative constraints

Within individual institutions, many administrative difficulties may be expected to arise. Despite superficial differences, there are often considerable similarities among institutions in such matters as the division of departments and faculties into disciplines, the time needed to complete a degree (in terms of years of study, number and length of terms per year, number of courses per term and so on). Innovative teaching practices that do not mesh with these administrative arrangements will face considerable obstacles to their implementation. Within national boundaries, there is an even more remarkable similarity in administrative structures. Indeed, in North America the credit transfer system virtually demands it. In fact, this often involves a confusion between 'class contact hours' (what elementary school teachers call 'seat time') and the amount of student learning that actually takes place (largely outside the classroom, even in the most traditional of courses). However, knowing this will not help ease the burden of an innovative teacher who wishes to experiment with a new instructional approach.

For example, many relevant teaching methods, such as project-based instruction, do not easily fit into a schedule that requires a class to meet for three separate hours each week over 13 weeks. Field-based teaching, to cite another instance, may depend upon students devoting concentrated blocks of time to learning that take place far from the physical structure of the campus, and this may well conflict with the demands placed on students by other, traditional courses.

In any case, simply 'putting in time' in the classroom may not result in the most effective study, and there is some evidence that heavy student workloads can result in shallower learning (Ramsden and Entwistle, 1981). Changing approaches to student assessment may also present difficulties for institutions that specify a range of possible grades from A to F, calculate grade-point averages to two decimal points, and have the tacit expectation that all instructors will provide a set of marks that is elegantly distributed along a normal curve. It will be seen, for example, that many of the innovations described in Chapter 5 are based upon the concept of 'mastery learning' and the achievement of certain minimum learning criteria in order to guarantee a satisfactory mark (what is known as 'criterion-referenced testing'). This produces skewed grade distributions that tend to disturb department heads and registrars even though in many cases the results of assessment are completely in accordance with the predictions of educational theory. In the case of some other learning approaches, it is regarded as desirable for students to act as assessors, by grading themselves and perhaps their fellow students. This is quite consistent with the way assessment is frequently conducted in non-academic work settings. Once again, however, it is likely to conflict with academic institutional norms.

Even institutional location and architecture can compromise certain educational methods and goals, and it is interesting that some innovative universities (such as Roskilde) have designed environments that break away from the traditional model of small seminar rooms and large classrooms with fixed tiers of seats. Hummel (1977) presented a number of examples of school design that he argued are more suited to lifelong learning concepts (such as the open classroom). We are talking here, however, not merely of physical structures but of a whole administrative ambience that guides the way teaching in higher education is organized. As McCabe (1978) commented, 'Nothing can be more frustrating than for faculty to develop a well-conceived and economically feasible plan for learning, only to find that their management systems are not designed to accommodate it'.

Financing

Departures from the traditional usually require extra financial resources, not only to initiate the new approach, but also to provide evaluative evidence that the innovation is successful compared with existing teaching methods. On the other hand, many innovations may actually save money. Savings in instructional costs for the institution itself have been the impetus for a variety of new approaches to teaching and learning, including individualized instruction and various types of instructional technology, reviewed in Chapter 5 (although the financial outcomes in many cases have been disappointing). In the longer term, if new methods are, indeed, successful in producing more effective learners who can operate more efficiently throughout their lives, then the general benefits to society, including financial benefits, are obvious. However, this is small comfort to university administrators who must cope with fixed or declining budgets at a time of general fiscal constraint. Hence, the proponents of lifelong education are faced with the extremely difficult challenge of demonstrating the longitudinal benefits of the changes they advocate.

The whole issue of financing can also be looked at from the point of view of individual learners. The ability to take advantage of higher education is limited by the costs involved, both direct (eg tuition fees) and indirect (eg loss of earnings while studying). Some nations, including Sweden, Australia and Germany, have experimented with the abolition of student fees entirely, and many countries provide student loans or, more unusually, outright grants (the latter generally calculated by a means test). However, fees have been reintroduced in Australia, although they can be deferred until after graduation, while introduction of fees has been proposed or even introduced in a limited way in some German states, once again linked to student loans. In North America, fees have recently risen considerably (to the point where they now cover the full costs of education in some institutions).

Even the opportunity to study without upfront fees may not be sufficient inducement for some potential students, who would have to face a reduced standard of living, disruption in their careers and, in the case of fees paid through student loans, a substantial debt at the commencement of their career, in order to take advantage of higher education. More radical means for encouraging participation in higher education by adults already in the workforce include the extension of the notion of 'sabbatical leave' for workers, coupled with free tuition and paid educational leave, exemplified by the Swedish concept of partial salary.

In discussing the issue of financing lifelong education, Kurland (1980) made two suggestions, both involving 'mixed' approaches. The first (p 172) is that an individual's educational entitlement in a system of lifelong education could consist of a mixture of compulsory schooling during the childhood years and voluntary participation beyond a certain age. However, in order to try and guarantee equal levels of public support for different people, a fixed entitlement to education (stated in the form of cost of the services to be provided) could be specified. This entitlement could then be taken up in different ways by different people. A second type of mixed financing (p 174) could be achieved by making provision for payment of the cost of lifelong education, partly from public funds and partly from private. The most obvious form of private contribution would consist of fees paid by learners, presumably beyond some specified age level (prior to which all provision would be paid for with public funds); another would be financing by employers.

A relatively simple device for realizing both these approaches would be a system of educational vouchers. This idea has been the subject of political debate both in the USA and the UK. It has been attacked as an essentially 'conservative' measure that would have the effect of promoting private education at the expense of the public system. The undoubted political ramifications of this sort of change in financing higher education reinforces our earlier comments about the difficulties of introducing radical innovations in existing educational structures.

5

Lifelong learning and instructional methods: some promising approaches

We have already argued for a system of higher education that would differ in many important respects from what is to be found in most traditional universities and colleges. These differences are philosophical, organizational and paedagogical. It is the latter that are the primary focus of this chapter, which is concerned with instructional methods that will help promote lifelong learning skills. Here we review some of the approaches that have been successfully adopted in higher education to promote the types of learning we regard as desirable for an effective system of lifelong education. These embrace teaching and learning methods, as well as means for 'delivering' instruction in ways that make learning opportunities far more accessible in terms of times, places and types of learners.

Distance learning

A major barrier for many potential students in higher education are the physical constraints imposed by the times and locations at which courses are provided. Unlike schools, in most countries institutions of post-secondary education are distributed fairly sparsely, and may not even be in the major centres of population (as in the case of some major state universities in the USA). In many instances, too, courses are offered primarily during the 'normal' working day (between the hours of 9 am and 5 pm), on weekdays only, and for only part of the year. In the past this has been on the whole convenient for institutional staff as well as for a population of students who wish to attend classes during the traditional working day, study at home in the evenings and at weekends, and perhaps take a paid job during the long summer vacation. Such arrangements are much less convenient for the growing populations of non-traditional students, described in Chapter 3, who must combine higher education with other responsibilities, which may involve a full-time career, family responsibilities, extensive community involvement and so on. Yet these individuals are a very important clientele for lifelong education, and it is essential that universities try to accommodate their needs. One response to the demand for more flexibility in provision of courses has been the growth of distance education.

Although the term 'distance education' is relatively new, the underlying concept has a long history, especially in primary and secondary education, where correspondence courses have been offered for many years, especially in countries where the population is geographically scattered, such as Australia and Canada. The notion of providing instruction to students physically remote from the teacher and educational institution was undoubtedly born of necessity. This necessity can, however, be translated into a virtue by providing recognition of the fact that a great deal of learning, even in conventional educational settings, takes place in the absence of a teacher. For example, although the typical three hours of lectures weekly may be seen as equivalent to 'the course', student learning is by no means confined to activities in the lectures, but also encompasses reading the text and other relevant literature, work on essays and preparation for exams, discussions with other students and the whole process of reflecting upon the material from these sources. Clearly, for most students, time spent in this type of learning activity is much greater than that spent attending lectures. Furthermore, a good deal of the learning in question (though not all) can be done without direct help from the teacher or educational establishment. In the case of more innovative learning approaches, such as problem-based learning or project work (discussed later), independent learning assumes even greater importance. As has already been mentioned in several sections of this study, it is even possible that such learning may in some ways be superior to face-to-face learning (Cropley and Kahl, 1986).

Models of distance learning in higher education

Smith and Stroud (1982) reviewed different approaches to provision of distance learning opportunities in higher education in various parts of the world. A major distinction here is between programmes or courses offered under the auspices of an otherwise traditional institution and those provided by special-purpose colleges or universities that exist solely or primarily to cater for remote learners. In the first category are such operations as the University of Waterloo's correspondence programme, the off-campus programmes of Deakin University, Australia and the external courses of the University of the South Pacific that are offered via satellite to students scattered over the vast geographical area of the South Pacific islands.

While most institutions begin by offering traditional (on-campus) instruction and later may go on to develop distance learning courses, at Deakin University the process was reversed. The university was established in the first instance to provide distance education, and when it later began to enrol students into on-campus courses, it was decided to make use of the materials that had already been prepared for remote learners, rather than having lecturers structure each course anew. Supplementary lectures and tutorials are provided for students who attend the university, but it remains true that the teaching of internal students is based on a system and approach developed for external students.

The most notable example of a special-purpose institution is the British Open University, while other models include consortia of institutions, such as the American Distance Education Consortium, based in Nebraska, or Consorcio-red de educación a distancia (CREAD), a consortium that links distance education providers in North, South and Central America. While early versions of distance teaching relied on print media distributed via the mail, with the passage of time there has been an increasing use of alternative communications technologies, in an attempt to make contact between teacher and learner more flexible and immediate. In particular, the rapid growth of information technology during the past two decades has led to considerable exploration of new approaches to communication as applied to distance instruction. In recent years this has included radio, telephone and fax, broadcast and cable television, microwave and satellite communication and audio and video links via phone lines. Indeed, all these technologies are being used today to offer distance education in some parts of the world.

However, by far the greatest interest in recent years is in the use of the Internet, including electronic mail and the World Wide Web. Development in electronic communication over the past decade has been seen as offering a whole new approach to tertiary education, free from constraints imposed by traditional institutions. Distance education has, indeed, been 'rediscovered' by institutions or entrepreneurs largely ignorant of its extensive history and current influence. The last few years of the century have seen the invention of the 'virtual university', based on networks (of students and teachers) rather than physical plant. So far, it is too early to say how well these initiatives will succeed – succeed both in the sense of fostering lifelong learning, but also in the sense of simply surviving. Meanwhile, many of the established distance education providers, such as the Open University, although making extensive use of new technologies, also retain many traditional structures and delivery mechanisms (such as print materials for teaching, and use of the postal system for communicating with students).

External degrees

Although it is often thought that distance education is a new phenomenon that requires sophisticated technology, in fact the basic idea of receiving higher education without actually attending a university goes back over 150 years to the foundation of the London University system of external qualifications. The basis of London's external degree programme is remarkably simple. In contrast to more recent approaches to open education, the university does not involve itself with teaching, but instead is set up primarily as an examining body. Students must register for an external degree, must meet minimum entrance qualifications, pay fees and study for a minimum period of time – usually five years. However, how they prepare for degree examinations is left entirely up to individual students.

In fact, many students elect to take formal courses related to the particular degree programme. These may be correspondence courses offered by commercial concerns or part-time evening courses taught by a variety of public and private institutions. In addition, a number of vocation courses are offered both by London and other universities. It is estimated that around 20 per cent of external students take no organized courses, but direct their own studies. To help encourage student-to-student interaction and peer contact, the university maintains a database network that is open to all external students. Many students have used the database to find others studying for the same qualification and have formed self-help study groups who keep in touch with each other by mail, telephone or the Internet. The university has also in recent years provided all registered external students with basic study materials, which include a calendar, subject guide and past examination papers, but these materials are not intended to be comprehensive. The programme recommends textbooks, but provides no tuition. In 1999, there were approximately 26,000 students studying externally out of a total of 128,000 enrolled at the University of London. Students live all over the world and the university arranges for exams to be taken in over 100 different countries, although they are sent to London to be marked.

About 20 years ago Sassoon (1982), who was secretary for external students at London University, criticized a report by the British Advisory

Council for Adult and Continuing Education that appears to equate studying with being enrolled in a formal course. Sassoon expressed concern that private study remains unrecognized as a method of education, implying that education is something that involves deliberate teaching, while what students acquire on their own initiative does not count. Supporters of lifelong learning would, of course, wish to encourage such self-directed study, but in many cases students need to have their learning validated by award of some type of credential. London's external degrees are interesting because the institution makes such a clear-cut distinction between its roles as accreditor and provider of instruction. Higher education institutions generally undertake both functions together, and while they generally make great claims for the quality of their teaching, they also jealously guard their degree-granting status. It would be interesting to see how many colleges and universities would survive without a virtual monopoly in granting credit to students who complete their courses and programmes. Yet, in a system of lifelong education accreditation, teaching and learning need not always take place at the same time and in the same place. Later in the chapter we shall explore the way in which academic credit may be awarded for learning and experience that has taken place outside the confines of a formal educational institution.

Open learning systems

The term 'open learning' has become very fashionable in educational circles, although the definition of the term is not always entirely clear. In some instances 'open' appears to refer to the system for admitting students; in other cases to the fact that instruction is widely disseminated over a large geographical area. Certainly, most systems that describe themselves as involved in open learning provide teaching at a distance.

The most famous institution of this sort is the British Open University (OU), which began as 'The University of the Air' but, in fact, teaches by means of a wide variety of different media, and provides an ambitious integrated and systematic approach to instruction. The media concerned include written study guides or modules, publicly broadcast television and radio programmes, video and audio cassettes and CD-ROMs, published books, specially manufactured apparatus for certain scientific courses, personal contact with the instructors, regional tutors and counsellors, telephone and computer links (eg via electronic mail and the World Wide Web) with tutors and sometimes with other students, and the opportunity to attend residential summer courses. OU courses are specifically designed for students studying in their homes or workplaces and in their own time, not only in the UK, but also since 1992 in Western Europe and beyond. Undergraduate courses are open to anyone, regardless of educational qualifications, and the OU has made a special effort to accommodate students with disabilities – at present there are over 5,000 in this category.

The OU was one of the first British universities to use a credit system, and in 1997 had over 164,000 students registered in its programmes, including 39,000 postgraduate students and some 20,000 students living outside the UK. The institution has granted over 200,000 undergraduate degrees. A key element in its work is the course team, which develops instructional materials within disciplines, and coordinates the teaching elements that go together to make a course unit. Teams comprise of academic staff, who write the basic material, television and radio producers, and an educational technologist who draws up course objectives and sees that they are logically related to the teaching material and methods employed. Developing a course this way takes at least two years, with a course life of four or five years.

The OU has inspired many imitations in other countries. For example, there is an open university in Germany and another in British Columbia, while Athabasca University in Alberta operates on similar lines. In some cases, the British OU material has been used or adapted and the OU has recently formed a US Open University and plans to offer courses up to the doctoral level in management, information technology, computer studies and international studies. In the People's Republic of China a 'television university' was founded in 1979, and in its first three years graduated in excess of 78,000 students (Marshall, 1982). Japan opened a university of the air in 1984, and similar institutions exist in Hong Kong and Thailand. More idiosyncratic examples include Open International University for Alternative Medicines, based in India, and the Maharishi Open University 'opening the gateway of Total Knowledge of Natural Law for everyone, everywhere, in their own homes via satellite... to create perfection in life for everyone'. While most initiatives in open learning have been at the university level, the success of the OU in the UK prompted the government to found an Open College and an 'Open Tech' to train technicians and supervisors, while an Open College of Advanced Education was established in South Australia in the early 1980s.

Psychological aspects of distance learning

Cropley and Kahl (1983) carried out a systematic comparison of distance and face-to-face learning in terms of the psychological factors involved. They argued that the difference between the two modes of learning is not qualitative but quantitative. In other words, features such as self-direction, internal motivation, learning in the absence of the teacher, and the like are not the exclusive preserve of one form of education or the other, but are present in both, the difference being one of degree. This led Cropley and Kahl to suggest that conventional learning could be improved by giving greater emphasis to certain elements of distance education (self-direction etc) which, despite the fact that they are usually regarded as highly desirable, are less common in face-to-face teaching, although not necessarily completely absent. To push the argument a little further, it may be true that in some cases the presence of a live teacher could actually discourage students from being more self-directed.

On the basis of their analysis, Cropley and Kahl reached the conclusion that what they called the 'psychodynamics' (p 36) of learning are somewhat different in distance students. They are required to take much more responsibility for their own learning than face-to-face learners and they must be self-starters who are capable of initiating and carrying through a learning activity without the direct supervision of a teacher. This implies that distance learners must be able to work without direct feedback and without external rewards (such as an encouraging word from a teacher), and they must ignore distractions (since they mostly work at home in an environment designed for family life, not for the promotion of formal learning). These properties are also valuable in face-to-face learning, but in distance education they are absolutely vital.

The 'psychodynamic' properties of distance learning mentioned above closely resemble the prerequisites for lifelong learning or the properties of the lifelong learner outlined in Chapter 3. Thus it seems, at least in principle, that distance education programmes have a great potential for the promotion of lifelong learning. In fact, however, much distance education may try to minimize students' autonomy in planning and guiding their own study. Indeed many 'packaged' distance courses tend to be extremely prescriptive, perhaps out of a conviction that conventional forms of learning are the best, and that less traditional teaching/learning strategies are second rate or, as Knapper (1988b, p 63) put it, 'back door' forms of higher education.

Knapper went on to give further examples of the way in which distance educators often strive to replicate face-to-face instruction to the maximum degree possible: by insisting that the same syllabus and examinations be used as in the on-campus version of the course, using a standard textbook, and sending out packages of highly structured lecture notes derived from the 'live' class. This is done in the interests of maintaining common standards between distance courses and those given in the more traditional manner. In doing this, however, distance educators may sacrifice the opportunity of challenging students to take more responsibility for their own learning instead of just relying on the authority of teacher and textbook writer. The communications technologies now used increasingly in distance education offer the potential for much more flexible, interactive and student-centred learning. Yet the great majority of distance courses continue to rely heavily on print-based materials that are conceptually little different from the old correspondence courses and often stress mastery of information rather than the sort of critical thinking, reflection and integration that are essential components of lifelong learning.

The set of prerequisites for lifelong learning presented in Chapter 3 can be applied to the special case of distance education, and Knapper (1988b) reviewed a number of distance teaching universities in terms of these criteria. He identified a tendency for such institutions to move towards more traditional teaching approaches and suggested this was mainly because faculty are more familiar with didactic, teacher-centred approaches, having themselves been educated in this manner. Despite the growth of distance education world wide, there are still very few programmes for training teachers in appropriate paedagogical strategies. In addition, for obvious logistical reasons, it is very difficult to involve distance students in course and curriculum planning, as recommended by advocates of lifelong learning.

Resistance from students also plays an important role. They may be overly respectful of established wisdom or sceptical about the worth of learning outside highly conventional settings. They may also be afraid of taking more responsibility for their own learning, doubtful about their ability to plan and guide it, lacking in necessary knowledge and skills, or simply too comfortable with the passivity and dependency often fostered by conventional teaching and learning.

Linking education and work

Brzustowski (1983) discussed a number of challenges to universities brought about by the changing nature of work, and the resulting need to forge much closer links between higher education and a wide range of work settings and employers. He reinforced the point made in Chapter 1 that while the number of people who work with material goods is steadily declining, the number of workers who are involved in processing information in one form or another is increasing. Furthermore, in many societies people can expect to change jobs – and careers – much more frequently than in the past. This means that university graduates will have to acquire new knowledge on many occasions during their working lives. Brzustowski here was not referring simply to the continuing education function that has existed for many years in professions such as medicine. In addition, there is a need to retrain for different occupations or for radical role shifts within occupations – what Pillay

(1998) termed 'multi-skilling' and 'cross-skilling'. She also emphasized that employees need to 'up-skill' because workplaces increasingly require workers with a deep understanding of *why* they are performing a task as well as just doing it, and this requires people to *restructure* what they know.

This may be accomplished by attending courses arranged by universities; on the other hand, much of the learning will necessarily have to be self-directed. Indeed, a series of in-depth interviews with practitioners in six professions carried out in the UK by Becher (1996) revealed that, while they all recognized the need for ongoing learning to cope with change, formal courses were often their least preferred strategy. Other modes of learning mentioned by respondents included professional interactions (exchanging ideas and experiences with colleagues in a reasonably structured way), networking ('knowing someone who knows someone who may know the answer'), consulting experts, personal research, learning by doing (ie on the job) and learning by teaching (eg running a course, writing an article). The study raises important questions about the role of higher education institutions in continuing professional development. While respondents saw universities as valuable sources of specialized knowledge and initial professional training, few had attended updating courses offered by university departments. Becher concluded that higher education plays only a 'marginal role' in continuing education for the professions, largely because of its tendency 'to regard formal courses as the most appropriate role of teaching provision, while in general practitioners take a different view' (Becher, 1996, p 54). He argued that his findings also have lessons for undergraduate education, and that 'recognition of the variety of ways in which practitioners tackle hitherto unfamiliar issues ought arguably to form part of initial training... Learning how to learn would certainly, on the evidence of this research, constitute a more effective use of time in undergraduate courses than instruction in specific skills' (p 54).

A somewhat comparable survey of employers in New Jersey (van Horn, 1995) found significant concerns about the quality of traditional higher education graduates, who were felt to be under-prepared in the skills most valued in the workplace. Employers overwhelmingly supported experienced-based programmes such as internships and cooperative education, and felt they should have more say in the design of the college-level curriculum. Most employers provided their own in-house training, with an emphasis on team work, creative problem-solving, decision-making and communication skills, both oral and written. They valued on-the-job learning and training by external consultants more highly than the typical education provided in an undergraduate degree. In addition, if higher education was to play a greater role in continuing professional development, employers wished to have more involvement in the design of courses and greater flexibility in methods of delivery. On the other hand, van Horn commented that academics complain that many employers demand training that is too focused on company needs.

Yet if changing skills and responsibilities are to be an increasing aspect of professional life, then it is obviously essential to have the means for individuals to continue learning throughout their working lives and to forge links between educational institutions and the workplace. One response to this need has been the development of 'work-based learning', which aims to forge links between the workplace and the educational provider, and offers students flexibility in what they study, in where and when they study and in how they are assessed (Brennan and Little, 1996; Trigwell and Reid, 1998). In its most radical form, students may even take responsibility for the curriculum, although more usually this is negotiated by three parties – the student, the university and the employer. Students are engaged in occupational tasks of increasing complexity and are provided with opportunities to understand the overall purpose of what they are doing, with advice from experts or coaches. Other workers also serve as models of good practice, and reflection on learning is encouraged. An important goal is encouragement of generic learning skills and the ability to manage one's own learning.

Work*place*-based education is an important example of work-based learning, and involves a partnership between an educational institution and employer to develop programmes aimed at employees of the enterprise concerned. The underlying educational principles of such programmes were described by Boud (1997) as follows:

- the learning tasks are not predetermined but depend on context and need;
- the starting point for curriculum planning is the nature of the work itself;
- learning normally takes place at the work site, though this may be combined with university coursework or independent study;
- to progress or graduate students must show they have met defined criteria;
- the assessment framework is usually provided and monitored by the university.

Other common forms of work-based learning include work placements, in which students enrolled in degree programmes take part in practica or internships that involve extended periods in work settings with the aim of gaining practical experience related to their more formal studies. We discuss one type of placement – the sandwich or co-op course – in more detail later in this chapter. A less intensive approach to linking work and university study is 'practice-based education' in which realistic work situations are brought into the classroom through such means as case studies or simulations, perhaps led by an outside practitioner. Here the university maintains control of the curriculum.

Candy and Crebert (1991) pointed out a number of important differences between learning in the workplace and in academic institutions. For example, academic learning in academic environments involves propositional knowledge, is decontextualized, encourages elegant solutions, and tends to be individualistic and competitive. In contrast, workplace learning involves procedural knowledge, is highly contextualized by the work setting, focuses on problem solving and generally encourages collaboration and team work. In addition, university students have more choice in what they have to learn, and focus on the understanding of abstract ideas derived from books and other authoritative sources, whereas in the workplace learning is performance-oriented and knowledge often has to be created on the spot.

One common theme in writing about the educational value of work-based education is that meaningful learning does not necessarily take place simply because the student is in a work setting, but has to be deliberately fostered. This, in turn, means faculty involved in work-based learning need to understand the nature of learning: for example, how academic principles can be translated to real-life settings, or how students can be encouraged to reflect on problems they encounter and formulate strategies for use in future situations. There has been increasing interest in exploring learning strategies for work-based learning on the grounds that if we knew what strategies were most effective, we could try to teach them (Warr and Allan, 1998).

While so far we have been discussing ways in which higher education can better equip students with skills they can use in work situations, other writers have made the point that the workplace itself can be seen as a 'learning organization' and must adapt to changing times and circumstances (Senge, 1990). Watkins and Marsick (1993) argued that a learning organization is one that:

- is in tune with the external environment in which it operates;
- promotes discussion, team learning and collaboration among employees;
- empowers employees towards a collective goal and vision;
- creates continuous learning opportunities;
- develops systems to document and share learning.

While this idea has achieved widespread currency, it is much harder to operationalize the concept in ways that would allow us to measure the extent to which a workplace really embodies the principles of a learning organization, or that offers guidance on how it may move towards that goal (Knapper, 1995). Clearly, however, the attitudes and behaviour of employees are the most important factor here, and a number of researchers have developed scales to measure learning approaches in the workplace (eg Kirby, Knapper and Carty, 1997) and workplace climate for learning (Martin, 1998). It appears from this research that many employees see learning at work as a perfectly natural activity. However, the learning strategies they employ (eg surface learning versus more imaginative and integrative approaches) are determined by the attitude of supervisors, support available for learning and clarity of goals and expectations (Knapper, 1995; Martin, 1998).

Experiential education

In Chapter 4 we commented on the predominance of the lecture method in higher education, which we criticized as encouraging a passive approach to learning. A second feature of the lecture is that it generally involves a 'second-hand' condensation and interpretation of facts or ideas. This may under some circumstances be an advantage, but it is obviously inappropriate where a major goal of learning is to provide students with direct experience and the opportunity to learn through their own active involvement in a particular task. To use an example from most people's childhood, we can only learn how to ride a bicycle by trying it ourselves, perhaps with sympathetic support from a parent or friend. No amount of reading about the task or watching others do it will do; the task has to be learnt experientially. Of course, 'learning by doing' has a long history in education; for example, it is the basis of the apprenticeship system for training craftspeople. While education of this sort is often more difficult to set up and manage than more traditional, didactic instruction, potential benefits to learners are considerable. Of particular importance (and of a special relevance to lifelong education) is the capacity to facilitate transfer of learning skills to real-world situations. It is these characteristics of learning by doing and forging close links with the world of work that form the basis of 'experiential' education.

The origins of experiential education go back to the 1930s with the appearance of John Dewey's classic book, *Experience and education* (Dewey, 1938). Since then, the term has been used in a number of different ways; for example, some educators have used it to refer to the process of learning self-awareness, while in other instances experiential refers to learning on the job or in some type of practical setting. Nonetheless, there are some common elements in the term as used within higher education. These include Dewey's notion of active learning (as opposed to passively listening to a lecture) and encouraging close links between learning and real life, especially work situations.

Indeed, in the USA experiential learning has acquired the status of a 'movement', and there are well-established associations to promote its aims. For example, the Council for Adult and Experiential Learning (CAEL) has several hundred institutional members and carries out a broad range of activities to fulfil the mandate implied by its title. The National Society for Experiential Education (NSEE) is a non-profit association of over 2000 educators, businesses and community leaders. It was founded in 1971 to serve as a national resource centre for the development and improvement of experiential education programmes through publications, an annual conference and a network of consultants. An early British equivalent was the Learning from Experience Trust, founded by Norman Evans. The importance of experiential learning as a legitimate component of higher education is now recognized in most parts of the world, and a number of systems have been established for awarding academic credit for such learning. There are even acronyms for the process. In the USA the preferred term is PLA (Prior Learning Assessment) while in Britain it is APEL or 'Assessment of Prior Experiential Learning' (Brennan and Little, 1996).

While Dewey was concerned with bringing real-life experiences into the conventional education system (as in the case of his famous laboratory school), for many US colleges experiential learning is equated with adult learning, and the experience referred to generally means experience in the world of work. Much of the work of CAEL displays a considerable preoccupation with the 'credentialling' of prior work experience, and the organization has developed complicated procedures for use by colleges and universities to assign appropriate credit hours for 'life experience'. This practice has been criticized on the grounds that it trivializes the purpose of higher education. For example, Sawhill (1978/79, p 7) asked, rhetorically, 'Can we name any human experience, no matter how recreational, private, or trivial, and be certain today that some institution of higher learning is not offering credit for it?' He went on to argue that institutions have abused the system of awarding advanced standing to adults who have engaged in years of work or reading by 'their willingness to offer credit for experience that does not have a normal academic parallel'. Brennan and Little (1996) reviewed the differences between assessment for academic credit and assessment of workplace competence (eg to meet national occupational standards) and concluded that such differences may be 'so great that most commentators suggest that dual accreditation is not possible' (p 136).

Despite such criticisms, the practice of awarding academic credit for learning outside the formal education is now widespread. For example, CAEL reports that almost half of all accredited colleges and universities in the USA award credit on the basis of comprehensive individualized assessment of prior learning, most of them on the basis of a portfolio.

This is a formal written document, compiled by the student, which identifies what learning has taken place and provides supporting evidence for learning outcomes and relevant competence. Portfolios are also increasingly common in the UK, along with learning contracts negotiated among student, employer and higher education institution. The contract typically reflects the needs of the learner and employer, the learning objectives and intended outcomes, the human and physical resources available to the learner (eg a mentor, a computer), a timetable for completing the contract and a method to assess that the objectives have been achieved (Brennan and Little, 1996).

The experiential learning movement has achieved such prominence in North America that efforts have been made to develop an underlying theoretical rationale derived from basic learning principles. The work of David Kolb is frequently used in this connection. His notion of the 'learning cycle' (Kolb and Fry, 1975) involves a series of sequential steps that include:

- experiencing;
- 'publishing' (sharing reactions and observations);
- processing (the systematic examination of commonly shared experience and identification of group dynamics);
- generalizing (inferring principles about the real world), and applying (planning more effective behaviour).

According to Kolb, an individual learns from concrete experiences, from reflecting on those experiences from different perspectives, changing or refining the learning experience on the basis of such reflection, and then testing out (applying) that learning either indirectly (eg through discussion) or by application to a real problem. Because of its emphasis on problem solving, reflection and self-direction, Kolb's theory has obvious attractions for proponents in lifelong learning. Its utility is not confined to work-based learning but can also apply to any learning situation where the emphasis is on application of skills and knowledge to solving problems or making decisions.

Sandwich courses and cooperative education

While experiential education and work-based learning are based on the notion of providing higher learning opportunities for those in the workforce, sandwich or cooperative education takes a somewhat different tack by, in essence, providing work experience for university students. Although in practice the two approaches may have common elements, the underlying principles differ somewhat. Furthermore, whereas experiential education has primarily involved adults in the workforce, most students in cooperative programmes have tended to be drawn from the traditional population of school-leavers.

This is true both of the British sandwich courses and the North American co-op programmes (the rather ambiguous term refers to cooperation between education and industry). A typical programme (there are many variations) involves a student in five or six work placements, each of four months' duration, alternating with academic terms. Placements are generally made by the academic institution. The students are involved in productive work (for which they are paid at normal job rates), and their performance is supervised and evaluated both by the university and the employer. Academic requirements and coursework are the same as for non-cooperative study, but an additional equivalent amount of time is spent in the work situation. Since co-op students generally work right through the year (instead of taking a long summer break), a complete co-op programme typically lasts only a year or so longer than a traditional academic programme.

There are obvious advantages to the system both for the employer (who is provided with a year-round supply of students and can screen potential future employees) and for students (who have a source of income, chance of a job later and the opportunity to try out practical applications of the theoretical knowledge acquired in their academic studies). Perhaps the greatest benefits accrue to the institution, which can use its physical and human resources more economically right through the year – although this generates some resistance from faculty who are used to having summers free from teaching – and which can enrol more students without increasing physical facilities on campus. Indirect benefits include the impetus provided by students who are in frequent contact with the latest technology and current industrial processes. Their experience provides a stimulus to faculty to remain abreast of current developments, and the curriculum can thereby be made more relevant to the demands of the workplace. In addition, the close contacts between academia and industry are useful in themselves (as a way of encouraging a two-way exchange of ideas and information) and also carry prestige.

In many countries cooperative education programmes have proved extremely popular with the business community and with government – presumably because they are seen as encouraging pragmatic, career-related (but at the same time high quality) higher education, as opposed to the popular stereotype of the university as an ivory tower. The University of Waterloo, which was founded as a cooperative institution in 1957 with 75 engineering students, today has 60 per cent of its 16,000 full-time students enrolled in co-op programmes, and makes placements in about 2,500 businesses and industries in various parts of Canada, and in other countries such as the USA, France, Germany, Australia and Japan. The university employs 36 coordinators to arrange suitable student placements and supervise the work experience. This type of activity makes for good public relations, and the institution has been singled out for praise by many leading industrialists and politicians. The idea has spread, and there are now more than 100 higher education institutions in Canada alone involved in cooperative education.

The discussion to this point has described cooperative education in North America, primarily because of the large number of different types of co-op programmes there and the rich documentation describing their organization and activities. However, as mentioned earlier in this section, the British equivalent to cooperative education – sandwich courses – has a very long history. The oldest British course was established at Sunderland Technical College in 1903, and there were 43 such programmes in existence by 1974. On the whole, the British sandwich courses and North American co-op programmes share a common philosophy, and are also alike in many organizational respects. The main differences (eg the notion of industry-based programmes as opposed to the institution-based programmes that are almost universal in North America) were described by Grant (1971). As elsewhere in the world, British sandwich courses tend to be most common in engineering, but they also exist in business, architecture and, less commonly, in the humanities and social sciences. There is an active World Association for Cooperative Education which holds an international conference every two years. One of the association's aims is to foster global collaboration by building international alliances among educational providers, industry and government, with a particular focus on connecting developed and lesser-developed nations.

While many of the reasons for adopting cooperative education seem driven by pragmatic considerations such as financial advantages to students and recruitment benefits for employers, there have been attempts to spell out underlying paedagogical goals and principles. For example, Ricks (1996) argued that cooperative education should:

- be student-centred and foster self-directed learning;
- foster reflection on practice;
- encourage transformational learning;
- integrate school and work learning experiences;
- be collaborative;
- be conceptually based (eg in adult learning theory);
- be relevant and meaningful;
- be documented and accountable.

It will be clear that these principles are highly consistent with the goals of lifelong learning we articulated earlier.

Other approaches

Students as consultants

Although cooperative education is by far the most common (and most documented) approach to providing students with appropriate work experience, there have been numerous other attempts to provide links between academic study and the needs and demands of business and industry. Some institutions and professional programmes have advisory councils drawn from business or government to provide input on curriculum and teaching issues. Other programmes have offered free consulting to local business that involves faculty and students working on real problems. The client gets solutions (or at least the chance to see the problem through fresh eyes), while students get genuine contacts with business and the chance to work on a real-world issue where a good solution can have tangible pay-offs.

For example, at the University of Waterloo, the Department of Applied Mathematics for many years ran a 'problems clinic' in which small groups of senior undergraduate students were assigned to work on industrial problems under faculty supervision. Clients included a steelworks, a railway company and a bank, and the project was able to attract matching funds from the government of Ontario. Another Canadian university, McGill, pioneered a 'value engineering workshop', a project-based approach that involved students in an in-depth analysis of an industrial product or process with a view to improving its design. The workshop began in the university's Department of Mechanical Engineering in 1973 and involved final-year students working in teams of five with an outside company representative. The project teams worked intensively over two or three weeks on an issue submitted by the company. The companies paid a small fee to the university to cover organizational expenses, but it was estimated that savings of millions of dollars in production costs resulted. For example, work for an aviation company on a costly fuel control system for aircraft turbine engines resulted in changes that had substantial potential savings. Another project to improve the performance of a scavenger pump for a diesel engine oil system resulted in a suggestion that the pump should be completely eliminated and alternative changes should be made to the design of the main oil pump instead. The potential savings here were a huge $1.2 million per annum (Breathnach, 1983). A similar approach has been used for many years at Aalborg University in Denmark, where teams of students work on problems submitted by local businesses. The client 'owns' the solution and on occasion has even taken out a patent on a particularly innovative idea. The reward for the university and students is the chance to work on a real problem in an authentic work setting.

Links with alumni

Another potential, but generally disregarded, link between higher education institutions and employers is provided by graduates or, in North American terms, alumni. Former students are already called upon to contribute funds by many North American institutions, and cooperative programmes frequently use alumni contacts to procure appropriate job placements. A further step may be to involve selected alumni in teaching – not by replicating the expertise of faculty, but by having them provide segments of instruction related to their own particular expertise in business or industry. This could have mutual benefits to higher education and employers, since the university could provide valuable help in updating the knowledge and skills of industry personnel by exposure to leading-edge research. Brzustowski (1983) talked about a relationship between former students and their university, using the metaphors of 'maintenance', 'check-up' and 'recall', reminiscent of the 'relationship between the purchaser of an automobile and its manufacturer' (p 7).

Volunteer work and service learning

So far we have talked at length about fostering lifelong learning through closer links between higher education and the workplace. However, it can be argued that preparing students for responsible citizenship is just as important as preparing them for future careers (Boyer, 1994). One way of doing this is to make use of student experiences as volunteers (Greenberg, 1982). It has been estimated that up 70 per cent of students in US colleges and universities are involved in some sort of volunteer activity in the local community, working on a variety of projects relating to health, education, the environment, community development and so on (Levine, 1994). Apart from self-initiated volunteer work, there are also campus-based agencies, such as the Public Interest Research Groups, originated by Ralph Nader to perform both an educational and activist or lobbying role. PIRGs are run and staffed by students, financially supported by student government, and have concerned themselves with a wide range of public issues, ranging from technology in the workplace to acid rain. The more successful groups have organized meetings, published newsletters and books, and their activities have involved students, academic staff and members of the general public.

In some cases, the volunteer activity has been institutionalized and integrated with academic programmes. For example, the University of Waterloo Psychology Department operated a volunteer programme for a number of years in which students received assignments related to their coursework – for example, students taking educational psychology might work in a school for retarded children. Reports were prepared on the experiences, and in some cases partial academic credit was awarded. This is an example of something now known as 'service learning', defined by Bringle and Hatcher (1996) as 'a credit-bearing educational experience in which students participate in an organized service activity that meets identified community needs' (p 222). However, this is not all. Students also need to *reflect* on the activity in order to gain a better understanding of both academic issues and broader societal concerns. In addition, there should also be *reciprocity*, meaning that benefits should accrue not just to the student volunteer but also to the agency and individuals being served (Jacoby, 1996). Service learning encourages volunteers to work *with* people, not just *for* them, in the expectation that everyone will benefit from the changes that result.

Service learning programmes currently exist in many hundreds of US higher education institutions, stimulated in part by the creation of Campus Compact, a national organization of university presidents established in the 1980s to encourage student involvement in the local community. Many campuses, in fact, have service learning offices to coordinate such volunteer activities. Although programmes vary widely, Morton (1993) identified a number of underlying conceptual goals relating to service and citizenship; promotion of liberal democracy (learning about relationships between individuals and the state), involvement in participatory democracy (political problem solving and empowerment) and fostering social justice and service as citizenship. Many proponents of service learning have been greatly influenced by the writings of Dewey and his stress on education for democracy and the importance of active involvement by learners in real-world issues. Service learning is seen as facilitating critical thinking through posing a problem, gathering evidence and analysing it, then forming, executing and evaluating an appropriate plan of action. Students must learn not just to answer questions, but to question the answers (Mendel-Reyes, 1998).

Service learning has been used in a wide variety of academic contexts. For example, students in a political science course at Swarthmore College worked together on a community service project and spent Saturday mornings helping a local group rehabilitate low-income housing. Students had to prepare a report on the experience and relate their impressions to themes being discussed in the academic component of the course (Mendel-Reyes, 1998). Service learning has also been used in writing courses (eg editing a newsletter for a local community group), in business courses (eg to develop a business plan for a local volunteer agency) and in science (eg working with local elementary school students on practical science projects). Other forms of service learning have involved 'participatory action research' in which student groups not only take on a community project but also try to introduce social and political change in the process. Two examples described by Reardon (1998) are involvement of students at the University of Illinois in the development of a community-owned farmers market in East St. Louis and in the formation of mutual self-help networks among subsistence farmers in Tanzania. Many more instances of service learning in US universities can be found in Rhoads and Howard (1998) and Jackson (1994).

In the UK, the term 'study service' has been used to describe voluntary community activities undertaken by students as part of their academic programme (Goodlad, 1982). At least two types of learning are thought to accrue from the community service activity. In the first place, it is hoped that students will acquire information directly related to their academic courses. Second, it is expected that they will become more self-aware, learn to question their own attitudes, assumptions, prejudices and so on. Goodlad reviewed this type of community service in various countries, and has commented that such volunteer work is by no means confined to the helping professions, but also exists in disciplines like law, management, engineering and the hard sciences – although, as expected, the volunteer work placements were primarily in government settings, especially social services departments.

Some of the benefits of volunteer organizations are obvious: for example, the organization receives a source of free assistance (and perhaps enthusiasm), while the student can learn a useful skill and also get the personal satisfaction of contributing time and effort to a worthwhile cause. A number of studies measured the effects of service learning on students, faculty, institutions and the community. Giles and Eyler (1998), on the basis of an extensive review, claimed that there are positive impacts on students' personal development (compared to students who do not take part), an increase in social responsibility, and a willingness to be more involved in social issues and to work for change over the longer term. Bringle and Hatcher (1996, p 223) also summarized research showing that service learning enhances classroom climate and 'has a positive impact on personal, attitudinal, moral, social and cognitive outcomes'.

Networking

A recent meeting of Canadian university presidents tried to explore what aspects of higher education contributed most to student learning and success. One the most senior presidents commented that perhaps the best things that happened in university was the chance for students to establish a network of contacts with their peers – contacts that would help them cope with the system while they were part of it and would continue to facilitate learning and career success long after they had graduated. In fact, this off-the-cuff comment receives some support from the research literature. The extensive research of Astin (1993) and

Pascarella and Terenzini (1991) showed that opportunities for peer inter-action and interaction with faculty were among the very few factors that predict cognitive development in college and university students. From the point of view of lifelong learning, we are interested not just in inter-nal networks, but in wider links with the larger community.

An early example was presented by Sarason *et al* (1977), who described the development of one such network (the 'Essex network'), involving hundreds of people in several states in the USA to mount edu-cational programmes that would otherwise have been impossible. Indi-viduals from schools, colleges and universities, as well as from public and private agencies, joined together to exchange resources on a 'bar-ter-economy' basis for their mutual benefit. Sarason *et al* claimed that the Essex network demonstrated that there are ways of dealing with lim-ited human resources to maximize community spirit, provide services and develop people's potential. While this sort of pooling of resources is relatively rare in higher education, the idea of the 'skills exchange' (in which members of the community offer their expertise in a wide variety of fields, either for payment or in exchange for someone else's expertise) has existed for some time in a number of Western cities, especially large North American centres such as Toronto and New York. The rapid growth of electronic networks through the Internet has created communities of learners, some on quite idiosyncratic topics (quilting, bee-keeping, the history of the abacus), that exist independently of for-mal educational establishments. The whole idea behind the concept of 'freeware' and 'shareware' (computer applications and software distrib-uted on the Internet) is to exchange products and ideas on the basis of shared interests rather than (primarily) commercial profit. Though cer-tainly not 'higher education', such networks incorporate many of the principles of lifelong and life-wide learning.

Innovative approaches to teaching and learning

Individualized learning

A criticism of many traditional teaching methods is that they necessarily adopt a uniform approach to instruction in which all students are taught the same way and receive the same information, regardless of their indi-vidual needs and characteristics. Yet, for the system of lifelong and life-wide learning that we are advocating, the need to cater to individual student differences is crucial.

The term 'individualized learning' has been used for many years, and was initially developed out of dissatisfaction with traditional methods (such as the lecture), but without any particular relation to lifelong learning. Knapper (1980) reviewed different types of so-called individualized learning and pointed out that the extent to which such learning was truly tailored to the needs of the individual varied greatly from one scheme to another. For example, the programmed instruction developed for teaching machines in the 1950s was supposedly 'self-paced', but often this simply meant that students could work through the material at their preferred speed, while the actual content and order of presentation were exactly the same for all students. In this sense the degree of individualization was no greater than would be possible in reading a book. Later versions of programmed instruction did attempt to structure the material in different ways for different students by 'branching', which made it possible for students who had mastered early parts of the programme to progress rapidly to more complex material, while students who were having difficulty could be routed through additional explanatory material with careful step-by-step explanation of tricky points. In the case of computer-assisted instruction, the potential for this type of individualization is considerable although, as we shall discuss in a later section on educational technology, attempts at truly individualized CAI have been largely disappointing to date.

Two popular types of individualized learning that had fairly widespread use in higher education are Keller's Personalized System of Instruction (PSI) and Postlethwait's Audio-Tutorial Method (Knapper, 1980). These methods were developed in the 1960s and reflect a behaviourist approach to learning and instruction that was extremely fashionable at that time. This involves detailed specification of course objectives, the preparation of instructional 'modules' or self-contained units and frequent testing of students for 'mastery' of the different units. While these approaches appeared to be successful in allowing students to learn subject-matter content, they were individualized only in the sense that students worked by themselves. Control of what was to be learnt lay firmly in the hands of the instructor and, indeed, assessment in most Keller Plan and Audio-Tutorial courses was confined to multiple-choice tests, where the repertoire of possible answers is obviously limited.

At the start of the new millenium, behaviourism is largely out of fashion, and although many distance education providers and commercial training programmes stress that their courses are individualized, the term is largely used as a slogan and mainly refers to the fact that students may select the particular modules they wish and study where and when it is convenient. In the present climate, there is also greater emphasis on collaborative learning and team skills, and the term 'individualize' often conjures up the image of a solitary learner. Contemporary concerns about individual differences are more likely to stress the need to cater to diversity and ensure that teaching approaches recognize that students may have different social and cultural backgrounds, life experiences and learning approaches. Such differences are, indeed, an important element in encouraging lifelong learning, and we return to this issue in Chapter 7.

Independent learning projects and self-directed learning

True individualization of instruction should facilitate lifelong learning by catering to different learner needs. Similarly, independent learning may be expected to fulfil the goal of encouraging students to direct their own learning and 'learn how to learn'. As in the case of individualized instruction, the concept of independent learning has been construed in different ways. To complicate matters further, a wide variety of different terms (including 'self-directed' and 'self-regulated' learning and 'autonomous' learning) have been used to describe paedagogical approaches that we have here labelled 'independent' learning.

Approaches that stress student problem-solving ability, decision-making skills and even creativity frequently use teaching strategies that share a common aim of promoting effective self-directed or independent learning. The precise terminology employed is less important than the underlying learning processes involved. For example, Morgan (1983) discussed the theoretical aspects of project-based learning in higher education, but his comments and conclusions have broad applicability to the whole field of independent and self-directed learning. Although there are more comprehensive reviews of the field (Candy, 1991), Morgan's framework offers a useful and concise way of describing different approaches, their differences and commonalities. Morgan's definition of project-based learning has two components: the first is a stress on students' responsibility for designing their own learning activities, and the second refers to active student involvement in the solution of a real-life problem as the best means of beginning to understand the topic or issue.

Morgan distinguished three promising approaches to the use of independent learning projects in colleges and universities. The first model, 'project exercise', involves a circumscribed project carried out as part of a traditional course, with topics generally specified by the instructor, and an assumption that the knowledge and techniques needed to complete the assignment will be those customarily used within the discipline and already familiar to students. Morgan's second model is the 'project component', where a project is not necessarily linked to an academic discipline, but is intended to fulfil broader, interdisciplinary aims, such as developing problem-solving skills and independent study. Here there is a stress on projects related to contemporary issues in the real world, and greater freedom of choice in choosing topics. The project component is not necessarily built upon knowledge and skills already acquired, and may indeed form part of a special-purpose course outside the discipline-based curriculum. Morgan's third category of 'project orientation' refers to the use of project work as the basis for an entire curriculum or institution, with conventional didactic teaching provided only occasionally as supplementary instruction. Institutions organized along these lines include Roskilde and Aalborg in Denmark and the University of Bremen in Germany.

The use in regular courses of small exercises closely tied to the methods and knowledge of a particular discipline (Morgan's first model) is widespread in higher education. Indeed, there are considerable resemblances between this approach to project work and the traditional laboratories and field work found in most science disciplines, which we discussed in Chapter 4. Although use of projects in this way is a useful supplement to more passive types of learning, it is likely that more ambitious implementations of projects (as in Morgan's second and third models) will be needed to encourage effective problem-solving skills that could be transferred to real-world situations.

Guided design

One such approach is 'guided design', developed by Wales and Stager (Wales and Stager, 1977; Wales, Nardi and Stager, 1993), which is generally used in a way that Morgan would classify as a 'project component'. The underlying philosophy of guided design is that effective problem solving or decision making is best learnt by confronting a student with carefully designed but open-ended problems. Each problem is planned in such a way that, to arrive at a solution, students must make use of the discipline-based subject matter they are learning. At the same time, decision making and problem solving are seen as skills in their own right, and are taught explicitly, guided by printed materials prepared by the teacher that break down the problem-solving process and allow students to gain insight into their own intellectual approach to decision making. According to its originators, guided design is intended to be used where some type of professional training is involved that includes decision making as a central component, where there is an established body of information on which students can draw to help them make their decisions and where the decisions made by professionals frequently have to be implemented by others. Hence, the teaching of guided design actually models the approach of a professional working in the real world. For example, it emphasizes learning from a wide variety of sources, working with open-ended problems, and concentration on issues that are drawn from real life.

Students work in teams of five or six on problems formulated by the instructor. They must identify the 'real issue' and set goals for their work, as well as list underlying constraints; they are then required to generate possible solutions, choose a most likely solution, analyse and evaluate the solution, and report their results. A key feature of the approach is the provision of feedback to students at each step along the way. It is also emphasized that there is no one correct solution and that the actual process of decision making and problem solving is more important than the particular solution arrived at. In fact, the guided design method requires students to examine closely the way in which they made their group decisions, and to try to learn from this experience and from the expertise of others in the team and the class.

The amount of time devoted to a problem very much depends upon the nature of the problem itself and the background knowledge and experience of the students. Simple problems may take two or three hours, while more complex issues may occupy 15 hours of class time. While these activities are taking place, students are also expected to study an appropriate amount of subject matter outside the class, and to make use of this material as and when appropriate. Wales and Stager claimed that learners not only acquire relevant knowledge in this way, but also develop an ability to learn independently, solve problems logically yet creatively, gather information from a variety of sources, make appropriate value judgements, work as part of a team and communicate their ideas to others.

Worksheets

A somewhat comparable approach to problem solving was developed by Finkel and Monk (Finkel and Arney, 1995; Finkel and Monk, 1978; 1979). They made use of a workshop format and 'worksheets' that can either comprise the basis of a course, or be incorporated into a conventional teaching programme. Their aim was to allow students to 'share the pleasures' of intellectual experience with instructors and with each other, in order to solve an open-ended problem included in the worksheet. Students work in teams that range in size from two to seven, and the teacher acts as a resource person – observing, giving guidance, asking questions and providing information in response to requests from particular groups or individuals. The rationale for this method of working is that students acquire cognitive skills by being directly engaged in intellectual activity, not merely by listening passively to lectures. The worksheet approach has been used in a variety of disciplines, and Finkel and Monk claimed the experience has an effect not only on students' thinking abilities, but also on those of teachers: instructors who become involved in planning workshops and writing worksheets may have to 'rethink many fundamental questions in their field' (Finkel and Monk, 1979, p 38).

Problem-based learning

A well-known implementation of what Morgan calls project orientation (use of self-directed independent learning in an entire programme) is the problem-based learning approach pioneered by the medical school at McMaster University in Hamilton, Ontario, which has served as the basis for a number of similar innovations in various parts of the world. The McMaster programme has the specific aim of producing self-directed learners who can recognize their own personal educational needs, select appropriate learning resources and evaluate their own progress in studying (Ferrier, Marrin and Seidman, 1988). The curriculum adopts an interdisciplinary problem-based approach in which students work in a sequence of small groups for three years. Students have to direct their own learning, and accept responsibility for the progress of the entire group in terms of objectives that are specified for the programme as a whole and for the individual segments. In each segment, students work in a tutorial group of five plus a tutor, and the group must decide on the methods and strategies for learning to be employed. Groups are confronted with sets of problems, clinical experiences and a variety of additional resources. They are also encouraged to identify further problems, find other resources and even to specify new objectives. The goals for the various segments laid down by the programme administrators stress general skills and concepts rather than acquisition of facts. Final responsibility for evaluation rests with the tutor, but self- and peer evaluation form an additional important component.

Problem-based learning is now dominant in Canadian medical education, and has spread to medical schools in Europe (eg the University of Dundee), Australia (eg Newcastle University) and the USA (eg Harvard). It has also been adopted for professional education in many other fields, including engineering, law, architecture and social work (Boud and Feletti, 1991; Wilkerson and Gijselaers, 1996).

Learning from peers

Earlier chapters have stressed the importance of learning from a variety of sources, and not relying upon the single authority of the teacher or textbook. Within educational institutions – as in the workplace and many other aspects of everyday life – colleagues can provide invaluable information and advice, yet learning from peers is often neglected, or even discouraged. In many of the attempts to implement lifelong learning, however, discussion with fellow students has been seen as an important component. We have already cited evidence that peer interaction is a major contributor to students' cognitive development at university –

more important, in fact, than time spent studying in formal classes (Astin, 1993; Pascarella and Terenzini, 1991). As with project work, such learning can comprise one small component of a conventionally taught course, or can form the basis of an entire programme. Usually the term implies students working in groups on particular learning tasks, but other aspects of the approach include use of peers for student assessment and, in some cases, involvement of student groups in the actual planning of the course or curriculum.

A number of rationales have been given for encouraging students to learn from each other. At one extreme, peer learning has been seen primarily as a means of saving the instructor's time, especially in large classes, where the teacher or tutor may have only limited opportunities for contact with individual students. There is perhaps an implication here that learning from fellow students is inferior to learning from the teacher, but the research just cited suggests tangible benefits of peer learning. Since much of what a student learns in college takes place outside the classroom (over 70 per cent according to Wilson, 1966), then it seems likely that fellow students will be a major influence (Lazar, 1995).

Some commentators – for example, Botkin, Elmandjra and Malitza (1979) in an influential report for the Club of Rome – have gone so far as to argue that learning from fellow learners (what they term 'participatory learning') is essential in order to solve the awesome problems currently facing humankind. They saw this as involving shared decision making, attitudes characterized by cooperation, dialogue, empathy, recognition of others' rights and acceptance of a mutual obligation to tackle problems confronting society. If, as Botkin and his colleagues believe, decisions should be made communally and not left to an élite, then the importance of learning from and with others is clearly crucial. A similar point was made by Schein (1972) in his report on professional education for the Carnegie Commission on Higher Education. He argued that the acute social, political and economic problems facing contemporary society would require more than specialist knowledge from individual disciplines, and could only be tackled effectively by interdisciplinary teams who were trained to integrate knowledge and work together. Over 20 years later, in their report for the Australian Board of Employment, Education and Training, Candy, Crebert and O'Leary (1994) concluded that peer-assisted learning and mentoring (along with self-directed, experiential and problem-based learning) are an essential component for developing lifelong learning in undergraduate education.

Peer learning has a long history in education, and many different terms have been used to describe the process, including 'cooperative learning' (not to be confused with the cooperative work/study programmes discussed earlier in this chapter), 'learning syndicates', 'learning cells', 'study circles' and even the confusingly named 'supplemental instruction' which involves trained upper-year students teaching lower-year students (Rust and Wallace, 1995). A more important distinction than nomenclature, however, involves the underlying objectives for peer learning.

In some instances students are used primarily as *counsellors* or mentors for their colleagues – what Goldschmid (1981) called *'parrainage'*. Advanced students volunteer to act as counsellors to first-year students on a variety of issues, including study methods, exam preparation and so on. They are also encouraged to draw the staff's attention to any learning problems that may be remedied by changes in the course organization. This type of programme may be organized through an office of student affairs, a faculty office, the student union or even through the university residences, which in North American universities have become increasingly involved with academic support services.

Another approach to peer learning has been to use students as *tutors* to their colleagues – as in the case of supplemental instruction mentioned above. In some instances this may simply mean better students serving as 'teaching assistants' for others in the class (Kabel, 1983). In other implementations the relationship between students is one of equality – for example, Goldschmid's (1971) idea of learning dyads or learning cells, in which small groups of students 'tutor' each other in turn in order to practise mastery of course material.

A more ambitious approach is the 'syndicate method' in which an entire course is organized on a group learning basis (Collier, 1983). In such a course the class is divided into groups (syndicates) of from four to eight students, and the main work of the class consists of assignments that are carried out on a cooperative basis by the teams. The teacher generally acts as a facilitator and resource person: students are encouraged to ask for consultation when necessary and also to seek out their own sources of information relating to the assignment. US versions of the syndicate method are termed collaborative or cooperative learning, and there is an extensive literature about the ways they may be used and on evidence of their effectiveness in promoting educational outcomes relating to the goals of lifelong learning (Millis and Cottell, 1998).

Somewhat more controversial is the practice of involving students in *assessment procedures*. Heron (1981) argued, however, that restricting assessment and grading to faculty encourages extrinsic motivation for study and denies students the opportunity for fully autonomous learning. He pointed out, for example, that peer evaluation is the norm for academic staff with regard to their research work, where its effects on standards of excellence, critical enquiry and personal development are often vigorously defended. Furthermore, peer and self-appraisal are common forms of assessment in the workplace. Heron went on to elaborate a number of approaches to the involvement of students in their own assessment: these embrace different mixtures of self- and peer assessment and what he calls 'collaborative' assessment, in which the task is shared between instructor and students. Heron admitted that having students rate themselves or colleagues requires a certain amount of affective and interpersonal sophistication, but argued that self- and peer assessment can have important benefits for the process of learning as well as for mastery of content. He advocated a careful series of steps for those contemplating the use of peer assessment. These include deciding what to assess, which criteria to use in the assessment, how to apply these criteria and, lastly, actually carrying out the assessment. Boud (1995a) is another strong advocate of involving students in assessing their own work and that of their colleagues and has prepared a practical short guide (Boud, 1986) that outlines the steps, and gives many useful examples.

Introducing such an approach to assessment and grading is likely to provoke some resistance from more traditionally minded colleagues – for example, on the grounds that students will not realistically assess their own work. A number of studies have examined marks assigned by peers and by a course instructor, and reported differences in assessment are remarkably few (Boud, 1995a; Boud and Falchikov, 1989). Furthermore, it is possible for an instructor to involve students in the assessment process without necessarily abandoning final responsibility for assigning a mark in the course. Kabel (1983), for example, had students in his chemical engineering course suggest items for inclusion in the final examination: not only were many of the questions, in fact, used on the exam, but students could also receive additional credit for submitting particularly good items.

Such approaches are not without problems. For example, Collier (1983) pointed out that syndicate procedures often tend to result in less coverage of the syllabus – although the knowledge acquired in the course tends to be about the same. Even a strong advocate of small-group teaching methods (Abercrombie, 1981) cautioned about the difficulties of introducing these approaches, especially in a fairly conservative academic climate or where the instructors have little experience and training in how to facilitate group work. However, given the potential advantages of peer group techniques for enhancing lifelong learning skills, it seems worth while to encourage staff to acquire the necessary expertise so that such methods can be introduced with the maximum chance of success.

Alternative roles for teachers

Although our focus in this section has been primarily on the learner, the success of many of the innovations discussed above depends heavily upon the skill and enthusiasm of instructors in higher education, most of whom have had no formal training in paedagogy. Many critics of traditional learning methods have emphasized the importance of teachers in changing educational practice, and have suggested ways in which the roles and duties of the instructor should be changed.

For example, Ernest Boyer's highly influential report for the Carnegie Foundation, *Scholarship reconsidered* (Boyer, 1990), argued for broadening the concept of scholarship to include not just empirical research (what Boyer called the 'scholarship of discovery') but also 'scholarship of integration' (synthesis and integration of knowledge across disciplinary boundaries), 'scholarship of practice' (application of knowledge to societal problems) and 'scholarship of teaching' (turning scholarly inquiry into the creation of meaning and effective strategies for student learning). Boyer's report received widespread attention across North America and abroad, and stimulated a series of well-attended annual conferences on faculty roles and rewards sponsored by the American Association for Higher Education (Edgerton, 1993).

In Canada, Boyer's ideas were reflected in the work of the Commission on University Education sponsored by the Association of Universities and Colleges of Canada (Smith, 1991), which recommended requiring training for all new entrants to the university teaching profession, better and broader documentation of teaching accomplishments and a reward system that was responsive to teaching effectiveness and innovation. In 1994 the Ontario Council on University Affairs commissioned a report on steps that might be taken to increase the emphasis on university teaching (Knapper and Rogers, 1994). Similar recommendations were made by Ramsden *et al* (1995) for the project on recognizing and rewarding teaching commissioned by the Australian Committee for the Advancement of University Teaching, and in Sweden by the Council for Studies of Higher Education (Jalling and Carlsson, 1995). In Britain, the Dearing Commission tried to put some teeth into the notion of training by recommending a credentialling body for university teachers similar to those that exist for other professions (NCIHE, 1997), and in 1998 the Committee of Vice-Chancellors and Principals established an Institute for Learning and Teaching that is intended to oversee the process. It appears that the new institute will place considerable emphasis on continuing professional development, reflective practice and preparation of teaching portfolios – strategies that are quite consistent with the goals of lifelong learning.

Some concluding comments

This chapter has reviewed a variety of instructional methods that appear to show considerable promise for the encouragement of lifelong learning in higher education. We have explored three rather different themes. The first focused upon broadening the clientele in universities and colleges through distance learning. The second focus was upon programmes that attempt to forge links between higher education and the workplace. The third theme dealt with a variety of instructional methods that share an emphasis upon self-directed, independent learning leading to effective problem solving and decision making.

In fact, we have only been able to touch upon a few of the many different instructional methods that may be relevant to the theme of this book. We have devoted most attention to work-based learning, project work, independent learning, and peer group methods, first because they represent broad approaches that encompass many specific innovations, and second because these techniques appear to offer particular promise for our goal of promoting autonomous, self-directed learning. Many other interesting teaching approaches have had to be omitted here. For example, the notion of learning contracts to facilitate independent study, the use of simulations and games in learning, the case study method developed in the Harvard School of Business and widely used in faculties of commerce and law and the many techniques intended to promote creative problem solving and so on. Indeed, our review of Huczynski's (1983) encyclopaedic listing of instructional methods used in education and business revealed that no fewer than 76 entries describe techniques that could be said to facilitate lifelong learning. A random selection from these entries provides a diverse list of methods encompassing 'action learning', 'buzz groups', 'critical incident analysis', 'flexastudy', 'instrumental team learning', 'lateral thinking', 'mathetics', 'process analysis', 'self-help groups', in addition to numerous approaches that have been referred to specifically in this study. These techniques emphasize active student involvement in the learning task, use of group resources in learning, the importance of processing and reflecting on learning material instead of just 'receiving' it, bringing in a variety of learning resources to reflect or simulate real-life situations, and forcing creative approaches or solutions to problem solving and decision making.

To summarize the main theme of this chapter, it is our contention that methods already exist that would encourage lifelong learning in colleges and universities. The next question is how the ideas discussed above may be implemented more widely, and this is the focus of Chapter 6.

6

Changing institutions to lifelong education

Chapter 5 reviewed a sample of the instructional approaches already used in higher education institutions that embody some of the principles of lifelong education. However, it would be a mistake to believe that lifelong education is already being practised on a widespread basis (even if known by another name), or that post-secondary education is on the threshold of a transformation to instructional approaches that will indeed equip students with the competencies outlined earlier in this study. On the contrary, despite these very promising trends, it is necessary to repeat the rather gloomy theme of earlier chapters: much teaching in higher education is of the traditional didactic sort, much learning is passive in nature, and the opportunities for horizontal and vertical integration of learning are limited.

This then raises the question of just how institutions of higher education may be transformed along the lines we are recommending, which is the concern of this chapter. The very fact that universities and colleges have used similar instructional methods for many years reinforces the likely difficulty of change, despite outside forces in society that make the need for new learning approaches increasingly urgent. Many studies of innovation, resistance to change and ways of surmounting this resistance have been carried out in higher education, and we describe some of this work below.

One approach to innovation is to bypass the traditional educational structures by founding entirely new institutions and, indeed, some colleges have been set up with goals that include the fostering of self-directed learning skills. However, there are also mechanisms within established colleges and universities that may be used to help transform teaching and learning practices. Such mechanisms include the work of instructional development units and study skills programmes, which have become widespread in many university and college systems during the past 25 years. Another development that has the potential to affect methods of teaching and learning in a profound way is information technology – in particular the use of computers to deliver instructional materials, relatively unrestricted by constraints of time and space. In this chapter we examine some of these initiatives and consider the question of whether, and how, they may move instructional practice within higher education in a direction that is more in keeping with the principles of lifelong education outlined earlier.

Special-purpose institutions

In the first edition of this book we commented with some enthusiasm on the emergence of new or radically transformed institutions that seemed to us to offer the prospect of a different approach to teaching that might better fulfil the goals of lifelong learning – for example, through greater emphasis on self-directed learning, broader student access through distance learning and closer links with the workplace. These new institutions included the British polytechnics, progressive liberal arts colleges (such as Goddard College and Evergreen College in the USA), the new distance institutions (the British Open University, Athabasca University in Canada, Deakin University in Australia) and the problem-based learning universities in Europe, such as Roskilde and Aalborg.

The situation has changed since our first account in 1985. Higher education worldwide has seen a lengthy period of financial retrenchment, and very few new institutions have been established, with the exception of the recent explosion of interest in 'virtual universities' that are intended to offer instruction through the Internet. The British polytechnics have been given university status and their programmes appear increasingly traditional; many of the more radical liberal arts colleges have closed or have abandoned their more progressive teaching experiments. Massy and Wilger (1996) commented on the dominant research ethos in US higher education that rewards conventional scholarship at the expense of innovative teaching and curriculum development, even in institutions that were intended to focus exclusively on undergraduate education. At the same time, there remain a number of institutions whose teaching programmes and methods support the goals of lifelong learning, and in this section we offer a brief overview of their approach and achievements.

The distance and open learning institutions we reviewed in Chapter 5 fulfil some of the criteria for lifelong education outlined earlier. In the first place they enable a much broader cross-section of the population to take advantage of higher education opportunities without the normal restrictions imposed by attendance at a conventional university. In addition, because distance education requires much more careful planning of instruction than is usually thought necessary in face-to-face teaching, many of the new open learning universities give a great deal of attention to the preparation of teaching materials. Furthermore, the resulting instructional process takes account of learner needs in a much more thoroughgoing way than is often seen in higher education, for the reason that if it does not, the instruction is incomprehensible and students drop out of the programme – the usual supplementary support systems being simply not available. Some of these institutions – the British Open University is an example – have formalized this interest in teaching and learning methods to the extent of setting up advisory services for the academic staff on the preparation of course materials. In some cases, too, the work of these agencies has demonstrated a concern with the principles of independent learning that are a major focus of interest of this book.

Institutions built around innovative curricula

Other institutions have been established specifically with the goal of fostering lifelong learning, although they may not have used this term. Some were founded during the time of great expansion (and radicalism) in the late 1960s and early 1970s – for example, Roskilde University in Denmark. Roskilde's programmes place considerable emphasis on independent learning skills, project work, and group interaction in student teams. Interdisciplinarity is also encouraged both for teaching and research, with the goal of 'stretching the borders of the classical disciplines'. Roskilde has about 7,000 students, and study is structured within units called 'houses', which comprise both a physical space and a social unit, each with approximately 100 students, four to six tutors and a secretary. In the house, students work in project groups of 5 to 10 members, and each group has its home base in one of the group rooms interspersed among the faculty offices. The university encourages strong links between research and teaching by involving undergraduates in faculty research programmes.

Another innovative Danish institution with goals that are of relevance to lifelong learning is the University of Aalborg, established in 1974, which has been a pioneer in making problem-based learning and team work central to its programmes. Aalborg, which has about 11,000 students, is primarily an engineering school, although it does have some programmes in management, social science and the humanities. All learning at all levels takes place in teams, who work on applied projects – initially these are design-oriented (familiar problems that can be solved on the basis of established methods); in later years projects involve tackling real, unsolved problems, often in actual workplace settings (Kjersdam and Enemark, 1994). There are close links with local employers, who not only make use of student groups to solve industrial problems, but also provide input on curriculum planning.

A few innovative institutions have much longer histories than either Aalborg or Roskilde – for instance, Goddard College in Vermont, founded in 1863, whose curriculum is based on the principles of self-directed, independent and experiential 'learning by doing' as advocated by Dewey. The aim is to produce students who are effective problem solvers in real-world settings. The college's mission statement contains an explicit reference to the goal of creating lifelong learners, which it defines as 'individuals who take charge of their own learning'.

Admission to the college is only partly based on traditional high school transcripts and grade point averages; it relies heavily on an autobiographical essay describing the student's educational motivations as well as a personal interview with college faculty. This emphasis upon oral and written communication is also an important component of the learning experience at Goddard. There is no set curriculum at the college, no fixed credit hours, very few lectures and no formal examinations. Rather, the stress is on learning as an active, evolving process, which leads to students gaining experience in a variety of practical projects. Students begin by working in faculty-led groups to explore particular issues, but later in the programme they are expected to formulate their own individual study plan, which typically involves a good deal of independent work. Students must all complete a final major project that could involve an empirical research study, a photographic portfolio or even a novel. Although most students are resident in Plainfield, the college also offers a 'short-residency option' to meet the needs of people with professional or family obligations. Here students attend a seven-day residency prior to each semester, but work for the rest of the time in their own community doing independent study in collaboration with a faculty mentor.

An extremely important element in Goddard's approach to education is evaluation, which is seen as an ongoing formative activity that is an integral part of a student's learning experience so as to make 'the whole process part of her or his life'. Learning processes are discussed explicitly, on the grounds that knowledge about educational development provides the student with a basis for self-criticism, self-insight and growth. At the end of each term students write a self-appraisal of what they have learnt and how they have changed. The teacher also provides an evaluation of the unit or class concerned, and these appraisals are discussed between student and faculty member. Great stress is placed upon involvement with the local community – for example, the college runs a volunteer fire brigade and founded the local community health centre. Links between work and study are also stressed, even to the extent of having students carry out many of the manual tasks necessary to run the college, such as helping in the cafeteria or cleaning the premises. Students take an active role in college administration: for instance, by their participation on the Goddard board.

Not surprisingly, Goddard College has not led an unruffled existence, and indeed it had to survive a major crisis that involved near bankruptcy and a threatened loss of accreditation. Such an intensive approach to lifelong learning goals is apparently difficult to sustain on a large scale. It has also proved difficult to find faculty who share the college's educational philosophy and have the qualities necessary to foster appropriate skills and attitudes in students. Nonetheless, there is some empirical evidence of the college's success in fostering lifelong learning skills in its students. Certainly, Goddard graduates are frequently successful after they leave the college: many go on to graduate school, and many succeed in the professions, especially in 'non-establishment' roles such as civil rights lawyers, environmental lobbyists, small business entrepreneurs and similar occupations.

Another small liberal arts college that has tried to implement rather similar educational goals is Evergreen State College in Olympus, Washington. Publicly funded, Evergreen has a student enrolment of about 3,000, and its teaching programmes try to foster problem-solving skills, self-reliance, cooperation, communication and personal integrity through interdisciplinary seminars that constitute the central mode of study. Other teaching approaches include internships and applied projects, and students are actively involved in assessing their own learning (Gray, 1990).

Goddard and Evergreen are unusual in that they have both survived and remained true to their original educational objectives. Other experimental colleges have not always been so fortunate. In 1982, Evergreen sponsored a conference on experimental and alternative approaches to higher education that was attended by a wide variety of representatives from institutions across North America. Many institutions had failed to survive, or their programmes had been modified to reflect a much more traditional concept of higher education. On the other hand, in many cases other institutions had sprung up to replace them. Furthermore, Bunting (1982), commenting on the Evergreen meeting, argued that the surviving experimental colleges had provided very important models for higher education, and had had a wider influence than the numbers of students enrolled would suggest.

Informal institutions

A much more informal approach to education than the ones discussed so far is exemplified by the 'free university' movement that sprang up in the USA in the early 1960s, and spread to many parts of the world. Free universities were organizations that offered informal courses to the general public, taught by citizens without particular academic qualifications other than a competence and interest in the topic to be taught. The 'university' served as a general (and very loose) organizational structure, but individual courses were autonomous, and responsibility for content and methods rested with teachers and students. Some of these programmes were in fact sponsored by traditional universities, perhaps as part of the student government or continuing education activities. Others were based on community organizations such as the YMCA or public library. Still other programmes were quite independent and organized by a few interested volunteers.

Free universities were initially set up on US college campuses as a reaction against traditional education. For example, they provided a forum to discuss and learn about social issues, and reflected a sense that education should be a community activity and that students should have a major input into what, and how, they learnt. Once the campus activism of the 1960s had died away, free universities began to take on a more community role as a way of providing an informal and inexpensive education for working adults. Classes typically took place in community centres, public libraries or private homes. Courses included many topics, ranging from arts and crafts to more academic subjects. In Toronto, for example, the 'Skills Exchange' served as a clearing-house for linking individuals with particular learning needs with others who wished to teach. A booklet listing a wide variety of courses (from philosophy to macramé) was widely distributed throughout the city free of charge; the Exchange offered no classroom facilities (classes generally took place in the instructor's home) but was responsible for disseminating information and monitoring the range of offerings. These administrative services were supported by levying a small additional charge that formed part of the course registration fee and was set in each case by the instructor concerned.

The skills exchange concept still survives in a number of North American cities, and there are still one or two 'free universities', such as the Colorado Free University in Denver which advertises itself as providing 'a range of community-oriented adult education classes for lifelong learners'. It seems likely that the social and political imperative that spurred the creation of the original free universities is no longer as relevant in the more materialistic 1990s. Meanwhile, the World Wide Web now provides many of the functions of the skills exchanges by allowing groups of enthusiasts to share information, expertise and new ideas across whole countries and continents. At the same time, these initiatives did exemplify some of the principles of lifelong learning – for example, that learning does not have to take place in special institutions, that learning from other people can be as important as learning from officially appointed teachers, that learning programmes should be self-directed and so on. Draves (1981) described the guiding philosophy of the free university movement in terms of the principle that 'anyone can teach and anyone can learn'. At the same time, these informal networks failed in some respects to meet the ideals of lifelong education, if only because they tended to attract students who already had a well-developed interest in education: typically, job holders with a college education.

Third age universities

Somewhat similar in philosophy, but catering specifically for older learners (typically those over 60 years of age), are the 'Universities of the Third Age'. The first 'Université du Troisième Age' was founded in Toulouse, France in 1972 and was an initiative of established universities wishing to provide educational opportunities for older adults. The aim was to promote and practise lifelong learning by providing low-cost and informal educational opportunities for retired people. There are no requirements for prior educational qualifications and no degrees are awarded. In Britain, the idea was adapted by a group in Cambridge who wished to form a movement based on self-help and mutual aid that would serve as a kind of 'intellectual democracy', unaffiliated with traditional higher education institutions.

The French and Cambridge models share the aim of encouraging older people to continue lifelong learning, but the former retains close ties with universities for provision of teachers and accommodation, while arrangements in the case of the Cambridge model are typically more informal, with participants sometimes acting as students, sometimes as teachers and often in 'study circles' rather than traditional lectures. Topics of study are extremely diverse and range from very practical issues of immediate concern to older adults, such as 'elder abuse' or appropriate use of medication, to strictly academic topics in history and science. Some groups also become involved in lobbying and social activism around issues of concern to both the elderly and the wider community.

Thompson, Itzin and Abendstern (1990) outlined some aspects of the Bath University of the Third Age, which had 350 members aged between 50 and 94. The Bath U3A was a cooperative, quite independent of local higher education institutions and received no state funding. The basic teaching unit was a 'study group' consisting of two or more people with a common interest. Although larger groups might appoint a coordinator, each student was expected to function as a member of a 'learning exchange'; for instance, by taking responsibility for the organization of one group meeting, or perhaps by writing a discussion paper.

It is estimated that the 'U3A' movement now has millions of members worldwide, although not all use that name. For example, in Australia, 30,000 people are involved in programmes offered in over 130 different locations. In North America, a very similar development has been the Elderhostel system in which older adults use university campuses during the summer vacation for a type of 'learning holiday'. U3A groups exist throughout Europe, North America, Asia and Australasia. There is an electronic network for third age groups based in Britain and an international association, based in France, that holds regular conferences. As with the free universities, the Universities of the Third Age tend to attract individuals with above-average educational backgrounds, as opposed to people who have had fewer opportunities to study (Stevens, 1983).

While some institutions have operated outside the formal educational system (the free universities), and some have been received with benevolent tolerance by the educational establishment (eg the Universities of the Third Age), others have provoked hostile reactions from their more conventional counterparts as a result of their incursions into non-traditional forms of higher education. For example, the University of Phoenix is a private, for-profit institution catering for mature working adults who want to earn their degrees quickly. It is the largest private university in the USA. Courses are taken one at a time and they are accelerated – lasting five weeks for undergraduates and six weeks for graduate students. Each class meeting, or 'workshop', lasts four hours and the 20–24 hours of time students spend in the classroom for each course are supplemented with at least that much time in required study groups.

In stark contrast to the traditional university course, the teaching of every course at Phoenix is guided by a 'course module' or detailed syllabus that spells out objectives, specifies assignments and prescribes quite precisely how the instructor should spend class time. Teaching is largely done by over 5,000 part-time instructors, few of whom have traditional academic appointments, and although the university is accredited by the North Central Association of Colleges and Schools, its attempts to offer its programmes in other states have been met with virulent opposition from faculty at traditional universities on the grounds of inadequate 'academic standards'. Despite this, there is considerable demand for Phoenix courses and there are presently over 50,000 students enrolled at more than 80 campuses and learning centres. From the point of view of lifelong learning it appears that the University of Phoenix has some positive characteristics (the ability to study at home) and some negative (an overly prescribed curriculum). While not endorsing its educational approach, Wolfe (1998, p B5) argues that criticisms of Phoenix by academics ring hollow: 'In short, long before the University of Phoenix came into being, institutions of higher education already had adopted many of the techniques that it would find so profitable'.

Certainly, any institution that is perceived as a direct rival to traditional colleges and universities is likely – for both good and bad reasons – to attract their attention and, on occasion, their criticism. The wide range of alternative higher education institutions (a small sample of which have been described here) is still very small in comparison to the higher education establishment. These alternative colleges may have profound effects upon enhancing lifelong learning skills in some individuals, but they are unlikely to bring about the transformation of higher education that may foster lifelong learning skills on a broad scale. At the same time, such experimental and innovative institutions often serve as an example and testing ground for ideas and practices that can later be incorporated into traditional settings. Changing teaching and learning practices within the educational establishment is discussed in the remainder of this chapter.

Changing teaching and learning methods

Educational development

In Chapters 4 and 5 we outlined some of the promising teaching methods and alternative roles for teachers that would be required in a higher education system that made lifelong learning a priority. We also discussed the dilemma that, although teaching constitutes the main *raison d'être* for most higher education institutions, few instructional staff ever receive formal training in methods of teaching and learning, and most are appointed almost exclusively on the basis of their expertise within a discipline, as exemplified by research publications. When universities were relatively small, student–staff ratios low, and only a few hours each week were devoted to formal classes, there were relatively few complaints about the quality of teaching. The highly selected group of students who entered higher education prior to the 1950s was, for the most part, well qualified and motivated; furthermore, most institutions and departments were small enough to allow considerable informal contact between staff and students, to the extent that any deficiencies in teaching methods were often masked.

This situation changed rapidly and extensively during the period of great growth in the 1950s and 1960s. Not only were there vastly more students, much larger classes and increased staff workloads, but the types of student entering college and university were different in terms of attitudes, knowledge and approach to the learning task. Hence, teaching methods that had served well in the past came under increasing critical scrutiny, as higher education expanded and changed. The 1970s and 1980s saw calls for institutions to be in some sense 'accountable', to demonstrate the value of university learning in terms of external criteria. This was linked to some criticism of prevailing teaching methods and – especially in North America – widespread use of student evaluations of instruction.

Between 1970 and 1975, over 1,000 colleges and universities in the USA began some type of activity to help staff members improve their teaching (Centra, 1976), while similar developments took place in Canada, the UK and other Western European countries. In Australian universities, a large number of teaching and learning units were established, many with substantial staff complements, and comparable activities were to be found in countries all over the world. In many cases these endeavours were fairly modest and were run on a voluntary basis – for example, they might involve organization of a series of seminars, or the appointment of senior staff members to act as 'mentors' to new instructors. In other institutions, formal offices or units were established, ranging in size from one or two part-time staff to operations that employed 20 or more professionals, and encompassed such diverse activities as consultation on teaching, induction courses for new staff, automated test scoring services, audio-visual aids and graphics services.

By the mid-1970s these services (which we refer to here by the term 'educational development') had become sufficiently institutionalized to constitute a type of 'movement'. It is perhaps premature to call educational development a profession, but there are many indications that it has managed to establish itself within higher education in many parts of the world (Knapper, 1998). The annual conferences on improving university teaching, sponsored by the University of Maryland, have been held in many parts of the world for almost 30 years, and attract several hundred participants from dozens of different countries; a large number of those organizing the conferences and presenting papers are professional educational developers. The International Consortium for Educational Development (ICED) includes member organizations from 15 different countries embracing five continents. ICED holds regular conferences, maintains an electronic discussion forum (listserv), undertakes research and sponsors a journal (*The International Journal for Academic Development*). There are several other national journals devoted to educational development issues, including *Higher Education*

Research and Development (Australia) and *The Journal of Staff, Program and Organization Development* (USA). These are publications that focus explicitly on the philosophy and practice of educational development – there are many dozens of general journals and periodicals on university teaching to which professional educational developers are major contributors. Although there are few practitioners with doctorates in educational development *per se*, post-graduate programmes do exist at some universities (eg the University of New England in Australia) and in the UK the Staff and Educational Development Association has for several years offered an accreditation programme for university-based developers.

Although there are different models of educational development across and within different higher education systems, there are also many commonalities. Most centres have as their overall aim the enhancement of teaching, which they promote through workshops, seminars and courses (in particular, courses for new faculty), a range of publications about tertiary teaching methods and individual consultations on instructional change and improvement. Centres are frequently involved with evaluation of teaching, sometimes in an administrative capacity, but more often advisory; nearly all have resource libraries, some offer help to departments with curriculum development and an increasing number are involved with educational technology. Some units have small grants programmes to encourage paedagogical innovation, and others serve as general consultants on institutional policy issues affecting teaching and learning – for example, concerning programme quality audits or ethical issues in teaching (Knapper, 1998; Menges and Mathis, 1988; Weimer, 1990).

Since, by definition, those involved in staff development have a commitment to the improvement of teaching, it is not surprising that many of them are concerned with the philosophy and implementation of lifelong education. Indeed, some substantial contributions to the understanding of lifelong learning have come from educational developers, such as David Boud, Philip Candy, Gay Crebert and many others whose names appear throughout this study. At the same time, political pressures within universities may deter educational development units from urging fundamental change in university teaching and learning practice. Since units are often regarded as 'marginal', their staff may feel they lack the freedom – or the political influence – to speak out frankly on fundamental issues without running the risk of criticism from the teachers who are their main clients. There is also some evidence that those least inclined to participate in educational development activities are faculty who are in the greatest need of improvement (Konrad, 1983). Furthermore, there is a danger that development activities will focus unduly on enhancing existing teaching approaches, that is, giving workshops to improve the lecture method, giving advice on how to construct multiple-choice examinations and so on (Geis and Smith, 1983; Gustafson, 1977; Gustafson and Bratton, 1983). This may actually hinder the acquisition of lifelong learning skills, which demand much more radical institutional reorganization and a move away from teacher-dominated learning.

It would be reassuring in a sense to think that this inability to make fundamental changes in instructional methods lies at the root of the educational development movement's failure to make the impact on university teaching and learning that some critics had hoped for. However, it seems more plausible that the slow rate of change has more to do with the general indifference of staff to the teaching function, the general university ethos that stresses research more than teaching and similar factors. In fact, when debates about educational reform are brought to the public forum, educational developers have often been leaders in calling for change and suggesting strategies for achieving it. For example, they were influential in the work of the Dearing Committee in the UK (NCIHE, 1997), the AUCC inquiry in Canada (Smith, 1991), the Carnegie report on the scholarship of teaching in the USA (Boyer, 1990) and the report on undergraduate education commissioned by the Australian Higher Education Council (Candy, Crebert and O'Leary, 1994).

Among the most promising activities of educational development units are their involvement in evaluation and in research on the learning process itself. Evaluation schemes have tended to focus primarily on student ratings of instruction, and many of the questions on rating forms relate to presentation techniques rather than opinions about the amount and type of learning that has taken place. In this sense, it is possible that evaluation reinforces traditional approaches to instruction (Wilson, 1987). On the other hand, information about how students respond to teaching is certainly better than no information (or data based on coffee-room hearsay). Furthermore, summative evaluation schemes that influence administrative decisions about promotion, tenure and so on, at least have the merit of reinforcing the importance of the teaching role. Many rating forms include at least some items that ask about the quality of learning, and more recent approaches to instructional evaluation – for example, the teaching dossier (Shore *et al*, 1986) – have considerably enlarged the scope of the process from a reliance on student questionnaires to a more general concern with learning outcomes. Hence, while teaching evaluation in its present form may not contribute directly to achieving the goals of lifelong education, it can serve as a basis for scrutinizing present teaching practices and appraising instructional changes that encourage a more independent type of learning. Educational developers have also been instrumental in encouraging formative and reflective evaluation by teachers that is certainly consistent with the principles of lifelong learning (Cross and Angelo, 1993; Weimer, 1990).

Research carried out by educational development units may not always be of relevance to the promotion of lifelong learning. However, there resides in the units considerable expertise (perhaps the principal expertise available at the institution) in conducting investigations into educational practices within the university and their effects upon learning. Research of this type has already gone some way towards revealing the shortcomings of traditional instruction (eg investigations of grading practices, studies of the effectiveness of the lecture etc, many of which are referred to in this study). It seems likely that in-house research of this type could provide an extremely useful basis for developing teaching and learning methods that may encourage practices consistent with the principles of lifelong education spelt out in earlier chapters.

Study skills

Just as instructional development units have collaborated with teachers in higher education to effect change, there have also been efforts to work directly with students to improve their learning skills. Study skills programmes exist in many universities around the world and there are numerous textbooks on effective study techniques aimed at the university and college student (Marshall and Rowland, 1998). In some cases training in study skills is part of the educational development office. A more usual model, however, is to offer such training through the university counselling service.

Typical programmes focus on improving reading skills, time management and effective organization of study, note-taking and preparation for examinations. In addition, they often offer instruction in effective writing, preparing essays and reports, and similar skills. Some courses include instruction in 'concept mapping' (creating a visual representation of material being studied) and/or 'self-questioning' (generating questions about what is to be learnt or done in an assignment). It may be thought that such activities are remedial and largely for weaker students, but in fact they attract many good students who wish to do even better. The fact that such programmes are popular with students shows, if nothing else, how little attention is paid in most discipline-based courses to learning *processes* (as opposed to subject-matter content), thus forcing learners to seek the relevant information from outside sources. As Hadwin and Winne (1996, p 693) put it:

> higher education should not merely teach students knowledge in curricular subjects such as history, chemistry, and sociology. Institutions should also provide means for students to develop adaptable strategies with

which to pursue knowledge and solve problems during and after post-secondary experiences. Having such skills contributes abilities and the motivation necessary for lifelong learning.

Just as educational development can be criticized on the grounds that it may focus too much on improving traditional teaching approaches, so study skills workshops that focus on note-taking, examination preparation and similar techniques could be said merely to equip students with ways of making the best of inappropriate instructional methods. On the whole, this is somewhat unfair to study skills advisers, since they are rarely in a position to change teaching practice within their institution, and have to respond to a reality in which students wish to perform well in the actual learning context that they encounter in higher education. Furthermore, some of the common components of study skills courses do deal with aptitudes that are perfectly consistent with lifelong learning – such as the ability to organize study, manage time, learn from peers, communicate with others, read and write reports and so on.

One approach to study skills that encourages students to be independent learners and continually question their own learning processes is outlined in the handbook prepared by Marshall and Rowland (1998). Although the familiar topics of taking better lecture notes and preparing for examinations are covered in the text, Marshall and Rowland encourage a generally critical attitude about the general purpose of education, and urge students to examine their expectations, choices and decisions. Students are told how to seek guidance from their peers (as well as from academic staff), how to ask questions and even whether or why material encountered in academic courses is worth remembering. The sections on examinations and grading are also somewhat unusual in that they focus on how students may derive personal benefit from the evaluation process and use it for their own ends.

Study skills programmes have also been criticized on other grounds. For example, it is argued that they are not fully integrated into the regular academic work of the student and are seen as 'quick fix' solutions to problems that require much more fundamental changes in attitudes and study habits. Hence, techniques learnt in a short course lasting a few hours will be unlikely to transfer to the different learning situations that students encounter in a variety of classes, tasks and subject matters. Hadwin and Winne (1996) reviewed 566 papers on study skills and learning and decided that only 16 provided convincing evidence of transfer of taught skills to other situations. Nonetheless, they did 'cautiously conclude' (1996, p 712) that concept mapping, self-questioning and monitoring time spent studying had positive effects on course success. They recommended blending instruction about study strategies with regular course work, with the aim of encouraging engagement 'in broader and deeper cognitive processing about *studying* [authors' italics], as well as about the content... Both processes are critical in establishing a fruitful base for students to engage in self-regulation of learning' (Hadwin and Winne, 1996, p 713). Hattie, Biggs and Purdie (1996) used the term 'situated cognition', and stressed the importance of teaching study skills that involve a high degree of learner activity and 'metacognitive awareness'. This they defined as the ability to manage one's own learning through planning, implementing and monitoring learning, and ability to use particular learning strategies in appropriate situations.

A common theme among these critiques is the need for closer links between study skills instruction and the subject matter being studied in academic courses, along with the elevation of study skills to a more prominent place in the curriculum, where they can receive more time and attention, attain a generally higher profile and greater credibility and, as a result, involve more students. This is the approach used in Murdoch University's foundation courses, mentioned in Chapter 4, which are required of all incoming students and include a major component of study skills techniques. The foundation courses adopt a broadly based interdisciplinary approach, and tutors are expected to teach learning skills strategies along with the 'academic' content. Since many of these tutors have no prior training in teaching language and learning skills, a staff development induction programme has been established. Specialist student learning staff have also developed study guides that include material tailored to the content and assessment requirements of each foundation unit and cover critical thinking, essay and report writing, numeracy, reading and study management, with an overall emphasis on encouraging peer learning. Specialist support is provided for students who require additional help with study skills.

In many institutions, however, it may be difficult to integrate study skills techniques into regular discipline-based coursework, as has been suggested by Marshall and Rowland, Hadwin and Winne and Hattie, Biggs and Purdie. In many cases the teaching staff will have little interest in taking time to cover basic study techniques, or may lack the skills to do so effectively. Despite the criticisms reviewed above, many study skills programmes do, in fact, try to relate the techniques they teach to the real academic problems faced by students – for example, by having students bring to the study skills workshops problems and examples encountered in their normal courses. It is also true that no amount of training will do any good if university courses actually devalue self-direction and reflection through emphasis on didactic teaching and assessment methods that primarily stress memorization.

Non-traditional students present a special challenge for study skills programmes: for example, foreign students, students from minority groups, and mature students all enter the special environment of higher education with backgrounds and aptitudes that may differ markedly from those of students who come from the traditional secondary school system. Since in many countries adult learners form an increasingly large segment of the student body, this group has been of special concern. Among the particular study problems identified are those of re-entering the education system, coping with mathematics and science subjects, combining academic work with other commitments, and integrating life experiences with what is learnt in the classroom. Many institutions have organized special study programmes for mature students, and a common element is the use of peers to help with the learning task and provide a mutual support system (Knights and McDonald, 1982). Other strategies have included pre-enrolment of adult students to enable them to 'try out' university education before formally registering, linked with special counselling (McDonald and Knights, 1979), and use of mentors to provide support with learning problems (Cohen, 1995). Before becoming too concerned about the special problems of mature students, however, it should be borne in mind that there is growing research evidence that such students are often actually more effective learners than their younger counterparts and, in particular, have better time-management skills (Trueman and Hartley, 1996) and demonstrate deeper learning approaches (Richardson, 1995).

Another special group is 'at-risk' students – those who experience difficulty with tertiary study during their first semester at university. At one time such students would simply have been allowed to fail, but in most universities today student retention is a high priority. Murdoch University, for example, offers a special course ('Introduction to university learning') for first-year students in danger of failing or withdrawing. The course is taken in conjunction with the regular first-year foundation programme, and aims to develop the students' skills as university learners by integrating their practice of fundamental learning skills with the study of concepts and theories from a range of disciplines.

Whatever the shortcomings of study skills programmes, it seems clear that many students do need help with the process and practice of learning, and that they cannot be expected to acquire by magic the techniques necessary for independent learning. This further implies a need to teach lifelong learning skills explicitly, and there have been some recent publications aimed at teachers that focus on instructional strategies for better learning. For example, Weinstein and Hume's *Study strategies for lifelong learning* provides teachers with a number of classroom aids to encourage strategic and self-directed learning and reflection about the learning process (Weinstein and Hume, 1998). Wisker and Brown's *Enabling student learning* (1996) explores a range of institutional and individual strategies to foster attitudes and skills relevant to better learning approaches. Hartley (1998) summarized recent psychological research on study skills and learning approaches and offered advice to both teachers and students on promoting more effective learning, including acquisition of lifelong learning skills. He pointed out, however, that encouraging effective learning involves all aspects of teaching and, in particular, the way that students are assessed.

Educational technology

At a time when there is widespread talk about an information revolution affecting the world as profoundly as the industrial revolution did 200 years ago, it is not surprising that information technology has been heralded as a force that will dramatically change the delivery and organization of education, including higher education. Indeed, the term 'revolution' has been used explicitly in the context of technology's potential effects on education. Thirty years ago, the distinguished academic, Lord Ashby, saw information technology as a fourth revolution – following three previous revolutions that encompassed the establishment of the formal school, the transition of an education based upon speech to an education based on writing and the invention of movable type and the printing press (Carnegie Foundation, 1972).

The term 'information technology' is relatively new, but the older concept of educational technology has a history that goes back to the 1950s, and included such innovations as programmed instruction, teaching machines and educational television. These developments did have at least a short-term impact upon educational practice. For example, the programmed instruction movement in the 1950s received a great amount of attention in schools and universities, and caused many teachers to examine closely their educational objectives and instructional methods. Educational television, while its low level of acceptance within the traditional school and university proved a major disappointment, has been used extensively in distance education (eg the Open University and its counterparts), although its relative importance here in relation to other more traditional media is probably much less than titles such as 'University of the Air' or 'Télé-Université' may imply.

Information technology links together the computer, with its immense capacity for storing and handling information, and electronic communication systems that enable the information to be sent over great distances and to numerous reception points, virtually instantaneously. The most common manifestations today are the Internet and the World Wide Web. The new technologies have considerable implications for educational practice – not only in providing new ways of delivering learning materials (eg increasing access through distance learning), but also in facilitating communication among learners, and changing the ways in which instructional resources may be organized and presented. Even more than that, technology is now an all-pervasive aspect of people's everyday lives. As Green (1999, p 11) stated:

> It's not just computers, the Internet, or the Web; it's the *aggregated presence* [author's italics] of technologies in all facets of daily life that has made the difference. Higher education's clientele – students from ages 17 to 67 – now come to college expecting to learn *about* technology and also to learn *with* technology.

In this section, we examine the implications of educational technology for lifelong learning, focusing on the use of computers to change teaching and learning methods, the way that communications technologies facilitate distance education and the extent to which lifelong learners need to know *about* relevant technologies and be skilled in their use. We examine the various technological developments in the light of criteria for lifelong learning spelt out earlier – in particular, the matter of *broadening access* to higher education, catering for *individual differences* between learners, making learning more *flexible, active, integrative and relevant to real-world issues*, and promoting more *collaborative, self-directed and reflective learning*.

Teaching and learning with computers

There is nothing very new about the use of computers for instructional purposes. It was an obvious step in the early 1960s to develop versions of programmed instruction for use on a computer which was, even then, a more reliable delivery device than the old mechanical teaching machines. Computer-assisted instruction and its variants (computer-assisted learning, computer-based instruction etc), using large mainframe computers, were the subject of much development and experimentation during the 1960s and 1970s, especially in North America. Although experimentation with computer-assisted instruction continued in many colleges and universities, it would be true to say that the great majority of the work remained on an experimental level, while traditional teaching practices remained largely unchanged.

Computer-assisted instruction on mainframe machines was frequently unwieldy and expensive. However, the advent of the microcomputer (personal computer or PC) in the late 1970s seemed to offer a new opportunity for computer-based teaching to make a major contribution to educational practice. Nowadays PCs are so inexpensive that they are ubiquitous in schools and homes, at least in the economically developed countries, and it is not uncommon for colleges and universities to require that all students have their own machine. Software can be produced with little, if any, knowledge of programming and distributed cheaply, and educational courseware can easily be made to combine text with graphics, sound and video. Connections with the Internet are available at modest cost in all but the most remote locations and offer the prospect of unhindered access to a cornucopia of educational resources. Small wonder that there is pressure on faculty to incorporate educational technology in their teaching or that there is (yet again) talk of revolutionary change in the way that learning takes place in higher education. There is no doubt that the educational community – and the wider community of learners – have considerable expectations of the role that computers will play in education at all levels. However, the exact nature of those expectations is not always clear.

How do these developments in information technology serve the need to equip students with lifelong learning skills? Two advantages often claimed for educational technology are that it promotes active learning and provides a means of individualizing learning (and hence perhaps offers prospects of more learner control). In practice, the degree of active learner involvement and individualization in computer-mediated learning (CML) varies considerably from one situation to another. Computer-based educational programmes embrace several different instructional approaches. They may involve 'drill and practice' exercises (eg in French grammar or arithmetic), 'tutorials' (largely didactic information presented electronically), diagnosis and testing of student ability or learning, and simulations.

The most common types of programme are probably *tutorials*, in which the computer is used to present material, in much the same way as a textbook or lecturer, but with the added feature that comprehension or mastery is tested at regular intervals, with failure to answer the test question correctly often causing the learner to be routed to a remedial sequence of instruction. Although modern versions of tutorial CML look much slicker, with graphics, video, links to self-test questions and glossaries of technical terms, the paedagogical underpinnings are mostly the same as those that guided early PC-based educational courseware 20 years ago, or – for that matter – the teaching machines of the 1960s. The 'activity' for the learner here is limited – indeed, it is generally equivalent to the active learning involved in reading a textbook and answering questions embedded in the text. Individualization can, in principle, be achieved to a quite considerable degree using complex branching sequences guided by sensitive diagnostic tests. In practice, this potential advantage of the computer has rarely been fully exploited, and a good deal of the 'individualization' that exists in computer-based learning courseware is no greater than was found in the much cruder, mechanical teaching machines of 30 years ago.

Drill and practice programmes are more common for school-age children (eg the very successful 'Roger Rabbit' applications to teach basic arithmetic and spelling), but they have also survived in higher education and are used widely in language laboratories to teach vocabulary and grammar. Certainly, they involve active learning and can be effective at teaching knowledge and simple skills, but they are hardly likely to revolutionize education in the manner suggested by Ashby.

On the other hand, the use of computers to *diagnose learner aptitudes*, knowledge and even learning style seems to have considerable promise. Because of their almost unlimited storage capacity, computers can generate diagnostic questions from a large bank of items in order to pinpoint what students already know about a topic, and then provide appropriate guidance. This approach appears to offer particular benefits for non-traditional students, who may have been out of the educational system for some years, but have acquired knowledge and skills from a variety of alternative sources. Since independent and self-directed learning is an important aim of lifelong education, it would be valuable to have a tool that could be used to help guide students' learning activities, and do so in a much more rapid and precise manner than is normally possible through the more traditional means of discussions between teacher and learner. However, the use of CML for such diagnostic purposes has never been fully exploited, perhaps because it requires a good deal of hard work to generate appropriate questions and develop the logic for linking patterns of answers to appropriate remedial instruction. It is even more difficult to go a step further and try to guide students on the basis of their study habits, preferred learning style and similar factors. Hence, the type of computer diagnosis we are describing here does not exist in the sophisticated form that would be desirable.

While many university texts now come with computerized banks of questions, they are mainly intended to provide material for fact-based quizzes. In contrast, considerable efforts have been put into *presentation software* that exploits the capacity of the PC to supplement text with sound, and graphics and video. It is often argued that contemporary students, used to constant visual stimulation (eg through television and computer games), need the extra stimulation of multimedia to attract and keep their attention. This may be so (although there is scant empirical evidence to support this hypothesis), but it remains true that a great deal of information – both in school and at work – is print-based, and most students will need to use written communication in the foreseeable future. In addition, the sophisticated presentation software used for instructional purposes is of no particular relevance to the promotion of lifelong learning, except in the sense that it can be distributed readily over great distances – but, of course, so can print.

A more promising use of computer-based instruction involves *simulation* of some task or situation that would normally be difficult to bring into the classroom or home. The effectiveness of simulations to teach complicated skills has been known for some time; for example, flight simulators used in pilot training. Computers are no longer limited to presenting text; they can also show video, play sounds and even provide a 'virtual reality' that includes sensation of touch, movement, all in three dimensions. The ability to manipulate a simulated environment is what makes computer games like 'Riven' so attractive, and the same capabilities can be used for educational purposes. These applications involve both active learning and individualization – in the sense that the learner controls the interaction with the programme. There are many examples of computer simulations for teaching in higher education. The most successful from the point of view of learning seem to be ones where a computer interface would be used in the real-life situation (manipulating financial information; controlling an oil refinery) rather than those where other essential non-computing skills are involved: for example, medical diagnosis (Tannenbaum, 1999).

Communications technology and distance education

It can be argued that the various forms of CML discussed above simply provide a more sophisticated and engaging means of doing something that was always possible in a simpler format through lectures and print. The advantages of tutorials on CD-ROM or of presentation software such as Powerpoint rest on the assumption that a major purpose of education is to 'deliver' information from an authoritative source, often in a largely linear manner (Creed, 1997). However, the new communications technologies, in particular the Internet and the World Wide Web, offer the possibility not just of presenting information, but of linking information sources with millions of individuals all over the globe; moreover, the users, too, become sources of information and expertise.

In the decade since the last edition of this book, the growth of the Internet has been staggering. Currently, it is estimated that there are over 74 million Internet users, 40 per cent of whom have never attended a higher education institution. Usage is much higher for those enrolled in college or university, and in North America students are routinely given their own accounts for access to the e-mail and the Web. Green (1999) estimated that 40 per cent of US college courses used some form of e-mail, while one-third used the Web, if only to post a course home page. Clearly, this offers the potential for reaching far more learners than are able to benefit from higher education by the traditional means of attending classes on campus. However, perhaps even more important from the point of view of lifelong learning is the opportunity offered by the Internet for students to learn from each other. Anyone who has browsed the Web for a just a few hours cannot fail to notice the huge amount of informal teaching and learning that already takes place through this medium, most of it quite outside the control of educational institutions and spurred on by the enthusiasm of participants who post information, ask for help and exchange ideas and information. Despite the abundance of commercial providers, many of the most fascinating Web sites are those run by groups who share a common passion for some topic, ranging from bee-keeping to hagiology. These virtual learning communities (Di Petta, 1998) have the advantage of being on the whole more democratic than traditional education; on the other hand, the accuracy and quality of the information posted and exchanged may at times be suspect. This has attracted the condemnation of many university faculty who find their students seeking information on the Internet that in times past would have been sought in the university library.

Higher education institutions have attempted to exploit these new technologies by developing and expanding distance education programmes. In Chapter 5 we discussed distance learning and its potential for facilitating greater educational access. While distance learning in higher education still makes extensive use of old-fashioned media, such as print, there is no doubt that modern communications technologies offer considerable possibilities for reaching new students and even for transforming the way learning takes place. In particular, the communications technologies promise to help overcome one of the main handicaps of traditional distance education – the difficulty of fostering interaction between students and between students and teacher. In a typical on-line course students use the Web to access course materials ('lessons'), assignments and tests; they communicate with their teachers through e-mail. Many courses have electronic discussion forums, and a few even allow links to a real classroom through 'streaming video'.

Distance education offerings have burgeoned so rapidly in the past five years or so that it is impossible to get any accurate estimate of the numbers of students involved. The US Department of Education claimed that in the autumn of 1998 distance courses were offered at 90 per cent of higher education institutions with enrolments of more than 10,000 students, and 85 per cent of those with enrolments between 3,000 and 10,000. In early 1999, the TeleCampus Web site listed over 12,000 classes offered by 700 colleges and other institutions located all over the world. Meanwhile, 14 of North America's largest research universities announced their intention to collaborate in marketing their distance education courses through a central directory (or 'portal') on the Web (Young, 1999).

This apparently massive growth has caused some commentators to forecast that information technology will allow distance study to become the norm, with the traditional school or university gradually being rendered obsolete. Twenty years ago, Masuda (1981) described an information society in which learning would take place primarily by computer-based systems. He argued that 'education will be freed from the restrictions of income, time, and place' (p 65), with unlimited educational opportunities and conditions that would make it possible for people to develop their full educational potential. Hence education, according to Masuda, would move out of the control of normal educational institutions, and be concentrated instead on individual learners, linked to each other in knowledge networks. Furthermore, it follows that this type of self-directed, individually tailored learning would not be restricted to the conventional years of schooling, but will be lifelong – 'to enable adults and elderly people to adapt themselves to the changes of the information society' (p 67).

Certainly, there is now considerable competition from private sector providers of distance courses and some analysts have postulated the 'emergence of a "higher learning" industry, dominated by commercial firms' (Katz *et al*, 1999, p xiv). For example, the Western Governors University (WGU) was founded by 17 US state governors and 14 business partners that include IBM, Sun, AT&T and Microsoft. It does not employ teaching faculty or develop its own courses but instead purchases on-line academic content from a range of providers, including colleges and business worldwide (Leavitt, 1997; Marchese, 1998). Sylvan Learning Systems of Baltimore, which for years has offered private classroom-based technical training, has announced its intention of becoming the leading provider of educational services to families and industry.

The publisher, Harcourt Brace, has announced its intention to open an on-line for-profit university using its own course materials and offering degrees up to the Master's level aimed at non-traditional students in business, health care systems and administration, information technology and general studies (Blumenstyk, 1999a). In partnership with a number of North American universities, IBM has established a 'Global Campus' to provide tools and services for distance education and 'distributed learning environments'. In addition, two universities in Michigan have collaborated with automobile manufacturers and the United Auto Workers to form the Michigan Virtual Automotive College which will provide comprehensive on-line training for the industry. Even the venerable Oxford University established a distance education programme in 1996 with the title of Technology-Assisted Lifelong Learning (Darby *et al*, 1998).

Marchese (1998) stated that so far alternative and distance education providers account for only 2 per cent of the post-secondary market – and enrolments so far at WGU have been disappointingly low. However, according to International Data Corporation, the number of people taking at least one college-level course over the Internet in the USA will triple by the year 2002 to about 2.2 million (Thornton, 1999) and there is no doubt that on-line learning offers a very real challenge to traditional forms of university teaching. Indeed, the potential for marketing distance education is seen as so great that it is now possible to attend (residential) workshops on 'Designing a virtual corporate university'.

While the examples above are drawn from North America, similar developments have occurred elsewhere – in Marchese's words (1998, p 7), 'from Peru to Malaysia'. For example, in Germany the University of Karlsruhe is spearheading a consortium of institutions to offer courses internationally using the Internet and other communications technologies, and the University of Hagen (Germany's open university) is in the process of replacing some print-based courses with Web pages and Internet-based audio- and video-conferencing. Interestingly, the language of instruction will be English. In India, too, there has been recognition that on-line education offers the prospect of globalization of higher education (Powar, 1998). The country's premier distance education institution, the Indira Gandhi National Open University, has experimented with courses that involve satellite-based interactive teleconferencing, although so far the number of students involved is small, and the experiment has encountered a number of technical obstacles, for example, due to inadequacies of the telephone system (Rao and Khan, 1998).

Despite the recent worldwide enthusiasm for on-line distance education, some experts have expressed scepticism about what Sir John Daniel, Vice-Chancellor of the British Open University, called the 'commercial hype and hope about distance learning' which he claimed was based on 'a very unidirectional conception of the delivery of instruction, where teaching is merely presentation and learning is merely absorption' (Daniel, 1998, p 11). The Open University (OU) has always used technology, notably television and radio, but its courses still rely predominantly on print material, with student support provided by a complex network of 7,000 tutors (about one for every 20 students). Blumenstyk (1999b) reported that OU courses are fundamentally different from a typical US distance course – they are longer, use a much wider range of materials (most specially written) and provide a much more elaborate support network for students. Not surprisingly, they are much more expensive to prepare – often over $2 million for a single course. At the same time, although considerable use is made of e-mail to communicate with students, so far only six OU courses are designed to be completely Internet-based, and they are in computing, or for a programme to teach principles of distance education.

Other commentators are more bullish than Daniel about the prospects for on-line education displacing traditional teaching approaches and, indeed, the university itself. The comment by Matthews (1998, p 49) is fairly typical of this line of argument:

The bedrock assumption that education must take place in classrooms in which a professor teaches a group of students underlies the entire organizational framework for higher education – affecting everything from course accounting and faculty workload to tuition and state funding. But this assumption is no longer valid, mainly because of advances in information technology.

Matthews believes that higher education will eventually be 're-engineered' around the technology; learning will be time and place independent ('asynchronous') and course *content* will no longer have much value since it is essentially just 'another form of data' and available free through the Internet. Courses will be customized according to the needs and schedule of the student, and quality will be judged in terms of student outcomes or 'competencies'.

While in some ways this vision supports our criteria for lifelong learning, as Daniel argues, it represents a very narrow view of learning that is based on 'delivery' of information ('modules'). There is little emphasis here on learner reflection or self-actualization, and it is no surprise that critics like Noble (1998) have described this approach as simply a form of 'commoditization of instruction'. Farrington (1999, p. 80) put the point well when he stated that 'a key challenge for distance education, just as for traditional residential education, is to stimulate students to go beyond facts and skills and create in themselves the deeper intellectual structures that define, however imprecisely, the goal of a true education'.

Educational technology and lifelong learning

What are the implications of these developments in information technology and distance learning for the lifelong learning criteria spelt out in Chapter 3? Knapper (1988c) selected a number of crucial characteristics of the learning process against which to assess the possible contribution of technology. The following is an adaptation of Knapper's list:

- *access and flexibility* (learning should be available to a wide range of potential learners at times and places that are convenient);
- *activity* (learners cannot be simply passive consumers of wisdom served up by teachers);
- *self-direction and democracy* (learning must be largely controlled by learners, not teachers);
- *collaboration* (learning should involve team work and communication skills);
- *regard for individual differences* (individual learning styles and goals must be taken into account);
- *relevance* (learning must be related to real life);

- *integration* (formal learning must take account of knowledge from different fields and in real-world settings).

Of course, these learning criteria are also important in conventional education with traditional learners. However, they are absolutely vital in the case of lifelong learning, because of the special needs and characteristics of adult students.

Knapper applied these criteria to various forms of educational technology. He concluded, for instance, that computer simulations encouraged active learning, were highly flexible and made learning relevant to real life; computer conferencing had all these advantages and in addition promoted collaboration. On the other hand, we could say that a CD-ROM programme to teach microbiology was largely teacher-directed (and hence not especially 'democratic'), allowed little integration of material from different areas, and offered little chance of collaborative learning, even though it may be quite flexible compared to attending a lecture, and demand a great deal of activity from the learner. Knapper's evaluation of instructional technology made it plain that, at least from the point of view of lifelong learning, not all applications of technology to education are equally successful or even desirable.

On-line distance education, for example, has been commended for broadening access to educational opportunity but, in fact, many people are technologically disadvantaged. For example, in many rural states in the USA, an average of 17 per cent or more of families do not have telephones, let alone computers (Tannenbaum, 1999). In addition, although there are over 74 million Internet users in the USA (about a quarter of all households), they tend to be younger and more educated than the general population. In 1998 households with incomes of $75,000 and higher were more than 20 times more likely to have access to the Internet than those at the lowest income levels (NTIA, 1999). While computer ownership has grown among members of minority groups in the past few years, black and Hispanic people still lag far behind the national US average of 40 per cent, and it appears the gap is widening. Even the OU tends to attract the more highly educated and its student body does not truly reflect the ethnic and economic diversity of Britain as a whole (Blumenstyk, 1999b). In the case of economically less-developed nations, the situation regarding access to computers and the Internet is, of course, much worse. For example, Cuneo (1998) reported that the percentage of the population with access to the Internet in 1997–98 was only 1.7 in Africa and less than 1 per cent in the Asia/Pacific region, compared to over 30 per cent for Canada and the USA. Cuneo also commented on psychological barriers to computer use and cited evidence that women and older people are much more anxious about using technology and often reluctant to use it for educational purposes. One final barrier to Internet access is language: information technology is dominated by use of the Roman alphabet and, in particular, by use of the English language, which puts it out of the reach of a majority of the world's population.

Another slant on the issue of technology and lifelong learning is to ask whether learners in the future will require knowledge of technology to function in a world that is increasingly technology dependent. For example, Oblinger and Verville (1998, p 79) argued that 'technology is becoming a required competency in the workplace; it has become another basic skill'. They reported that about 65 per cent of all workers in the USA use some type of information technology in their jobs and forecast that this will soon increase to 95 per cent. In earlier editions of this book, we included a section on 'computer literacy' and described efforts by higher education institutions to teach students appropriate computing skills. At least in the case of North American higher education, this is no longer so much an issue, since most traditional-age students have extensive computing experience already, own their own PC, and use it regularly for such tasks as word processing, data analysis, communicating on the Internet and searching for information on the Web. Many universities require their students to own a computer (in some cases a laptop that can be taken into the classroom and the library), although it is not clear whether the instructional methods used in these institutions really exploit the ongoing availability of access to technology. Assuming that ability to use technology (and computers in particular) is an essential life skill, then we are left with the dilemma of how learners can best acquire such skill, and at what cost. This will be especially problematic for the technologically disadvantaged groups we have referred to above.

Technology and paedagogy

One by-product of the recent surge of interest in educational technology is that it causes us to think about fundamental goals of teaching and learning and about the role of higher education institutions in a world that is rapidly being transformed by technology. For example, in the opinion of a recent Australian report on university financing, the changes wrought by the digital revolution will be so pervasive that universities will be forced to fundamentally rethink every aspect of the way they provide their services (CRHEFP, 1997, p 11). There is a tacit assumption in academia that educational technology will produce serious institutional reform and 'revolutionize the teaching–learning process' (Baldwin, 1998, p 9). However, this will not necessarily produce environments that are conducive to lifelong learning. Privateer (1999) commented that higher education to date has been dominated by 'reproduction technologies... characterized by a technology to transmit duplicated information' (p 69). He argued that the predominant teaching approach of lecturing and testing 'largely defines academic value by examining students on their ability to reproduce information within a fixed time period', with tests being 'echoes of lectures'. Privateer was concerned that technology will simply be used in the same way (what he calls 'elaborate versions of portable slates') instead of to develop 'learning management strategies... capable of uniting new ways of knowing with new ways of learning' (p 75).

Talbott (1999, p 26) made essentially the same point when he referred to a 'fact-shovelling model of education' that is easily and cheaply provided by computer-mediated instruction. This may diminish the role of traditional educational providers and Talbott goes on to speculate rather provocatively that eventually perhaps students too will become superfluous, since 'it's much more efficient to transfer information from one database to another than from a database to a mind' (p 26). In this context, it will be a major challenge for proponents of lifelong education to articulate ways in which information technology can be used to serve relevant learning goals.

7

Evaluating lifelong learning

The importance of evaluation

The terms 'evaluation', 'appraisal' and 'assessment' have cropped up repeatedly in our discussions so far, reflecting the central role of evaluation in any educational system. For example, we argued in Chapter 4 that the assessment of students (by means of examinations and grading procedures) is perhaps the greatest single influence on student learning in formal institutions of higher education, even if its importance often goes unrecognized by instructors. Elsewhere in this study we have touched on the appraisal of particular institutions, learning approaches and support systems for lifelong learning. In other words, the topic of evaluation is a recurring theme throughout this study. This chapter picks up the threads of these earlier discussions and focuses on the evaluation of procedures and approaches that aim to promote lifelong learning – hence the focus is on lifelong education itself.

One aim in this study was to make a case for the importance of fostering lifelong learning prerequisites and skills. We thus devoted the early chapters to describing the conceptual underpinnings for a system of higher education based on lifelong learning principles. Our argument was based upon philosophical, social, paedagogical and, in part, political premises that we believe will be shared by educators. However, whether or not this is so, it is important to recognize that our beliefs are in themselves not amenable to empirical evaluation. A second aim of this study was to outline what kind of practical changes in higher education might lead to the promotion of lifelong learning. Here evaluation is possible – for example, by examining relevant procedures and methods, using lifelong education principles as appropriate criteria.

In this chapter, then, we describe some of the types of evaluation that have been carried out and try to appraise some of the practical attempts at introducing lifelong learning methods in colleges and universities – especially approaches that have been described earlier. Equally important, we examine methods through which such developments may be judged. This will shed light on the question of whether the institutions and innovations concerned do indeed produce in students the skills, personal characteristics and values that we have claimed are essential for effective lifelong learning. Finally, we offer guidelines through which university teachers can examine some common instructional procedures and organizational arrangements in order to evaluate their own teaching in terms of our criteria for lifelong learning.

It is possible to identify two broad approaches to evaluation, as the term is used in this chapter. The first involves the assessment of individuals, usually students, and the second focuses on evaluation of systems and programmes. These approaches are not, of course, mutually exclusive. Indeed, to study the effectiveness of a programme, it is nearly always necessary to assess the students who are taking part, to see what they learnt and how their learning changed over time, in the hope of extracting general principles that can be applied in other educational contexts.

Difficulties of evaluation

The topic of educational evaluation is one that has been dealt with exhaustively in the professional literature, and it is not possible to do more here than outline some of the ways in which evaluations have been conducted, and draw attention to the stumbling blocks that will be encountered in any attempt to carry out assessments of procedures that aim to promote lifelong learning. It is important to review these obstacles, however, if only to explain the relative dearth of good evaluative studies in the area.

Despite these cautionary comments, the fact that it is often difficult to evaluate educational programmes and determine precisely their long-term effects on students does not mean that attempts at evaluation should simply be abandoned. On the contrary, we believe that it is essential to monitor relevant educational developments on a continuing basis. We believe further that such evaluation needs to be of a 'formative' nature, whereby the system, institution or innovation can be assessed on an ongoing basis, with a view to revealing those aspects that appear to be successful in promoting lifelong learning, as well as factors that mitigate against it. In effect, we wish to broaden the approach to assessment of lifelong learning programmes to emphasize not simply a retrospective and summative judgement on whether the programme 'worked' or was 'better' than the traditional programme, but also to provide information rich enough to improve the programme. This is especially important when the data gathered include information on student performance. Such data should be seen not primarily as a comment on the students' inherent abilities, but as an indication of what sort of learning took place and how it was facilitated by the instructional activities and educational context.

The results of evaluation

Those who look to particular instructional approaches as ways of implementing a deeply held educational philosophy – such as one emphasizing lifelong learning – may have to take a great deal on faith. Although this may seem to constitute a rather fragile basis for suggesting radical change in educational practice, it is important to bear in mind that the research evidence for the effectiveness of many traditional approaches to teaching is also equivocal or, in some cases, seems to demonstrate the limitations of traditional practices. Examples are research on the effects of the liberal arts curriculum (see Chapter 2) or the lecture method (see Chapter 4) on student learning, thinking skills, motivation and attitudes.

Given this caveat, what conclusions can be drawn from the existing evidence about the effectiveness of some of the alternative approaches described in earlier chapters? We will deal with this issue in following sections.

Evaluating teaching and learning approaches

Despite the problems that beset educational research, efforts to understand learning processes continue and, in particular, to determine how students' learning strategies are affected by teaching approaches. Of special relevance to lifelong education are the recent attempts to examine what may be termed the 'anthropology' or 'phenomenology' of learning, by means of naturalistic in-depth studies of how students go about this task, the factors in the academic environment that influence their approach to academic study and the cognitive changes that take place in students during their years at college and university. This research, instead of focusing upon the content of learning (which was the primary interest of early psychological investigations in the field), has tried to describe the different ways in which students understand and structure the information, concepts and principles they encounter in their courses.

Among the earliest research of this sort was the series of longitudinal studies carried out at Harvard by Perry (1970), who postulated a developmental model of learning in which students can progress from an 'absolutistic' view of knowledge (seeking the 'right answers'), to a more relativistic way of reasoning, and eventually to the development of personal commitment and the ability to take responsibility for personal choice. In the context of mathematics and science learning, Resnick (1983) took up a similar theme in observing that many students who did well on textbook problems were often unable to apply the laws and formulae they had mastered to the interpretation of real physical events. Beginning students tended to use their own 'naïve' theories to explain real-world phenomena and still resorted to these theories in attempting to solve new problems that lay outside the scope of textbook examples. Resnick argued that learners persist in trying to 'construct' understanding and are dissatisfied with simply mirroring what they are told or what they read. Hence, successful problem solving in science and mathematics requires a type of 'qualitative reasoning' in which alternative relationships among variables must be carefully considered. Unless teaching recognizes these qualitative aspects, and students are guided to make sense out of procedures and formulae, it will be impossible to achieve the problem-solving skills that most academics see as desirable. A similar argument was made by Brown, Collins and Duguid (1989) in their criticism of 'decontextualized' learning that takes place in most classrooms. As explained in Chapter 2, Brown *et al* called for the introduction of more 'authentic' learning, and suggested an approach for achieving this that they called 'cognitive apprenticeship'.

The British psychologist Pask (1976) offered some insights into this dilemma with his account of the different ways in which students attempted to build structures to explain the concepts and phenomena they encountered. He distinguished between 'serialists' and 'holists' (Pask's original terms were rather more evocative; holistic learners were referred to as 'lumpers' and serialists as 'stringers'). Serialists concentrate on one aspect of the task at a time in a step-wise fashion, and advance only simple hypotheses to explain what they perceive; holists look for whole structures and use more complex hypotheses in which several aspects of the problem are considered simultaneously.

While Pask was concerned with student performance at learning tasks, Marton and his associates at the University of Göteborg in Sweden focused on students' approaches to study in their handling of learning materials. Their research made use of interviews, diaries and similar techniques. Marton distinguished between a 'deep' approach to studying and a 'surface' approach. In the deep approach, the student actively strives for meaning and understanding in order to make sense of what has been learnt, tries to identify central principles and ideas, relates concepts and arguments to evidence and data and forges links with previous knowledge and experience. In the surface approach, there is a passive concern with rote learning, memorization and isolated details and facts, in order to reproduce the material rather than understand it. Such learners may solve problems, but in a mechanical way that may often be inappropriate. Marton and Saljo (1976a, 1976b) gave an example of students studying a text with a surface approach who focused on the words of the text rather than on the underlying message. In contrast, students adopting a deep approach seemed to focus their attention beyond or beneath the text in an attempt to identify the basic ideas being presented. These ideas have clear relevance for our earlier discussion (see Chapter 4) about the frequent discrepancy between the high-level learning objectives espoused by many university teachers and the more trivial types of learning performance often required in examinations. In this context, it is interesting to note that students who are capable of functioning at a deep level may not trouble to do so if the demands of the situation encourage surface level performance, as demonstrated by the work of Watkins (1984) and Ramsden and Entwistle (1981), mentioned earlier.

Miller and Parlett (1974) introduced the notion of cue-seeking in students. 'Cue-seekers' actively look for all the hints they can obtain about what is required in a learning (or examination) situation, and successfully adapt to the demands of the 'hidden curriculum'. 'Cue-conscious' students are able to do this too, but have a more critical and independent approach and can demonstrate deep learning if required to do so. Miller and Parlett's third unfortunate category of the 'cue-deaf' refers to students who are simply not aware that there are any cues to respond to.

Another research team that adopted a similar approach was the Study Methods Group at the British Open University (Morgan, Taylor and Gibbs, 1982), who followed a group of 29 students enrolled in an introductory social science course, interviewing them on three occasions to probe various aspects of their learning experience. They were able to identify differences consistent with the Göteborg group's distinction between deep and surface approaches to study. Morgan *et al* recommended that educators design activities and methods of student self-assessment that would encourage learners to engage in more deep level, active ways of studying, and to change their conceptions of the learning task if necessary. They cautioned, however, that this goal would be frustrated if university teaching neglected the important task of developing appropriate study skills, and urged the development of models of learning that are based upon a sympathy for the student's perspective, as opposed to experts' notions of appropriate discipline-based knowledge and skills.

Marton (1983) argued that 'the very amount of textual material assigned to students makes an extreme surface approach impossible' (p 328). He also made the point that a good deal of learning is interpersonal, and that students quickly learn to recognize which of their teachers are convergent thinkers and which are more likely to encourage the type of critical approach inherent in deep learning. As Hounsell (1983) and Ramsden (1982) pointed out, faced with an overloaded syllabus and assessment procedures that stress powers of memory rather than understanding, students may be discouraged from undertaking deep and critical thinking. An important factor here is the general departmental ethos in which students find themselves, which can have profound effects upon methods of study.

Ramsden and Entwistle's (1981) classic study examined the learning approaches of 2,208 students from 66 academic departments in a number of British universities and polytechnics. Deep learning was found to be associated with the learning climate the students encountered in different departments. In particular, the following factors seemed to encourage deeper learning approaches:

- *good teaching* (teachers are well prepared, confident);
- *opennesss to students* (teachers are friendly, flexible, helpful);
- *freedom in learning* (students have a choice in what they study);
- *clear goals and standards* (assessment standards and expectations are clearly defined);
- *vocational relevance* (courses are seen as relevant to future careers);
- *social climate* (there are good relations between students and staff, both social and academic).

In addition, two factors seemed to encourage more surface learning (or what Ramsden and Entwistle called a 'reproducing orientation'):

1. *heavy workload* (especially where this entailed many assessment tasks that focused on content coverage);
2. *formal teaching* (a perception that formal classes, as opposed to individual study, were the main source of learning).

Bertrand and Knapper (1991) repeated the study on a smaller scale in a Canadian university and found similar results.

The influence of teaching on learning approaches has also been demonstrated by a quite different line of research undertaken in the USA. Astin (1977, 1993) has for several decades been conducting a massive study involving 20,000 students, 25,000 faculty and 200 higher education institutions. He found that the characteristics and behaviour of teachers had major implications for student development. In particular, opportunities for student–teacher interaction had 'positive correlation with almost every self-reported area of intellectual and personal growth' (p 383). Of even more importance from the perspective of lifelong learning, there were similar positive effects associated with opportunities for interactions with other students. In contrast, the sheer number of hours spent in classes was unrelated to cognitive development, suggesting that it is the quality of faculty-student contact, not the quantity that is of critical importance.

In another major meta-analytic study, Pascarella and Terenzini (1991) analysed the results of 2,600 empirical investigations dealing with the impact of higher education on student learning and development. They found that learning was 'unambiguously linked to effective teaching, and we know much about what effective teachers do and how they behave in the classroom' (p 619). Key factors include the teacher's ability to establish rapport with students, teacher accessibility to provide personal guidance, quality of feedback on student work, active learning strategies, opportunities to interact with peers and a 'curricular experience in which students are required to integrate learning from separate courses around a central theme' (p 619). Writing about the implications of their analysis for policy and practice, Pascarella and Terenzini concluded that higher education institutions should strive to create environments that 'attract and engage students in both intellectual and interpersonal learning' (p 653).

Of course, fostering a climate for effective lifelong learning is highly dependent on the attitudes, beliefs and behaviour of teachers. This is a subject that has received relatively little attention, perhaps because undergraduates provide a much more amenable population of subjects for investigation than do academic staff. However, Beers and Bloomingdale (1983) investigated the epistemological beliefs of college teachers, using a framework similar to that suggested by Perry. They concluded that the system of values and beliefs held by instructors involves many attributions about student difficulties in learning – for example, some teachers may ascribe student learning problems to inherent lack of talent or personality factors, while other instructors see the cause as lack of experience or opportunity. (Beers also discovered a relationship between discipline and the nature of course objectives, with lower-level objectives being associated with the natural sciences as opposed to the social sciences and humanities.) Since such attributions may cause some instructors to shrug their shoulders and 'give up' on unsuccessful students, this seems a topic that is ripe for further research.

In this connection, Knapper (1988a, 1990) studied teaching-related attitudes of university faculty in Australia and Canada. He found that respondents espoused quite sophisticated learning objectives that were consistent with the principles of lifelong learning. However, there was also a tendency for teachers to see students as lacking learning skills needed to fulfil such objectives. More recently Kember (1997) undertook an analysis of all the studies he could find (13 in all) on faculty conceptions of teaching, and developed an instrument that attempted to operationalize some of the constructs he identified. The scale measures two teaching orientations: the first Kember called 'teacher- or content-centred' (the emphasis is on imparting information) and the second he labelled 'student- or learning-centred' where the teacher is concerned with promoting conceptual change and intellectual development. Kember and Gow (1994) showed that learning approaches were, indeed, affected by the orientations of individual teachers – in particular, the teacher's ability to encourage discussion and interaction proved to be a key factor in promoting deeper learning. They argued that one of the major challenges for educational development programmes (see Chapter 6) is to move faculty away from reliance on didactic methods towards approaches that are more student-centred and encourage dialogue and discussion.

What is interesting about findings reviewed above is that so many of the aspects of teaching that appear to facilitate deeper learning and cognitive development are also factors that have an obvious connection to lifelong learning, such as collaboration, links between work and school and emphasis on student control of the learning process. For many faculty, it would be helpful to have a list of good teaching practices that facilitate lifelong learning in their students. Chickering and Gamson (1987) tried to distil 'seven principles for good practice in undergraduate education', based on consultations with some leading experts and researchers in the field – many of them people we have cited above. The resulting publication was issued as a news sheet and widely distributed to North American academics free of charge by the Johnson Foundation. The seven principles are listed and described, with examples of how they may be implemented in colleges and universities. According to Chickering and Gamson good practice:

1. encourages *student-faculty contact*;
2. encourages *cooperation* among students;
3. encourages *active learning*;
4. gives *prompt* feedback;
5. emphasizes *time on task* (ie students should spend time on the most important learning tasks, not busy-work);
6. communicates *high expectations*;
7. respects *diverse talents and ways of learning*.

Our own attempt to identify good practice for promotion of lifelong learning appears in Appendix 1.

Effects of work/study programmes

An important area of interest in Chapter 5 was the forging of links between higher education institutions and the world of work. Although the benefits of experiential learning and cooperative education may seem self-evident to the proponents of lifelong education, it is more difficult to find empirical evidence for their effectiveness. One relevant study by Somers and Bridges (1982) investigated the effects of such programmes on postgraduate success of students, including personal development, subsequent employment opportunities and involvement in continuing education and graduate study. Results indicated that experiential education is seen as providing preparation for subsequent study that is equal to or better than traditional programmes, and that the graduates of non-traditional programmes have no particular difficulty in obtaining employment.

Hayes and Travis (1974) carried out a comprehensive national (US) study of employer experience with cooperative programmes, sponsored by the US Office of Education. The study was intended to provide a cost-benefit analysis of cooperative education, and obtained data from 70 employers based on their experience with several hundred co-op students between 1964 and 1974. Results suggested that 'recruitment yield' (proportion of people hired as a percentage of those interviewed) was 13 times higher for co-op students than for college graduates in general, and that recruitment costs were on average dramatically lower for graduates of co-op programmes than for other recent college graduates. Although there were no significant differences between employer ratings of work performance for co-op students and other graduates, the former received more promotions to supervisory positions, and did so sooner than other college graduates. Co-op students frequently were offered and accepted jobs within the organization that they had worked for during their programme, and the likelihood of their remaining with the firm was greater than for other graduates.

While such tangible benefits are clearly important, it is also necessary to examine the effects of work/study programmes on the quality of student learning (Breathnach, 1983). An early attempt to study the benefits of cooperative education was carried out in the 1960s, and involved a comparison of 22 cooperative programmes and 16 conventional programmes in a variety of US higher education institutions (Wilson and Lyons, 1961). Data gathered were based upon interviews and opinion surveys with students, faculty and employers. The Committee concluded that cooperative education yielded the following benefits:

- links between theory and practice gave a greater meaning to study;

- student motivation for study was enhanced;
- students achieved a greater degree of personal independence, responsibility and maturity;
- students showed greater interpersonal skills;
- students were better able to understand the demands of the work situation;
- there was greater access to higher education by a broader range of students;
- there were closer contacts between academics and employers, with resultant benefits for curriculum planning;
- there was more efficient utilization of institutional resources in higher education;
- cooperative education provided a means for business to attract and screen potential employees.

It is not clear that the study did, indeed, provide unequivocal evidence to support all these conclusions. Whereas some of the outcomes could be measured in fairly straightforward ways, others were more a matter of perception and opinion. Furthermore, a particular problem arises because of the self-selection of students who enter work/study programmes – such individuals are quite likely to place a high value on the unique characteristics of cooperative education, and thus it is not particularly surprising that they stress the benefits of their experience. Nonetheless, whether or not the conclusions reported by Wilson and Lyons provide the empirical support for cooperative education that they claim, their list of outcomes certainly offers a useful set of criteria against which such programmes could be evaluated.

Evaluative studies of this sort show that there are definite economic benefits to students who participate in work/study programmes; the research also provides some evidence of academic achievement as measured by, for example, college or university grades. However, studies of cooperative education are hampered by the sorts of methodological difficulty reviewed at the beginning of this chapter. Furthermore, they do not really speak to many of the criteria that we have emphasized as especially important for promotion of lifelong learning skills – such as, for example, a demonstration of students' ability to learn from a variety of sources, evaluate their own efforts, plan and guide their own learning, choose among various learning approaches and similar qualities.

More recently, Knapper (1995) attempted to determine whether approaches to learning in university (specifically, deep and surface approaches) were transferred to the workplace. He developed the 'Workplace Learning Questionnaire', based on the 'Approaches to Learning' instrument that was originally devised by Ramsden and Entwistle for use with university students. Knapper measured the learning approaches of co-op students while they were in classes at the University of Waterloo and then later while they were in four-month work placements. He found that there were, indeed, significant correlations between learning approaches in the two situations. Equally important, students had no difficulty describing their work experiences in terms of the learning they did on the job. However, the dominant approach in the work setting was affected by aspects of the work climate – in particular, the attitudes of supervisors. Further work has been undertaken to refine the scale and investigate factors affecting learning approach in a range of work settings, including hospitals and a major Canadian bank (Kirby, Knapper and Carty, 1997).

Effects of instructional innovations

Chapter 5 also examined a variety of innovative teaching methods, including various approaches to individualizing instruction, methods intended to promote independent learning, project work of various sorts and methods that stress learning from peers. Many of these instructional innovations have been the subject of numerous research studies; in many cases there have even been studies (meta-analyses) of the studies themselves. In the section above on teaching and learning approaches, we already mentioned the finding in some major studies that interacting with fellow students had important benefits for cognitive development. This would seem to reflect the conventional wisdom that much learning in the outside world is based on informal contacts with colleagues.

Other research has focused more specifically on peer learning approaches. For example, Collier (1980, 1983) reviewed a large number of studies that examined the impact of peer learning techniques on the development of higher-order skills. He found evidence that these approaches resulted in heightened student motivation and increased involvement with their academic work. There was also evidence that students were able to apply principles they learnt to new situations (eg in individual learning), synthesized diverse materials, and gained a more sophisticated and systematic approach to problem solving, including facility at interdisciplinary collaboration and the ability to deal with conflicting viewpoints. Other research has focused not just on whether peer group methods result in learning, but on the precise conditions under which peer learning is most effective for particular groups (Larson, Dansereau and Goetz, 1983).

The benefits of peer group learning may not be restricted to the student. Several writers have commented on important advantages to the instructor or tutor. For example, Annis (1983), in a study of the effects of peer tutoring, found that although both tutors and those being tutored showed content-specific and more general cognitive gains than students not involved in the tutoring process, the improvement was significantly greater for those acting as tutors. This seems to confirm the popular notion that the best way to learn something is to teach it. Bouton and Garth (1982) concluded that the effect of learning groups on altering the role of the teacher – from sole authority to resource and guide – was beneficial in allowing an instructor to truly observe, perhaps for the first time, the student learning taking place in the course. In this way, learning groups became a spur to thinking about the nature of teaching and learning itself.

The McMaster University medical programme, which combines peer learning with project work, and was described in Chapter 5, has been the subject of extensive evaluation to assess the competencies of its graduates in relation to those of students from other, more traditional medical schools. There are regular entry and exit surveys of McMaster students, and data are collected annually from graduates of the programme. Performance on national licensing examinations is monitored, and records are maintained of the certification rate for graduates in the various medical specialties. In addition, the career paths and attitudes of students are systematically checked on a continuing basis. Data from these surveys are used not only to evaluate the success of the programme, but also as a basis for planning changes in curriculum and approaches to teaching. There is evidence that McMaster graduates (who write no formal examinations during their programme) perform close to the Canadian national average in licensing examinations, and have similar success rates in being accepted into internship and residency programmes compared to the graduates of other medical schools (Ferrier, Marrin and Seidman, 1988; Woodward and Neufeld, 1978). Surveys of graduating classes indicate that former students place a high value upon the problem-based orientation of the curriculum in preparing them for medical practice.

In addition to studies of individual programmes like McMaster, there have been attempts to evaluate the effectiveness of problem-based learning more generally. A notable example is the meta-analysis by Albanese and Mitchell (1993) who undertook a comprehensive review of the international literature on problem-based medical education published between 1972 and 1992. Although they confirmed some of the positive outcomes described above, they also found that PBL (problem-based learning) graduates sometimes had gaps in their knowledge base, and 'tended to engage in backward reasoning rather than the forward reasoning experts engage in' (p 52). They were also critical of the lack of a research base, notably studies that would help pinpoint which aspects of problem-based learning contribute to particular learning outcomes. (The same might be said, however, for the effects of different components of traditional education.)

Hence, despite the useful insights yielded by the studies reviewed above, a good deal of the research on educational innovations is rather unsatisfactory from the point of view of demonstrating that the approaches in question foster effective lifelong learning as we have defined it. Most investigations focus on what, from the point of view of our preferred criteria, are rather narrow – or even trivial – learning outcomes, such as scores on multiple-choice tests, estimates of time taken in learning, measures of students' preference for the instructional approach compared to traditional teaching and so on (Knapper, 1980). Some of the reasons for these inadequacies are easy to understand, and have been discussed above.

Effectiveness of special programmes and institutions

An underlying assumption of all higher education is that it will produce some type of change in students, and various attempts have been made by researchers to measure the effects of studying in college and university on subsequent behaviour and attitudes. Over 40 years ago, Jacob (1957) reviewed a large body of empirical research, focusing particularly on the impact of universities and colleges on values, attitudes, and cognitive abilities – including a number of skills that are of direct relevance to lifelong learning, such as independent and critical thinking, emotional and aesthetic experience, 'liberal' attitudes, interpersonal sensitivity and similar factors. His conclusions were rather pessimistic and caused considerable controversy in academic circles (Barton, 1959). Jacob found that while some opinions change as a result of going to college, and while some colleges have a major impact on students' values, on the whole most basic values and cognitive skills do not change for most students at most institutions in a way that can be attributed to the teaching they have received. Barton (1959), however, in an incisive critique, concluded that Jacob's findings were attributable primarily to the methodological problems that beset research of this type.

More recently, Terenzini, Pascarella and Lorang (1982), who used a sophisticated statistical approach to take account of effects of extraneous variables on student learning, reached the more optimistic conclusion that attendance at university did lead to cognitive gains that could not be attributed simply to normal maturation. The research by Astin (1993), mentioned above, also found some effects of teaching on cognitive development, although given the huge number of variables examined, it is interesting to observe how many aspects of university programmes did *not* seem to yield any measurable change. It should also be noted that the seminal studies by Astin (1977, 1993) and Pascarella and Terenzini (1991) looked primarily at students still in college. It is much harder to follow students over time after they have graduated. There is considerable evidence from government sources (eg census data) showing that university and college graduates are more successful in the job market and have greater lifetime earnings than those who have no higher education. However, this fails to allow for factors of ability and motivation. Moreover, there is almost no evidence on the learning aptitudes that people show in their lives and work that might be traced back to particular educational experiences at university, other than anecdotal data from alumni.

In Chapter 6 we reviewed various mechanisms for facilitating lifelong learning in higher education institutions, such as educational development and study skills programmes. In a sense, it would be surprising if there was definitive evidence about their ability to achieve lifelong learning in students, since most of the 'facilitating mechanisms' we reviewed were not specifically put in place to fulfil the criteria we believe to be of primary importance. Hence, most evaluations have concentrated on rather modest (and easily quantifiable) aspects of these programmes' performance, such as the number of clients they serve, perceptions of their success among members of the university community, effects on student evaluations of teaching and so on. Nonetheless, the reviews by Hadwin and Winne (1996) and Hattie, Biggs and Purdie (1996) do provide evidence that taking part in a study skills course or 'learning to learn' programme can produce modest and effective changes in students' learning strategies. In the case of educational development programmes, the evidence is inevitably indirect, since developers do not usually work directly with students. Certainly, there are studies that show the effects of taking part in educational development on changes in conceptions of teaching (eg Ho, 1998), and other evidence showing that conceptions of teaching affect students' learning strategies (Kember and Gow, 1994). Presumably, it will be necessary to wait until universities truly (as opposed to rhetorically) embrace the goal of promoting lifelong learning before study skills programmes and educational development units devote major attention to the difficult task of demonstrating their success at promoting relevant changes in student learning approaches.

Despite what has just been said, some institutions (such as those mentioned in the first part of Chapter 6) have adopted a deliberate philosophy of lifelong education, and in a few cases there have even been attempts to carry out systematic evaluations of the extent to which these guiding principles have been fulfilled in practice. Three cases will now be reviewed in some detail.

Goddard College

Goddard has been remarkable for its attempts over the past few decades to evaluate the success of its programmes in effecting change among students. The most ambitious study conducted by the college was a six-year experiment in curriculum organization that took place from 1959 to 1965 supported by funds from the Ford Foundation. The research focused on three aspects of student learning at Goddard that are of particular relevance to the concerns of this study. These were students' ability to 'learn how to learn', the extent to which they developed a capacity for independent study and their success in relating classroom learning to life outside the institution (Beecher *et al*, 1966). The curriculum was oriented towards promoting student problem-solving skills and their capacity for independent study. It stressed the forging of links between the college and outside agencies and work settings, learning from peers as well as from teachers, and self-evaluation by students of their own progress in learning and development. All these goals accord well with the principles of lifelong education. Seven aspects of student development were used as criteria:

1. the development of competence;

2. development of autonomy;

3. development of identity;

4. freeing of interpersonal relationships;

5. development of purpose;

6. management of emotions;

7. development of integrity.

Change in each of these seven areas was assessed by administration of questionnaires, interviews with faculty and students and an ambitious battery of tests and inventories. Students who entered the college in 1959 and 1960 were followed for several years, so that their progress could be monitored on a long-term basis.

Although the research suffers from the lack of any control group and the fact that students entering Goddard are likely to have very special backgrounds and motivations, the richness of the longitudinal data makes the study almost unique. In brief, the findings indicated that there was consistent change over time in the development of competence and autonomy, formation of interpersonal and emotional relationships, development of integrity and identity and so on. All these changes are consistent with the notion that the experience at Goddard facilitated the acquisition of lifelong learning attitudes and skills.

Alverno College

A somewhat similar approach was adopted in a longitudinal study of student change and cognitive development carried out at Alverno College in the early 1980s (Mentkowski and Strait, 1983). Alverno College is a small, Catholic liberal arts college for women in Milwaukee. It offers professional programmes in nursing, management, music and education, and has achieved something of a reputation for its system for assessing student competence. This is related to a specific set of learning objectives that were devised for assessing the college as a whole as well as individual programmes. An underlying theme of Alverno's curriculum is the encouragement of lifelong learning skills, promotion of the ability to transfer college learning to outside settings and a recognition of the influence of the 'informal curriculum' on student learning and development. Great emphasis is placed upon what Alverno refers to as 'valuing', by which is meant the ability to make moral and ethical decisions (Earley, Mentkowski and Schafer 1980). Among the other student competencies stressed by the college are communications skills, the ability to analyse and solve problems, facility in interpersonal interaction and aesthetic understanding.

This case study adopted both a cross-sectional and longitudinal approach, with over 750 students (the Alverno student body is approximately twice that size) completing a battery of instruments to measure cognitive development, skill in 'experiential' learning and other skills related to professional performance after leaving college. Sophisticated statistical procedures made it possible to account for background characteristics and programme differences, and to conclude that cognitive development and learning style were, indeed, affected by the college's programme. One interesting aspect of the Alverno research was that the results of the tests and measures were fed back to students on a regular basis following administration and scoring, along with advice about how to use these indicators of their performance to profit from their education and become more effective and insightful lifelong learners. This idea of using the results of research on education to facilitate the educational process itself seems as commendable as it is unusual. It is also highly consistent with principles of lifelong learning as we have articulated them earlier.

Aalborg University

Aalborg is not a liberal arts college, but primarily an engineering school that is planned around problem-based learning. Its programmes were evaluated and compared to traditional engineering education by two international panels on the basis of several internal studies as well as reports from external examiners and data from students, graduates and their employers. Graduates from the Aalborg programme were found to be stronger in problem solving, communication and general technical knowledge, whereas traditionally educated engineers had stronger specialist knowledge and skills. It was found that the problem-based learning skills taught at university transferred well to the first job, and were still being used after three years of employment. Summarizing the research, Kjersdam and Enemark (1994, p 11) concluded that 'the combination of problem-oriented and project-organized education in Aalborg has proved to be an effective educational system, which produces readily adaptable graduates with strong qualities in problem solving, communication and general technical knowledge'. A further study by Pothof (1995) compared a sample of Aalborg graduates with graduates from a traditional engineering school at the University of Twente in the Netherlands. Data were gathered from both alumni and their work supervisors in industry. Danish supervisors tended to prefer Aalborg students as employees because they were seen as having better analytical skills and were more pragmatic, more flexible and better able to put problems in a broader context. In comparison, Dutch supervisors had no special preference for Twente graduates over those from other universities.

The conclusions to be drawn from the Aalborg, Alverno and Goddard studies are not definitive. Nonetheless, it can be said that there is at least some tentative evidence that the educational approaches at these colleges did, indeed, help to foster lifelong learning skills. While the studies are by no means the only such research investigations that may be cited, it remains true that many of the innovations we have described have not been subjected to any detailed empirical evaluation. However, the fact that a number of the proponents of lifelong learning in higher education have taken the trouble to mount complex research studies, such as those briefly described above, is an encouraging sign – especially given the fact, already mentioned, that the research evidence for the effectiveness of traditional instruction is often lacking.

A framework for evaluation

We turn now to the question of how to evaluate existing institutions and teaching and learning strategies in terms of fostering lifelong learning. In such an evaluation, as with any other type of assessment, the process is much aided by the existence of a clear set of objectives or goals that can be used as a yardstick against which to measure the effectiveness of a particular system, approach or innovation. Both the Goddard and Alverno studies were commendable in that they began by specifying what types of effect on students their programmes may be expected to produce, given the underlying educational philosophy espoused by the college. These outcomes were then defined operationally and measures devised to determine different aspects of student learning and other changes over time. In evaluating lifelong education, then, it is important to begin by specifying appropriate evaluation criteria.

In fact, we have already referred to such criteria in earlier chapters, both in terms of the outcomes we would expect in students, as well as the characteristics of educational systems and organizations. For example, to distil some of the prescriptions from earlier chapters, we have emphasized that the system of effective lifelong education should lead to:

- closer links between higher education institutions and work settings;
- emphasis upon self-directed, independent learning;
- greater flexibility in logistical and administrative arrangements in universities (eg to permit teaching and learning in different formats, at different times and in different places);
- greater cooperation between colleges and other institutions where learning occurs (eg museums and libraries etc);
- a stress on interdisciplinarity and integration of content and skills from a variety of subject areas;
- the encouragement of broad participation and greater diversity in higher education institutions, possibly linked to the decentralization of higher education.

Candy, Crebert and O'Leary (1994, p xiii) also suggested criteria for assessing how far an institution has moved towards adopting lifelong learning as its guiding principle. These overlap to some extent with the criteria just stated, but add new dimensions to them. Institutions should:

- have an explicit policy on lifelong learning;
- have the development of lifelong learners as the core objective of all courses;
- evaluate all aspects of their own work in terms of lifelong learning;
- make access readily available to non-traditional students;
- recognize not only formal but also non-formal prior learning;
- provide appropriate forms of staff development;
- recognize and reward appropriate teaching;
- make use of teaching and learning procedures that encourage 'self-managed' learning;
- support learning to learn, and information literacy programmes.

Although he was writing about education in general, and not specifically about higher education, Gelpi's (1980, pp 29–30) 'indicators' for ascertaining the extent to which lifelong learning principles have penetrated a functioning system can also be applied to higher education. Different indicators may be more difficult to implement in some countries than in others, while some may be more or less significant in particular societies, according to the educational objectives of the country in question. Gelpi's suggestions derive from his orientation as a sociologist with a very strong interest in what he understands as democracy, emancipation, equity and fairness, and thus focus on only some aspects of the possible effects of implementation of lifelong education. Furthermore, they are subject to a considerable degree to earlier criticisms that many writers incorporate reforms they regard as desirable into the concept of lifelong learning. Nonetheless, his findings provide useful insights into evaluating universities. Among the indicators Gelpi (1980, pp 29–30) mentioned are:

- participation of workers' children;
- participation of workers themselves;
- use of instructors who are not professional teachers;
- active participation of workers as teachers or facilitators;
- decompartmentalization of the different streams of education;
- introduction of folk culture as an integral part of formal curriculum;
- integration of general and vocational education;
- incorporation of work experience;
- participation of students in management;
- significant development of self-instructional procedures and of research in this area;
- provision of appropriate facilities (suitable learning materials, appropriate teaching methods, financial support) to groups with special needs.

Teaching and learning criteria

Application of the sorts of criteria just listed to the various educational approaches and innovations described in this study could provide a framework for the evaluation of educational practice relevant to a system of lifelong education. Table 7.1 attempts to exemplify how such a framework might be constructed. Before discussing this table in more detail, it is important to stress that our interest here is not in testing the underlying principles of lifelong education which were spelt out in earlier chapters. For us, these principles are 'givens' – basic premises for a system of higher education and yardsticks against which existing systems may be judged. The intention of Table 7.1 is thus to assess a number of the approaches already discussed in terms of selected fundamental criteria for lifelong education. For reasons of space, the number of criteria included in the table is limited, and the list is intended to be illustrative rather than exhaustive.

Table 7.1 Educational approaches and teaching–learning criteria

Criteria	Approach					
	Lectures	Guided design	Distance learning	Cooperative education	Problem-based learning	Computer-mediated learning
Vertical integration						
1. Students plan their own learning	Low	High	High	?	High	?
2. Students assess their own learning	Low	High	?	High	High	?
3. Formative rather than summative assessment is stressed	Low	High	Low	?	High	?
Horizontal integration						
1. Active rather than passive learning is stressed	Low	High	Low	?	High	High
2. Learning in both formal and informal settings is encouraged	Low	High	Low	High	High	Low
3. Peer learning is encouraged	Low	High	?	?	High	Low
4. Students integrate material from different subject areas	Low	High	?	High	High	?
5. Different learning strategies are used in different situations	Low	High	?	?	?	Low
6. Knowledge is used to tackle real-world problems	Low	High	Low	High	High	?
7. Learning process is stressed at least as much as learning content	?	High	?	?	High	Low
8. Self-evaluation against real-world criteria is encouraged	Low	High	?	High	High	Low

The table is divided into two main parts. The first section includes criteria relating to the principle of 'vertical integration' (which stresses learning throughout the life span), while the second section comprises criteria that involve 'horizontal integration' (links between formal school learning and learning in other settings). On the left-hand side of Table 7.1 are listed a variety of properties of teaching and learning that we have discussed in connection with the promotion of lifelong learning. These properties comprise our criteria, since for us they represent a priori desirable aspects of educational practice. The same applies to the selected teaching approaches. The columns of the table represent either innovations in teaching/learning that have actually been applied in higher education (such as problem-based learning, computer-mediated learning), or else broadly based educational approaches (such as distance learning or cooperative education). Also included is one teaching approach (the lecture) that we have argued is not supportive of lifelong learning, purely for comparison purposes.

Relating each of the approaches to the various criteria, it is possible to see in what respects they facilitate lifelong learning, and in what respects they fail to do so. We have provided, in each cell of the matrix, a rating of 'low', 'high' or 'uncertain' (indicated by a question mark). These estimates are based partly on research studies (when they are available) and partly on intuition. In most cases, the question marks do not mean that it is difficult to apply the criterion in question, but that whether or not the innovation fosters lifelong learning depends upon the way it is implemented. (In fact this reservation applies to all the cells of the matrix, in the sense that it is possible to 'misapply' virtually any educational approach.)

Organizational criteria

Table 7.2 presents the same set of educational approaches in terms of selected lifelong education criteria for the organization of teaching.

It is apparent that not all lifelong education principles of organization can be easily applied to the educational practices listed, as is indicated by the presence of a question mark in the column concerned.

Some additional organizational criteria are listed separately below. These are not applicable to the six examples of educational practice used in Tables 7.1 and 7.2, since they are concerned with the organization of institutions and educational structures. In fact, it would be perfectly possible to develop a comparable table for these criteria. However, since the focus of this study is on teaching and learning, rather than on organization per se, we have not taken this analysis any further here. These additional criteria include:

- existence of overriding educational policies that encourage life-long learning;
- provision of a diversity of higher education institutions;
- trend towards debureaucratization of higher education;
- ease of student transfer between educational departments or 'streams';
- provision of facilities and organizational structures that encourage maximum participation in lifelong learning;
- broad participation (by students, alumni etc) in decisions affecting education and management;
- provision of necessary logistical support systems within institutions (suitable classrooms, freedom from grading restrictions etc);
- existence of advisory services for faculty related to teaching and learning;
- encouragement of research on lifelong learning;
- encouragement of educational innovation (eg through development grants, relief for staff from some regular duties etc).

Tables 7.1 and 7.2 provide only the bare bones of a guide to the evolution of educational practice, especially since the various lists of criteria do not go beyond the special concerns of this study. We hope, nonetheless, that they offer a basis for assessing the effectiveness of particular educational approaches from the point of view of fostering lifelong learning. Although the ratings in the cells of these tables are admittedly crude and somewhat subjective, they provide some food for thought about the various teaching and learning approaches we have discussed. In particular, it is interesting to note that innovations that look extremely promising when gauged against some of the criteria often seem inadequate or uncertain in terms of others. In addition, although the tables may indicate that a particular learning method is almost ideally suited to promoting lifelong learning, other criteria could be taken into account that may make it seem less desirable – perhaps time involved, convenience, cost, skills and knowledge possessed by teachers and so on. In a similar vein, the list of practical innovations could be expanded – the six depicted in the tables are merely examples. Nonetheless, we believe that the approach described here shows how the necessary evaluation could be carried out for other innovations and with an enlarged list of criteria.

Table 7.2 Educational approaches and organizational criteria

Criteria	Approach					
	Lectures	Guided design	Distance learning	Cooperative education	Problem-based learning	Computer-mediated learning
1. Broad participation of population in education (in terms of age, socio-economic class, etc)	?	?	High	?	?	?
2. Integration of general and vocational education	Low	High	?	High	High	?
3. Flexibility in curriculum/course content and organization	Low	?	Low	Low	?	?
4. Award of academic credit for life	Low	Low	Low	?	Low	Low
5. Incorporation of outside work experience into formal curriculum	Low	?	Low	High	High	?
6. Use of instructors who are not professional teachers	?	?	?	High	Low	?
7. Development of self-instructional procedures	Low	High	High	Low	High	High
8. Provision of advice to students on appropriate learning	?	High	?	?	High	Low

The construction of such an evaluative schema is an essential step in the conduct of research on lifelong education – something which is a prerequisite for the reform of educational practice.

8

A stocktaking: continuing problems in implementing lifelong education

At the beginning of this book we cited the positive conclusion of Hasan (1996) that lifelong learning was finding ever greater acceptance as a guiding principle for the reform of education on a worldwide basis. However, in their review of progress in recent years, Candy, Crebert and O'Leary (1994, p 84) identified a number of 'lamentable lapses' to be found in many undergraduate programmes:

- either not having lifelong learning as a goal of curriculum or, possibly worse, having it but ignoring it;
- overloading the curriculum;
- imposing too much detail;
- making excessive use of lectures;
- failing to link learning with the real world;
- basing assessment to an excessive degree on knowledge of facts, and thus promoting 'reproductive' learning;
- not giving appropriate feedback;
- viewing the library as a place for storing books;
- viewing university as essentially vocational training.

We share many of the misgivings of Candy *et al*, and agree with Neice and Murray (1997, p 186) that 'for many countries [implementing lifelong education] will require vigorous and highly directed policy attention. The obstacles to its achievement are formidable'. The aim of this chapter is to take stock of the progress that has been made by higher education institutions in achieving lifelong learning goals since the first edition of this book appeared in 1985. In particular, we try to compare the claims made for the benefits of lifelong learning by its many proponents with the documented evidence of success. We also consider obstacles to the achievement of lifelong learning goals and discuss what steps would have to be taken for these barriers to be overcome.

Weaknesses in the theoretical base

Problems with the concept

About 25 years ago, Pucheu (1974) concluded that lifelong learning was a 'rubber' concept that could be stretched to take on any desired shape. Unfortunately, this still seems to be true. Many conferences on lifelong learning leave the disappointing impression that a substantial number of proponents of the idea proclaim its virtues as an act of faith, in the spirit of true believers. Learning is good and, therefore, lifelong learning must be even better. Since lifelong learning is self-evidently a good thing, it is necessary to be an unequivocal booster of the concept, without asking too many questions. To ask for a tighter definition or expect psychological, sociological, paedagogical, organizational or financial evidence is almost an act of heresy.

The various measures that such proponents of lifelong learning support are also seen as self-evidently good and are incorporated into the definition of lifelong learning, even where the connection is at best tenuous. The converse is also true. Since lifelong learning is good, it must lead to everything else that is good. An example is the assumption that lifelong learning would automatically arise from and lead to environmentally green attitudes, or that it would of necessity emancipate the socio-economically underprivileged. (Since there is a well-documented connection between how much a person has learnt in the past and how well that person learns in the future, it seems quite possible that lifelong learning would widen the gap between the *educationally* privileged and the underprivileged, but this is only occasionally discussed.) In effect, lifelong learning is in danger of becoming all things to all interested parties, with the result that the term could degenerate into nothing more than a catch-phrase capable of justifying anything.

A second and closely related issue is that discussions of lifelong learning often have a hidden agenda with political or ideological undertones. For example, it is assumed that lifelong learning automatically implies liberal or 'progressive' views, and that anything that is part of these views is part of lifelong learning. An example is the assumption that lifelong learning would automatically be based on generalist, interdisciplinary studies. Yet we know of no compelling empirical evidence that unequivocally demonstrates a connection between learning throughout life and non-specialization. In fact, narrowly qualified specialists are quite capable of adaptation to new situations even in old age, and it appears that factors such as personality or self-image may be more important in such adaptation than the degree of specialization itself (Cropley, 1999b). It is also possible to imagine, as a mental game, a repressive, totalitarian society that promoted lifelong learning. Indeed, the illiberal regimes of the former Soviet Bloc enthusiastically supported the idea.

That the dominant humanistic/liberal view is not shared by all commentators can be seen in the position adopted by Tweddell (1998). In a discussion of the future of the university, he made the now familiar point that lies at the core of most discussions of lifelong learning: the 'challenge of change' will require a different kind of institution, and the university in its present form will need to change 'at a staggering rate and in non-traditional directions'. However, Tweddell's critique departed from others by adopting what is essentially a human capital approach, and emphasized the university's responsibility for 'providing the skilled people to drive the growth in all aspects of our society'. He also rejected the popular vision of 'the multipurpose generalist', and argued that universities will need to become single-purpose institutions that specialize in either vocational training (the great majority) or in research (a small number of élite institutions). Tweddell's vision of the new university is radical and oriented towards lifelong learning, but is at odds with the position automatically adopted by many thinkers in the area.

Such contrasting views on the implications of lifelong learning for higher education imply that the various commentators have not yet adequately defined what they are talking about. In fact, positions like that of Tweddell are in the minority and there is otherwise a fairly high degree of unanimity. However, this is mainly because, to a considerable degree, the relevant discussion has been hijacked in a fuzzy-minded way by educators who often simply use the term 'lifelong learning' to add authority to educational ideas they regard as good, and who may even regard the call for more precision as narrow and rigid, if not heretical. It is disappointing to read very recent publications that still cling to the view that the implementation of Marxism would automatically mean achievement of a system of lifelong education, or see the overthrow of capitalism as a prerequisite for lifelong learning. In our view, this hidden agenda hinders the emergence of a well-defined concept of lifelong education that may embrace worthwhile ideas from both the right and the left.

Domination by abstract theorizing

The modern literature on lifelong learning (ie since about 1970) has been dominated by philosophical, sociological and political discussions. As a result, much has been written about, for instance, the importance of lifelong learning as something that is intrinsically good and a major factor in the development of a humane and just society, about its role in improving the lot of disadvantaged social groups and reducing socio-economic inequities both within and between societies, and about its ability to bring about democracy, peace and a healthy environment. This is hardly surprising in view of the fact that the initial impetus for the modern discussion of lifelong learning came from the United Nations Educational, Scientific, and Cultural Organization (Unesco), with other socio-political organizations such as the OECD and the EU later joining in. However, this state of affairs has had the unfortunate result that discussions have remained at an abstract, idealistic level, and have been dominated by what is now called 'political correctness'.

One consequence is that, from the point of view of practitioners, statements about lifelong learning have largely been confined to praising apple pie, and fail to describe how the relevant ideas may be implemented in real situations. Several years ago we wrote a paper that spelt out some of the implications of lifelong education principles for schools (Cropley and Knapper, 1982). The editor of the journal that published the paper felt compelled to introduce it with the comment that the authors had taken the highly unusual step of discussing lifelong learning and educational *practice*. Although this occurred almost 20 years ago, we are still not aware of any substantial programmes of research on the actual practice of lifelong education. The one partial exception is the programme of the Unesco Institute in Hamburg, which yielded a large number of books and papers in the 1970s and 1980s, but is now far less active. Several of the institute's projects went beyond theoretical expositions and looked at pragmatic issues (Dave and Cropley, 1978; Goad, 1984; Skager and Dave, 1977). However, other Unesco Institute publications (eg Lengrand, 1986), despite promising much, focused on extolling the unproven virtues and benefits of lifelong learning, rather than offering practical strategies for its implementation.

The complaint that statements about lifelong learning are mainly abstract and theoretical may easily create the impression that they have a rich theoretical foundation, for example, in the psychology of adult learning. Unfortunately, this is not the case. Semlak *et al* (1991) conducted an analysis of over 3,000 relevant publications, and came to the conclusion that no 'grand theory' of adult learning has yet been worked out. They concluded that while theoretical statements do exist, they fail to provide a framework that defines learning needs, specifies educational demand or predicts participant behaviour in a manner that is not only plausible but also empirically testable. For example, classical models in developmental psychology such as those of Erikson (1963), Havighurst or Maslow (1954) predict that people aged 55 or over will be disengaging from career and work concerns and confronting new developmental tasks. However, empirical evidence in Neice and Murray's (1997) large-scale study of 20,000 people in six countries ranging from Poland to the USA showed that even in this age group work is the dominant motivation mentioned by almost all older learners. It appears that existing theoretical constructs about human development as it affects lifelong learning are not robust enough to predict or explain behaviour in the face of the substantial societal changes that have taken place over the past few decades.

Lack of a research base

A second major weakness in the scientific basis for lifelong education and lifelong learning is that empirical evidence is very scarce. With the exception of essentially demographic studies on factors such as participation rates, data are usually confined to results of questionnaire studies in which people state their reasons for participating in a course or programme. For example, in Chapter 5 we discussed cooperative education as a promising means of forging links between university and the workplace. However, while the goals of cooperative programmes as outlined by Ricks (1996) are quite consistent with the principles of lifelong learning, there is a worrying lack of studies that show the psychological effects of participation in cooperative and work-based learning. Certainly, there are surveys that show students generally like co-op programmes and are placed at an advantage in subsequent job seeking, but there is scant evidence of changes in learning outcomes of the sort mentioned by Ricks.

Even though students and employers may have positive attitudes to programmes like cooperative education, we need to caution that people's perceptions of their own attitudes and motives are modified by a number of psychological factors such as social desirability, avoidance of cognitive dissonance or selective perception. Self-reports unaccompanied by observation of actual behaviour are notoriously inaccurate, and are the subject of a considerable methodological literature (see Knapper, Cropley and Moore, 1977). A simple example from a completely different domain is that 5 per cent or more of people actually observed wearing seat belts report in questionnaires that they *never* use them.

An appropriate programme of research on lifelong learning would need to provide empirical evidence of higher motivation or improved learning resulting from the implementation of teaching and learning methods based on the principles of lifelong learning. A few research studies have been done, even though they are seldom mentioned in the literature on lifelong learning: for example, Dave and Cropley (1978) observed appropriate changes in the behaviour of students in a teachers' college after they had attended lectures on lifelong learning. In addition, however, research is needed to provide evidence of 'systematic validity', that is, that graduates' ability to adapt to change – or become innovators – is enhanced. Crucial issues are those of how lifelong learning competencies develop under different circumstances, and how this may vary from one person and situation to another. Also needed is information about how emerging competencies can be recognized and evaluated, both within institutions of higher education and also in life and work settings.

The first difficulty in demonstrating empirically the value of educational approaches thought to foster lifelong learning is that many of the teaching methods that may be expected to be relevant (eg those reviewed in Chapter 5) were not necessarily developed within a lifelong education framework. This means that evaluation criteria relevant to the sorts of objective laid out in earlier chapters have, in many cases, not been articulated. An innovation that offers the promise of encouraging lifelong learning (eg an experiment in student self-assessment) may be introduced for many different reasons – for example, to save instructional time, or to cope with an institutional problem such as the lack of suitably qualified instructors. Hence, if an evaluation takes place, the data gathered may not reflect students' acquisition of lifelong learning skills, but instead deal with outcomes such as time spent on the learning task, success on a multiple-choice examination, preference for this method over a conventional lecture approach and so on. It is not that these outcomes are necessarily unimportant, but rather that they are not in themselves adequate criteria for deciding whether or not a particular teaching approach fulfils the goal that we regard as important – fostering lifelong learning.

This limitation applies to some instructional approaches more than others. For example, in the case of educational technology, the goal is often one of providing a more 'efficient' system of teaching, and criteria for success often involve achieving the outcomes of conventional instruction, but with demonstration of a greater amount of learning, at less cost, and in a shorter time. These may well be important achievements, but they are not central to our aims as outlined in this study.

Frequently, in fact, innovations have as their main intention making what already exists better for achieving conventional goals that do not include fostering lifelong learning, except perhaps in an incidental way. Educational technology is a case in point. A great deal of effort has been expended in applying educational technology to making lectures more entertaining or capable of being delivered to greatly enlarged audiences. However, in our view this is counter-productive, since lectures are inherently flawed as the major form of instruction. Another example is provided by many applications of technology in distance education which actually seek to make distance learning more like the conventional face-to-face classroom and to eliminate the very aspects that we regard as favourable to lifelong learning, such as learning that is truly independent of an ever-present instructor to provide instant and constant feedback (see Chapter 2).

In the case of other innovations, for instance project-based learning, the theoretical underpinnings of the approach do specify objectives of greater relevance to our criteria, such as enhanced problem-solving skills and more student self-direction. Even here, however, the existing research is frequently inadequate to instil confidence that students have developed appropriate lifelong learning attitudes and skills. One major reason is that there is a shortage of appropriate instruments through which to measure these attitudes and skills. There are, for instance, few convincing measures of autonomous, self-directed learning, especially ones that allow some insight into how such skills develop, persist over time and transfer to other situations.

The ideal research study would be longitudinal and would monitor a cadre of students as they progress through their studies, to examine not just immediate effects at the end of a course but also whether, and how, they are able to build on their learning experience in subsequent courses and in their later careers. Longitudinal research is, however, notoriously difficult to conduct, and there is a paucity of studies of this sort in education in general, let alone in the area of lifelong education. Long-term research is expensive, presents problems in maintaining contact with the students involved and requires specially trained investigators. Given the fact that many of the innovations described here were developed not by educational researchers but by practising teachers with other more pressing responsibilities, it is hardly surprising that a good many innovations have not been evaluated at all, or have been studied rather superficially on a 'one shot' basis.

Another major difficulty is that of controlling all the variables affecting learning outcomes. For example, some studies of educational innovations have demonstrated change in the participating students (in terms of increased learning, different attitudes and values etc), but there is no way of telling whether similar changes might have taken place if the learners had been exposed to traditional types of instruction. Other studies have used control groups in which the progress of students' learning during exposure to some unconventional procedure is compared with outcomes for students who remained in the traditional environment. A major problem with such studies, however, is that learners are very rarely randomly assigned to the experimental and control groups. In circumstances where students voluntarily select a particular type of learning, it seems quite likely that they would have different attitudes and motivations compared to learners who opt for conventional instructional approaches. Even in those studies where some attempt is made to control for this factor (by random assignment to groups or careful matching in terms of a wide range of variables), there is the possibility that various motivational factors can arise within the experimental group simply because they are the object of special attention (the so-called Hawthorne effect). This possibly accounts for the fact that in the early years of an innovation many studies seem to show its superiority over conventional instruction. This was certainly true for programmed instruction and many types of educational technology. (Another likely reason is that research that fails to show a superiority, or at least a significant difference, does not get published.)

On the other hand, some studies may underestimate the effectiveness of the new technique, simply because the interest surrounding the experiment causes special efforts to be made even by the control group. For example, in some of the early British studies of the effectiveness of teaching machines, students in both the experimental and control groups appeared to be learning particularly well. Detailed examination of the 'traditional' lessons revealed in some cases that they had been planned with much greater care than usual. The necessity of specifying instructional objectives for the project and of planning careful tests of student learning had presumably caused teachers to think about lesson planning and to structure their material in a way that was different from their normal practice.

Not only can all these factors operate in individual studies, but they can also colour the general picture that emerges from overviews of research on a particular innovation. Even meta-analysis, which was devised specifically as a means of summarizing conclusions from a broad range of studies, is not immune from these problems (Slavin, 1983). This technique, which has been widely applied to studies of educational innovations, aims to extract the commonalities in published research reports in order to permit generalizations about whether, and under what circumstances, particular treatment effects can be demonstrated. Especially in more recent meta-analyses, an attempt is generally made to exclude research that is methodologically unsound or inappropriate in some other respect (Hadwin and Winne, 1996, chapter 6). This is certainly a great improvement on the earlier analyses that often gathered research studies on an indiscriminate basis, regardless of methodological flaws. Whatever the approach used, however, it is difficult to compensate for many of the problems listed earlier, such as the failure to report negative results, the Hawthorne effect, lack of longitudinal data and so on.

Yet another difficulty that plagues research in this area is that of proving a link between the 'treatment' and the measured outcome. For example, students who participate in a particular type of education may, indeed, demonstrate enhanced learning, distinctive values, increased motivation and so on, compared to a matching group of students who were taught in a different way. Assuming that some of the previously mentioned methodological difficulties had been overcome, it is still extremely difficult to be sure that the differences observed are really attributable to the different types of educational experience: differences in outcomes could be due to factors that are quite unknown to the investigators. While this problem exists in all studies outside the laboratory, the problem increases as the complexity of the research setting increases. Hence, it may be plausible to talk about controlling most of the variables in a small-scale study of a particular innovation (eg a peer learning component of an introductory sociology course), but in cases where a whole course or programme is involved, so many factors could potentially affect students' experiences that attributing changes in behaviour or attitudes to a particular learning method becomes problematical at best.

Many of the instructional approaches we described in earlier chapters, such as peer learning, computer-aided instruction, project methods and so on, have been written about at length in the educational literature. Quite reasonably, a question that frequently arises in connection with any innovation asks what evidence exists for the effectiveness of the new approach compared to existing instructional methods. In view of the difficulties of carrying out definitive studies of the effects of instruction on learning, it is not surprising that much of the evidence for the effectiveness of approaches reviewed here is lacking, or has serious shortcomings. Thus, we cannot turn to the research literature and find large numbers of carefully designed evaluations that provide precise guidance on choosing teaching methods for particular students, for particular learning goals or in particular social contexts. Rather, the picture that emerges from reviewing the educational research literature reveals a large number of developments and innovations implemented in relative isolation, sometimes not evaluated at all, and sometimes assessed with good intentions but amateurish methods, often appraised incompletely. The evaluations, as summarized in Chapter 7, are the exceptions rather than the rule, and all the more noteworthy for that.

Practical problems

The implementation of lifelong education would have sweeping implications for schools and universities. Among other things, certain elements of the external social system would assume new importance because of their obvious connection with the fostering of lifelong learning. Some familiar institutions would be seen in a new light, as would the roles of the people in them. For example, the workplace would be seen as one of the major educational sub-systems of society; one in which a great deal is already learnt and even more could be learnt if its potential were adequately acknowledged and emphasized. However, it is also apparent that cooperation among the different elements of an educational system could not be based purely upon conventional teaching and learning strategies. In other words, the system discussed here could not be based solely on traditional school learning. This means that implementation of lifelong education would require considerable changes in the role and activities of both teachers and learners.

Barriers to implementing lifelong education

At present there are substantial barriers to the emergence of such an educational system. The constraints are structural, institutional and individual; they also involve the nature of learning itself.

Structural barriers
Fundamental structural problems include general issues such as the different levels of access to education enjoyed by groups of differing socio-economic status, lack of finance and lack of visible political will – despite the many rhetorical calls for the implementation of lifelong learning from educational leaders, legislators and business leaders. There are also more specific problems such as the difficulty of movement between learning fields: for example, many German universities offer no recognition of part-time status, despite the fact that up to 75 per cent of students in some faculties are employed part- or even full time. Students may be required to take seven or more final exams within three months. These are the only exams the students take (ie there are no exams in individual classes) and comprise the sole basis of the students' final grades: a serious blunder can lead to an unfavourable average grade with serious consequences for chances of employment. Yet students who have outside jobs must complete these examinations within the same narrow time span as those studying full time. This cannot be changed, even if the universities wanted change, because curricula and examination conditions are specified in state law. German politicians show no interest in the

issue, while teaching staff understandably have no stomach for the long political struggle it would take to make a fairly simple administrative change, such as distributing the examinations over two terms.

Such factors have particular implications for older learners, and there is evidence that barriers of this kind are having a negative effect on participation of this group. A 1998 report of the Australian Vice-Chancellors Committee showed a drop of 4.1 per cent in applications for places at universities in that country, caused largely by a very sharp reduction in applications from mature-age students – the very people who should, according to the lifelong learning approach, be enrolling in greater numbers. In one state, South Australia, for instance, there was a drop of 40 per cent from 1997 to 1998 in applications from this age group. This fall was attributed by one authority to changes in the system of paying fees – not to an increase in fees but to an administrative change in the way they are collected.

Institutional barriers

These include problems of the *supply of learning opportunities* outside the formal framework of lectures held on campus between 9 am and 5 pm on weekdays (2 pm on Fridays), *access to learning supports* (a library, for instance, that closes at 5 pm and is not open at weekends does not support horizontal integration) and *lack of support from university teachers*. The old idea of the nature of a university and the associated faculty self-image as scholar/researcher is still dominant. Critics such as Steiner (1998) complain that even in applied disciplines with strong links to industry, such as engineering, university study frequently fails to develop in students the competencies they need for success in the professional world. This comment should not be interpreted as an attack on research, which we regard as a major aspect of the university teacher's job, but as a commentary on the tendency for scholarship to be carried out at the expense of professional practice and in isolation from it.

Learning barriers

Individual learning barriers centre on students' attitudes to university study and their view of what constitutes 'real' learning, their motivation and their self-image. Many people leave school with the feeling that institutionalized learning is unpleasant or divorced from their own needs and interests. In other words, they possess negative attitudes to institutions of learning. Motivation is too narrowly understood as a collection of vague goals that seem more likely to be achieved by means of schooling (a good job, autonomy at work, a pleasant lifestyle, wealth), even though the relationship may be perceived only in a global way. With the emergence of graduate unemployment and the realization that a degree does not automatically guarantee a good job, a diffuse, largely extrinsic motivation is not sufficient to activate lifelong learning or even foster acquisition of the necessary learning skills. Finally, experience of failure – or even of success, but only through highly dependent, teacher-centred learning – encourages learners to see themselves as incapable of learning, except perhaps under close supervision. It goes without saying that a combination of negative attitudes to learning, lack of intrinsic interest in the contents of learning, seeing it instead only as a means to fuzzy ends, and unfavourable self-image is not conducive to lifelong learning.

Learner attitudes can also be a significant hindrance to lifelong learning in another way. This is because of what can be called 'tactical studying': choosing known and conventional courses – especially if they are perceived to be easy – in order to obtain guaranteed credit, even if only limited advances in knowledge or skills can be expected. Learners may prefer such classes to ones that are potentially more challenging and rewarding when there is a risk of a poor grade or a greatly increased workload (or both), since the strategy guiding studying is obtaining the good grades and a diploma at all costs, and the best tactic for guaranteeing this is the 'safe' class.

Ironically, our experience is that, when asked to evaluate conventional classes, students often call for more self-direction, active learning methods and greater involvement in assessment. However, when such classes are actually offered, students often expect the innovative teaching and learning methods to be accompanied by guaranteed high marks. Otherwise they avoid them, preferring instead classes offering familiar material taught by conventional methods and making use of traditional, thoroughly predictable evaluation methods (eg a written exam at the end of the term). This is, of course, not true of all students, and those characterized by a 'deep' approach to learning (Entwistle, 1998; Marton and Saljo, 1976a, 1976b) are more likely to be intrinsically motivated to pursue learning for its own sake, rather than just getting a good mark in an easy course.

Researchers such as Entwistle (1998), and Kember and Gow (1994) also believe that institutions and faculty are themselves complicit in encouraging shallow learning approaches, and that learning is markedly affected by 'teaching ethos' and departmental learning climate. Candy, Crebert and O'Leary (1994) also emphasized the role of teachers as models, and implied that many teachers lack the necessary passion for learning. Just as with students, there may be a discrepancy between rhetoric and practice, with many staff stating they believe in student autonomy and active learning, while teaching exclusively by means of set-piece lectures and assessing through exams that mainly test memorization.

Learning-based barriers are both individual and also institutional in nature. At the individual level, many students do not possess learning techniques needed for vertical and horizontal integration, such as an ability to plan, skill in learning without direct supervision (or even willingness to do this) or skill in using information technology (see the more detailed discussion in Chapter 3). However, this is not solely the fault of individual learners or instructors. Few institutions provide a foundation for lifelong learning. For instance, teaching approaches seldom encourage personal reflection, make use of personal development plans or employ evaluation based on achievement of personal growth targets. Yet according to Hasan (1996) such activities are an important part of 'value-added learning'.

Indeed, most universities make little or no provision for opportunities to engage in lifelong learning. For instance, in attending classes or writing essays and reports, many students deliberately avoid referring to their own practical experiences in work settings, and feel that these are treated as irrelevant to the prescribed academic agenda. As one man with considerable work experience put it in a conversation, 'It took me a while to realize that this (his university studies) has its own rules that must be obeyed. Once I got this and learned to ignore my practical experience, I began to get good grades'.

In Chapter 5 we reviewed a range of instructional methods that seek to encourage lifelong learning by focusing on real-world problem solving and encouraging students to take more responsibility for their own learning. Use of such approaches has a number of implications for the management of education and instruction, in particular a change in the role of the teacher. In self-directed learning the instructor's primary responsibility is to give support and guidance, and help provide a framework for discovery and dialogue that will involve all members of the class – as opposed to merely telling students the right answers. A second, and related, consequence of self-directed problem solving is that the process of learning takes on more importance than the instructional content.

Such methods are often criticized on the grounds that standards will fall because less information is assimilated; that it is faster and more efficient to use teacher-centred methods, especially where structured factual material is involved; that many students are unable or unwilling to take responsibility for their own learning; that independent learning causes difficulties in conducting objective assessment of students; and that the special expertise of instructors is not properly utilized when education places the major emphasis on students directing their own activities. All these criticisms contain a grain of truth, and it is no doubt true that many enthusiasts for the various approaches outlined earlier unfortunately fail to take account of these issues in planning their learning activities.

Henry (1994), Woods (1994) and Heller, Reif and Hungate (1983) provided some useful guidelines that may help overcome such problems. Important strategies involve making tacit processes explicit, encouraging students to talk openly about learning processes, providing carefully guided practice in problem solving, ensuring that students master the component procedures involved (through carefully structured exercises), emphasizing both qualitative and quantitative thinking, and designing evaluation procedures that really test understanding and thinking skills.

Lack of consensus

The ideas proposed here challenge the basic concepts of learning that dominate thinking about higher education. They may even be seen as questioning its fundamental nature. Universities in the Western European/North American tradition originated as centres for the preservation and expansion of expertise, and the handing on of the responsibility for this task to a group of selected students. These institutions have come to control the credentialling system for many occupations, and their graduates have had a wider choice of jobs and enhanced lifetime earnings, even in the case of non-specialized, non-vocational programmes in the Arts and Humanities. Institutions of higher education thus function in a social context and not in isolation. They contribute dramatically to their graduates' advancement and recognition, and as a result have a major impact both on people's lives as well as on the power structure of society. They arouse strong expectations from the public, which they are called upon to satisfy, especially since universities consume large amounts of public funding. Because of such factors, they are the subject of intense political discussion, and are strongly affected by political forces.

Higher education institutions also serve as workplaces for a large body of teachers and researchers, plus support staff and a large bureaucracy; indeed, they are major contributors to the economy in many communities. It is hardly surprising that universities have a very substantial investment in preserving the status quo. Their clientele comprises many thousands of students who are aware of the power they have to enhance students' life prospects, and hence institutions are likely to resist changes that threaten their own chances of profiting from this power. The same students usually have parents who may themselves have benefited from the status quo and wish to see their children share in the advantages higher education can bring. Thus, the political system and the power structure on the one hand, and the individual people involved in higher education on the other, all have a vested interest in keeping things as they are, and calls for dramatic changes conflict with this interest. Brennan and Little (1996) made the predicament of universities particularly apparent. They pointed out that the place of universities in a true 'learning society' is so far unresolved. For example, if all businesses were, in fact, transformed to learning organizations of the type discussed in Chapter 5, it is not clear what role would be left for universities in providing education for the future workforce.

Another illustration of the difficulties of change was recently provided in a dramatic way by the public reaction to new selection procedures for admitting students to the medical school of the University of Adelaide, already touched upon in Chapter 4. The failure of some candidates with extraordinarily high matriculation grades to obtain places became a matter of public controversy and considerable bitterness, along the lines, 'We are driving the brightest and best out of our universities', on the one hand, versus, 'It isn't the eggheads who are most successful in life', on the other. Parents of unsuccessful candidates with exceptional high school grades asked the South Australian ombudsman to investigate the admission procedures, which they saw as discriminatory and unfair, despite the fact that an earlier investigation found the procedures to be 'based on cogent reasoning and not discriminatory'. It is apparent that there is no consensus on changing the criteria for distributing a scarce resource – access to expensive, exclusive university programmes that usually lead to a high income and high social status, as well as a life well stocked with creature comforts.

Substantial changes in higher education can only occur if there is a high level of agreement on what needs to be done. Unfortunately, so far this consensus is lacking. Missing are:

- a philosophy of education;
- a model for the implementation of lifelong learning;
- a body of knowledge on teaching and learning methods that foster lifelong learning;
- empirical evidence that the whole thing works.

The philosophy would have to be clear and compelling, and acceptable to all. As has already been pointed out, this would involve agreement on the purpose of higher education and the values that guide it. What should students learn? Who should receive priority? Associated with this would be agreement on how to provide the necessary financial resources. Who should bear the costs? How?

This lack of consensus is a major problem even in a national context, but is of overwhelming importance for the worldwide application of lifelong education that is foreseen by, for instance, Unesco. An appropriate implementation model would need to protect the traditional core of education as it is understood in each particular society. It would also need to offer sufficient flexibility for implementation in a wide variety of settings, without becoming so vague as to be no more than a statement of good intentions. For this reason, the idea of lifelong education as a paradigm (see Chapter 1) is helpful. But, in addition, the model would need to specify the necessary changes in a clear and practical way.

Institutional factors

Attempts to implement the principles of lifelong education in institutions of higher education are confronted by formidable difficulties. Organizations are inherently passive, tending towards bureaucracy and ritualism, and the goals and support mechanisms for higher education are basically conservative. The socialization of higher education staff is extensive and effective, and academics have great latitude in their work activities. In addition, the processes of university governance can often be an obstacle to change.

Management problems

The most fundamental problem is the fact that, as Walker (1980) pointed out, the idea of deliberately setting out to bureaucratize an innovation is in itself 'inherently obnoxious', that is, bureaucracies as we have come to know them are not usually regarded as ideal bodies for promoting change. There seems to be a contradiction between the call for innovative and flexible forms of education and the belief that this can be achieved through a system or organization, especially where the educational system concerned is to be both lifelong and also 'life-wide', embracing all settings in which people learn. There thus seems to be an irreconcilable contradiction between the desire to foster lifelong learning as an instrument of emancipation and the actual provision of organized educational services capable of achieving this goal. It is obvious, nonetheless, that some degree of organization of lifelong education is unavoidable, and that its proponents will have to learn to live with this apparent paradox. At the same time it will be necessary to remain continually on guard against the danger that the machinery of lifelong education could become so cumbersome as to defeat its own purposes. In other words, it is important that the systematization and organization of lifelong learning should not translate into excessive control or rigidity (Pineau, 1980).

Implementation of the principle of horizontal integration also means that differing forms of post-school education would have to be coordinated with each other. Each of these already has its own philosophy, goals, forms of governance, financing arrangements and jurisdictional basis. Thus, rationalization of financing, development of policy, hiring and firing of staff, administration and provision of leadership and the like would all raise special difficulties.

Planning problems

Implementation of lifelong education would naturally raise special issues in the area of planning (Schiefelbein, 1980). Existing methods to determine which elements of the total system should be expanded might well be no longer effective. Little is known, for instance, about participation rates in lifelong education (except that they are, as yet, disappointingly low), about reaction of employers to further learning, about effects of learning upon motivation for more, about payoffs of lifelong learning in the form of career benefits and so on.

A related issue concerns the demand for education at various ages and in various forms. The key questions here would have to be identified, and appropriate methods for obtaining the necessary data developed. For instance, it is possible that there would initially be an enormous growth in requests for educational services but that, as the overall level of education in a society rose, the demand might fall off. This might well occur if, among other things, the benefits resulting from increases in knowledge become smaller and smaller. It could also occur if self-directed learning became the norm, a result that would be favourably regarded by most proponents of lifelong education.

Further possible problems include conflicts between different ways of delivering education, or over priorities for different learner groups. Planners would be called upon to give advice about what forms of investment would yield the greatest benefits to society and which learners should be most strongly supported. For instance, should priority be given to those with the least prior education, those with the most (since they have already proved their ability to benefit from learning experiences), those with the largest amount of unrealized potential and so on? Whatever the choice, there is likely to be vehement protest from those overlooked.

Integrating and coordinating all forms of post-school education would also raise other crucial questions. Universities, for example, would be reluctant to give up any of their independence, or to sacrifice their right to be the sole arbiters of what is academically worth while and what is not. Post-school education as it is offered in universities is traditionally regarded as superior to non-formal education, and employers typically define job qualifications in terms of courses, certificates and the like, acquired in traditional institutions. Many university staff members would probably be loath to accept new definitions of competence, or to work side-by-side with practitioners who may have limited formal qualifications and no research experience. Issues of this kind mean that traditional institutions of higher education would be confronted by problems not only of a straightforward management kind, but also by questions of status and power. At present, virtually no knowledge exists about how to organize a system of education encompassing both formal and non-formal institutions, although in the USA the Council for the Advancement of Experiential Learning has begun to address such issues in ways that were touched upon in Chapter 5.

Academic attitudes

It follows, then, that a key factor in the introduction of lifelong learning in higher education is the attitudes of teaching staff (Nordvall, 1982) and the need to change preconceptions about educational goals and methods. Faculty resistance to change often reflects a general conservative stance among the professions, with a tendency to prefer known methods (Evans, 1968). In the profession of teaching, the role model is frequently cautious and traditional, and – as we have pointed out earlier – is generally unmodified by initial training or continuing professional education, since university graduate schools have paid little attention to instruction in methods of teaching and learning (Gaff, 1978). Indeed, in graduate training, loyalty to the discipline is generally presented as of more importance than teaching (Hefferlin, 1969).

University teachers are trained almost exclusively as researchers in a narrow specialization, and generally know little about educational theory, innovative teaching methods or curriculum development. They receive no initial preparation for teaching, and are recruited on the basis of research accomplishments (usually published papers). Once hired they generally work and teach in isolation, and career success depends on obtaining research grants and continuing to publish in recognized journals in their field, often discouraging interdisciplinary collaboration. In these circumstances, many academics struggle to cope with the demands of traditional teaching (lecturing, marking tests), and it is not surprising that they have little energy or incentive to become engaged in teaching and learning practices that might better foster lifelong learning.

In this connection, Cahn has argued that those in charge of graduate programmes 'have the responsibility to provide courses in methods of teaching for students intending to enter the profession. And these courses should be required of all to be recommended for teaching professions' (Cahn, 1978, p x). A similar proposal was made by the Commission of Enquiry on Canadian University Education established by the Association of Universities and Colleges of Canada (Smith, 1991). One innovation along these lines was the Doctor of Arts degree in the USA in which students not only specialized in a discipline but also studied the teaching of that discipline. Although the degree still exists in a handful of US universities, it has not succeeded in having the impact on graduate training that was hoped for by its originators. This seems to be partly due to the greater prestige of the traditional Ph.D. degree, but also to the recent tight academic job market.

Stiles and Robinson (1973) commented that, since teaching is regarded as a highly independent and personal pursuit, lecturers tend not to be exposed to the ideas of colleagues, and may be reluctant to adopt new approaches. Indeed, adoption of ideas used elsewhere may even be a tacit admission that teaching can somehow be 'standardized', which may, in turn, lead to the notion that it is possible to rely on package courses, teaching by television and so on, without the need for the individual control of instructional situations that many professors value very highly (Hefferlin, 1969). It can also be argued quite plausibly that change for its own sake is not necessarily a good idea, and hence some resistance may be perfectly logical.

Certainly faculty attitudes towards innovation can be inhibiting to someone who wishes to experiment with a new approach. Innovation may provoke antagonism from colleagues who interpret the change as an indirect criticism, and hence few instructors find it easy to adopt teaching practices that are radically different from those of their colleagues (Cohen and Brawer, 1977). The influence of traditionalism is strong. 'There is a reassuring simplicity in the old ways of teaching. They may not work well, but they are a solid tradition to fall back on... The irony of this order is not simply the static knowledge it produces, but also the alienation it provokes' (Shor, 1980, p 22).

In contrast, Bruenig (1980) made the point that anticipation of faculty resistance to change may be a self-fulfilling prophecy. He argued that, with some encouragement, staff involved in an innovative project that he studied were, in fact, willing to improve their performance, and he traced these attitudes to their high level of education, idealism, sense of vocational stability, professional interests and exposure to the optimism of their students. Failure to embrace innovation may also be due, in part, to lack of information about alternative methods. For example, in a comprehensive study of teaching at the University of Alberta, department heads reported a great many teaching innovations, yet they were largely unknown to colleagues in other academic units (Knapper, 1988a). It remains true, however, that academics in general tend to place high value on objective evidence, and the beneficial results of educational innovations are often hard to pinpoint precisely (Sikes, Schlesinger and Seashore, 1974), as we have argued above.

In the past decade there has, in fact, been increased attention to teaching in colleges and universities, in part brought by external political pressures for accountability (Knapper and Rogers, 1994). In some states of the USA, for example, funding has been directly tied to demonstration of learning gains on the part of students (the notion of 'value-added' education). Hence, 'assessment' has come to be seen not just as a way of evaluating students, but as a means of appraising higher education itself (Blumenstyk and Magner, 1990). In the UK and Australia, the notion of 'performance indicators' has become fashionable, and governments have said that they will make funding conditional on demonstrated achievement in both research and teaching (Cave, Hanney and Kogan, 1991; Johnes and Taylor, 1990). In 1990 the British Committee of Vice-Chancellors and Principals set up an Academic Audit Unit for universities to review the ways that institutions were monitoring their teaching function and to recommend good practice. Insofar as this encourages attention to teaching and learning, such developments seem hopeful. Whether or not they will lead to increased emphasis on lifelong learning, as opposed to traditional teaching goals, depends on the way performance assessment is implemented. Clearly, proponents of lifelong education must be aware of the ideological implications of change, and not simply rely naïvely on public pressure to effect a transformation of traditional practices. Emphasis on 'good' teaching has led to a revival of interest in training programmes for faculty. While the Doctor of Arts degree has largely disappeared, many universities (eg in Australia, Canada and the USA) do offer credit courses and certificate programmes on university teaching aimed at graduate students and sometimes new faculty. In addition, in some countries, there have been cautious moves towards the accreditation of university teachers (Cottrell, 1996). For example, this was a recommendation of the recent Dearing Commission in the UK, and the proposal was endorsed by the Committee of Vice-Chancellors and Principals, who have recently established an Institute for Teaching and Learning to oversee the process (NCIHE, 1997). Voluntary certification has existed for some time in the UK, under the auspices of the Staff and Educational Development Association, and several hundred academic staff have now been accredited on the basis of a combination of formal study and preparation of a comprehensive teaching portfolio (SEDA, 1994). However, a major obstacle to better training for university teachers is the academic reward system which continues to place the greatest emphasis on research productivity (Knapper, 1997). Teaching ability and the conceptual basis for teaching practice is rarely explored when making academic appointments, granting tenure or making promotions.

Lack of a system of instruction

Nearly all universities are organized along disciplinary lines, with teaching and research controlled by discipline-based departments. Professional rewards for teaching staff are also very much bound up with the discipline and department, and there is often little encouragement for lecturers who wish to collaborate with colleagues outside their home unit in, say, the team teaching of an interdisciplinary course. Since personal prestige and success is very much influenced by scholarship and publication, it is of further significance to note that here, too, disciplinary ties are extremely strong. Trotter (1977) commented that most university staff see themselves as owing first loyalty to their discipline, not to the institution where they teach. He contended that they see themselves primarily as physicists, lawyers or psychologists, and not as university teachers. This obviously serves to hinder cross-disciplinary collaboration, let alone true integration in teaching, especially since such values are undoubtedly communicated to students, both directly and indirectly. Nuttgens (1988) argued forcefully against the dangers of being trapped by disciplinary boundaries, and went so far as to contend that certain disciplines only exist because they are taught in universities. He criticized a system of higher education that rewards those who are 'imprisoned in their disciplines, narrowed into their specialisms', while 'any real problems and any real innovation demand that we cross those boundaries and work together' (p 121).

The problems just outlined operate at what may be called the 'macro-level'. However, there are also problems at the 'micro-level of interactions between students and teachers. To date, lifelong education has lacked a coherent prescription for a system of instruction and assessment. Although we have tried to spell out some elements of such a system in this study, a good many practical teaching and learning problems remain. They can be summarized as follows:

- In practice, teachers do not know how to link learning to real life, even if they are interested in doing so.
- It is not known what model is most appropriate for developing lifelong learners (eg explicitly embedding the necessary concrete experiences in the curriculum versus laying down essential, general foundations).
- There is no real consensus on what students should know and be able to do that can be operationalized for curriculum planning purposes.
- Teachers do not know how to assess the knowledge, skills and abilities that are necessary for lifelong learning.
- Despite honourable exceptions, most institutions of higher education are at best apathetic (or even antagonistic) about instituting the necessary changes in curriculum and instructional methods.
- One result is that few faculty take advantage of opportunities to develop their own knowledge and skills as lifelong learners and as teachers who might promote such learning with their students. Despite the availability of educational development centres and even sabbatical leaves for professional development, faculty tend to increase their expertise in a relatively narrow disciplinary field rather than as lifelong learners and educators.

- Many faculty, even if made aware of the possibility for such development, may be simply not interested.

Problems connected with assessment

As long ago as 1982, at a conference on US higher education sponsored by the Association of American Colleges, criticisms were heard that the bachelor's degree had become an almost meaningless credential that was not serving the needs of society (Scully, 1982). Degree programmes were attacked as lacking coherence, and the view was expressed that the paper qualification needed for job entry had become far more important than the quality of learning taking place. A decade later many of the same criticisms were still being voiced by writers such as Gaff (1991) who concluded that 'the national debate has not culminated in anything that approaches consensus... All critics agree with only one thing: We are not doing well, and we can – and must – do better' (p 27).

The value of academic qualifications for predicting occupational competence has frequently been called into question, and North American research has shown repeatedly that the relationship between college grades and success in a profession is extremely small. The overall variance accounted for by grades makes them almost useless in predicting occupational effectiveness or job satisfaction outside certain occupational settings such as the armed forces (Cohen, 1983; Samson *et al*, 1983).

The area of student assessment is characterized by a massive discrepancy between stated goals and actual effects of teaching and learning activities. As Boud (1995b) stated: 'There is probably more bad practice and ignorance of significant issues in the area of assessment than in any other aspect of higher education' (p 35). When asked about their aims for a particular course, university-level teachers will frequently mention learning skills of the kind outlined in Chapters 1–3, such as analysis, synthesis, creativity and critical thinking. In practice, however, an examination of the tasks students are asked to perform in many courses (examinations, tests, assignments etc) reveals that the learning involved may often be at a much lower level, often requiring simple memorization of facts. Milton (1982) made a good point about what drives student learning with the title of his book, *Will that be on the final?* The factors that Milton believed encourage poor examination practices include the preponderance of multiple-choice tests supplied with many standard textbooks, and the fact that so much testing of students in North American universities is left to teaching assistants who receive no training in the purpose and practice of evaluation of learning.

Farago (1982) also indicted the conventional grading system for discouraging students from pursuing independent, idiosyncratic educational goals. He admitted, however, that students themselves may prefer a finely discriminating grading scale that enables them, as they see it, to compete successfully in the job market. Whether or not that is true, some empirical support for Farago's criticism of assessment practices comes from a classic study by Watkins (1984). In a longitudinal study of students at a major Australian university, he found that most approached learning in a *shallower* way at the end of their programme than on entry. He attributed the change largely to the fact that most assessment tasks appeared to discourage 'deep' learning. Similar findings were reported for Hong Kong students by Gow and Kember (1990).

Elton (1982) explained the 'quite unreasonable stress on low-level abilities' in exams by reference to the knowledge explosion and the difficulty of devising assessment tasks that test relevant and useful skills, especially in the science areas. He went on to say that, nonetheless, 'teachers must search their consciences and discover whether they really want to produce walking encyclopedias rather than active human beings' (p 117). Elton called for a system of assessment that would be less stressful than the final examination system used in most British universities, and which would also be more relevant to the knowledge and skills needed for real life. This would include a move towards the use of self- and peer-assessment by students which, he argued, would help develop student autonomy in learning. He pointed out, however, that to achieve such changes would be difficult given the attitudes and level of understanding of many faculty with respect to the underlying philosophy and psychology of learning evaluation. He ended with a recommendation that teachers in higher education should receive formal training related to student assessment.

Kloss (1982), in his critique of German medical education, mentioned earlier, reports particular dissatisfaction with the examination structure. He pointed out that most of the final state examination in medicine consists of multiple-choice tests; there is in addition a brief oral examination, but this, according to Kloss, does not reflect the students' experiences during the practical year. Reforms in medical education in the 1970s (the *Approbationsordnung*) were intended to make the learning experience more practical, to foster closer contacts between medical students and patients, and to introduce some new subjects, such as sociology and psychology. Kloss maintained, however, that the efforts have been virtually nullified by the examination system being used. He reported that written exams tested factual knowledge in a disjointed manner, failed to evaluate students' clinical skills in dealing with patients, and did not allow students to demonstrate their ability to apply theoretical knowledge. In North American medical education, despite the reforms described earlier, reliance on inappropriate student assessment methods continues to be a problem, and the 1992 report by the

Association of American Medical Colleges called for urgent steps to devise valid methods for evaluating the clinical skills they will use as practising physicians (AAMC, 1992).

Moving towards lifelong education

It is apparent from the foregoing discussions that the actual implementation of the principles of lifelong education in higher education is beset by considerable difficulties. After completing their comprehensive review, Candy, Crebert and O'Leary (1994, p 88) concluded that '... for most universities [in Australia], there is much more that could be done to promote lifelong learning'. Indeed, an overnight wholesale change is hardly to be expected. More likely is a piecemeal implementation of certain elements of lifelong education over a long period of time – what Duke (1976) described as *implementation by degrees*. The question now arises of how to encourage moves in the right direction.

Changing the system

Although institutions of higher education function in a world that is rapidly evolving, universities and colleges themselves are often slow to respond, and introducing many of the changes implied by a move to lifelong learning will encounter many obstacles. One barrier to effecting change is likely to be the conservative institutional climate that prevails in many colleges and universities with respect to instructional methods (see Chapter 4). Little (1983) suggested a number of strategies for introducing teaching innovations into higher education. First, he recommended efforts to support individual initiatives by identifying staff who are likely – and able – to act as educational entrepreneurs. A second strategy was to 'cut one's losses' by ignoring the small number of teachers who would be adamantly opposed to innovation under any circumstances, and instead give support to those who can lead innovation effectively. Third, Little advocated that those interested in promoting change should work directly with students, who often welcome the opportunity to make their learning experiences more meaningful and relevant – although he may underestimate the ability of the secondary school system to encourage student preferences for passive, traditional teaching approaches!

Lindquist (1978) and Berg and Ostergren (1977) suggested factors that can aid the introduction of innovation into educational settings. These included:

- *linkage* (bringing people together and confronting them with new information and ideas);
- *openness* (active searching for new ideas and information);
- *gain/loss* (providing rewards of security and personal satisfaction or self-realization);
- *ownership* (giving individuals a stake in initiating and developing the innovation);
- *leadership and power* (sustaining and institutionalizing the innovation).

Taylor (1998), talking in a context of introducing technological change in universities, argued that it is easy to convince a small group of enthusiasts (the 'lone rangers') to adopt new ideas, but much harder to introduce change on a wider scale. He used the term 'appropriation' to refer to the process whereby faculty can be encouraged to adopt innovations pioneered with more adventurous colleagues. Based on the work of Kolb (see Chapter 5), he proposed a five-stage cyclical process that involves orientation, adoption, evaluation, innovation and institutionalization, and suggested the types of support that are needed for each step in the cycle. Slowey's (1995) monograph contains 10 detailed accounts that document change processes in British higher education, and attempts to extract some general principles that may serve as guidelines to change agents. She concluded that it is much more difficult to effect change in universities than in business and industry, but that increasing financial and political pressures affecting higher education have stimulated the motivation for change and the likelihood it may be successful.

However, moves towards change can only succeed if there is support from leaders in higher education, along with administrative structures that will facilitate lifelong learning. The latter include many of the characteristics of institutional organization reviewed in Chapters 3 and 4, such as flexible logistical arrangements for timetabling and for provision and use of physical space, appropriate services for mature students, and a general emphasis on quality of learning as opposed to more easily quantifiable indices such as the number of hours a class meets for formal lectures. Other crucial aspects of administrative procedures concern systems of assessment (reviewed in detail in Chapter 4), opportunities for group and peer learning, team teaching and interdisciplinary courses. Such changes in institutional policy may, in turn, require a shift in philosophy at an even higher level, such as the ministry of education, grants commission, accreditation agency or similar body. Despite the considerable autonomy which individual universities and colleges often enjoy, national education policies have in some cases had profound effects upon the organization of higher education in relation to the concerns that are the focus of this book.

Also of great importance is the whole matter of the institutional reward system, which in many colleges and universities is heavily weighted in favour of staff involvement in scholarship and research. If lifelong learning is to be encouraged, then it is essential that energy devoted to the improvement of teaching and learning be rewarded by the same tokens (tenure, promotion, in some cases merit pay) as are now accorded for demonstrated scholarship. Furthermore, there needs to be a recognition that research on teaching and learning itself is every bit as valid a scholarly contribution as more traditional research within the bounds of the discipline. At too many institutions today, it appears that research on the teaching and learning of, say, chemistry, as opposed to research in chemistry itself, constitutes a less significant contribution to the work of the department and institution. Indeed, Knapper's studies of faculty attitudes to the institutional reward system in Canada and Australia indicated that faculty perceived traditional research to be given twice the weight accorded to teaching, despite what may be stated in official policies. This is regarded as a major obstacle to enhancing the quality of teaching or introducing new instructional methods (Knapper, 1988a, 1990).

Finally, transforming universities and colleges to a system that will promote lifelong education will require the adoption of a common goal that focuses on the *process* of learning instead of just the content. The most important participants in the lifelong learning process are, of course, the learners themselves. Research on student learning is yielding promising insights, and various programmes to improve the quality of teaching and learning, reviewed in this book, represent a useful beginning in moving higher education towards a greater emphasis on lifelong learning skills. At the same time, it remains true that in many universities and colleges, teaching takes place without explicit attention being given to the learning processes that students will need not only in formal institutional learning, but in the problem solving and decision making they will encounter throughout the rest of their lives. While special programmes outside the formal curriculum may aid students in this respect, it seems essential for learning skills to be taught explicitly as part of the regular curriculum. We are convinced that most university teachers have a sincere desire to see their students master not only the basic concepts of their disciplines, but to go further and apply these insights in tackling a broad range of real-world issues. However, instructors may often lack the knowledge about how best to help their students go about this vital process.

This means that, despite our repeated emphasis on student autonomy in learning, and our criticism of didactic instructional approaches, university teachers have a key role to play in fostering lifelong learning. This is especially urgent in view of the fact that many students may, indeed, have to unlearn previous study habits and attitudes to education. In particular, there will be a need to communicate new values: for example, that students' own learning is more important than blind respect for authority, and that active learning is more useful than passive learning even though it may be initially more difficult. Since a great many instructors in higher education have no formal training in teaching, it will be a difficult task to move away from the prevailing didactic approaches to instructional roles that emphasize students' taking responsibility for their own learning. One encouraging factor, however, is the large numbers of university and college staff who have already demonstrated a lively interest in innovative teaching approaches that could facilitate lifelong learning skills in their students. We hope that this book will support them in their efforts.

Appendix

Promoting lifelong learning: some practical ideas for academics

Strategies for change

This book has attempted to develop a type of 'working philosophy' of higher education, based upon the guiding principle of lifelong learning. We have argued that lifelong education should be a major goal for universities and colleges and, to this end, have presented a critique of prevailing paedological and administrative practices.

Preceding chapters contain numerous instances of educational approaches that we believe are consistent with the concept of lifelong education, and in Chapter 7 we provided criteria against which such examples might be judged. Here we turn to some practical steps that individual university teachers might take to encourage lifelong learning in their own institutions and classrooms. The suggestions given here are in many cases not especially radical, and indeed may already be used by some readers of this book. The list is not comprehensive, and the ideas are not fleshed out in detail. Rather, they are intended to provide a set of examples that might stimulate instructors to consider changing their approaches to course planning, classroom teaching, and administrative practices, so as to help achieve the lifelong learning goals we believe are so important.

The ideas that follow relate to many different aspects of teaching and academic organization. They are categorized into two broad divisions: the first group is concerned with the academic as teacher, while the second focuses on the academic as institutional decision-maker. We hope that at least some of the suggestions here can provide a starting point for new instructional initiatives. Even better, we hope to provoke readers into developing their own suggestions for fostering lifelong learning in higher education.

Changes in teaching methods

For the most part, the suggestions here are all within the control of the individual teacher. They encompass the different aspects of instruction we have discussed earlier in the book – setting learning goals, choosing appropriate teaching and learning techniques, and assessing student competence or progress. For the sake of brevity, ideas are presented rather cryptically in point form, without full explication. This is partly because the suggestions hinge on approaches that have been discussed in some detail earlier in the book and also because most readers will wish to be highly selective about ideas they might try. Hence as a teacher you might do the following:

Learning goals

- Develop a set of course goals that are consistent with the principles of lifelong learning and get the help of a colleague in matching goals with student assessment tasks (exams, tests, projects) to see how the ways students are graded reflect expressed learning objectives.
- Communicate (and discuss) the learning objectives for the course with students.
- Ask students about their motives for taking the class, for example by administering a short questionnaire at the first meeting that asks about their expectations, attitudes, needs, and goals; consider how you might modify the curriculum in the light of what you find out from the survey.

Learning and study skills

- Find out about how your students learn, perhaps by administering one of the inventories that measures learning styles or study strategies (see Kolb and Fry, 1975; Ramsden and Entwistle, 1981), and discuss the results, and their implications, in class. Be prepared to modify how you teach in the light of what you discover about student learning preferences.
- If your institution has a study skills adviser, ask what steps might be taken to help your students learn more effectively, and suggest running a session on study skills for your class.
- Ask students for study problems they encounter, and their suggested solutions, especially in the context of your assessment tasks (assignments, exams, etc).

- Consider teaching study skills explicitly (eg how to write up a good lab report, how to prepare for an exam, what you expect in an essay) instead of focusing exclusively on course content.
- Teach information-finding skills as part of your course, such as conducting a search in the library or on the Web, finding appropriate information sources, selecting key words that describe the issue or topic, and using relevant data bases. Be sure to deal with the issue of evaluating information sources for accuracy and credibility.
- Consider setting assignments or projects that students can work on in small teams of three or four partners, and provide some prior instruction on how to work effectively in small groups. (Call on your educational development office for advice if necessary.)

Teaching methods and active learning

- Provide opportunities for active learning in the classroom, such as class projects, use of small group discussion, debates, role playing, etc.
- To allow more time for teaching cognitive and learning skills, disseminate course content other than by lecturing, eg by providing copies of course notes, using a Web site, etc.
- Develop (or find from another source) a self-instructional module (eg printed work-book, set of Web pages, perhaps even a CD-ROM) for a part of the course you find difficult or boring to teach. Make it available on a supplementary basis, and ask students to evaluate its utility.
- Try to introduce some element of peer learning, if only on a small scale – for example, make student pairs responsible for certain course topics and have them make brief class presentations.
- If students will make individual or group presentations, provide some prior instruction on how to do so effectively (get help from a professional educational developer if necessary). Consider poster presentations as an alternative to a traditional student-led seminar.
- Use case studies and similar real-life material as a major learning activity, with preparation done outside class (possibly by student teams) and results brought to class for fuller discussion.
- Even in a large class, try to arrange some opportunities for individual contacts between instructor, students (and, if appropriate, teaching assistants). This could range from conducting an informal 'clinic' after class to arranging a voluntary get-together at a local café or pub.
- Organize weekend seminars or workshops to extend or replace the officially scheduled classroom contact hours. Such events can offer an excellent means of promoting self-directed and peer learning.

- Use undergraduates as teaching assistants to help run the course (eg to lead discussion groups), or even as research assistants on a project of relevance to the course that can later be discussed in class.
- Encourage older people to enrol in your courses, and discuss (critically if necessary) the way in which class material applies to real life, and how what is learnt in the classroom might be changed or extended by incorporating examples and principles they have gathered from experience outside.
- Be willing to accept younger learners, for example those in early entrance programmes. Encourage younger and older students to work together, for example on projects or in study groups.
- Get students to discover sources of information about the course material apart from traditional library resources (eg a museum, government office, local expert), and provide an opportunity to make use of such material in a project, essay, or test.
- If you make use of visiting speakers, have students identify appropriate resource people, make the necessary contacts, and plan the in-class session (eg by gathering questions from other students and arranging for a panel to put the questions to the speaker).
- If appropriate, try to relate the course to some practical applications/implications in the work-place or local community, for example by a site visit or field trip.
- Emphasize the connection between the work of researchers and theorists mentioned in class and aspects of their private lives or characteristics of the society in which they lived. Even better, have students get the information for themselves, perhaps by contacting the individuals by letter, phone or e-mail.
- Bring practitioners into your classroom to describe the way in which theoretical knowledge can be applied, how it might be extended by knowledge of the real world, and what problems remain that new theories could help solve.

Values

- Take some time in class to discuss underlying values and ethical considerations of relevance to the course and discipline. Discuss your own values with the students and explain how you came to your position. Be prepared to debate such issues with students, and perhaps have them debate each other on a controversial issue of the day.
- Bring something of yourself to class by use of relevant personal examples, experiences, and anecdotes about the course material, and have students (especially older learners) describe their own experiences and attitudes.

Student assessment

- Set regular 'challenge' assignments and tests throughout the course, not necessarily for credit, and let students mark their own work; discuss answers in the light of your own solution and suggest steps for further or better work in the future.
- Have students assess one of their own assignments and/or assess the work of a fellow student (even if you retain the right to make the final decision on the grade). Discuss in class the evaluation criteria that will be used, and ask for feedback on the quality of work when the assessment has been completed.
- In grading exams or assignments, give bonuses for material not taken directly from the lectures or text book.
- Give bonus marks for cross-disciplinary material and examples.
- Give higher grades for appropriate references to practical issues, such as real-life examples of theoretical points.
- Set assignment or exam questions taken from real life. For example, ask students to show how a particular aspect of theory might be applied in a real-world setting.
- If students work in teams, try to ensure that they generate a team *product*: a presentation, poster, written report (or some combination). Have other members of the class assess the product as well as all team members. If necessary, have team members assess their own and others' contribution to the work on the assignment.
- Try to set assignments that require integration of concepts and material from different areas, and award part of the mark for the successful integration of ideas. Be prepared to provide students with examples of assignments where integration was done well.

Instructional evaluation

- Invite a colleague to review your teaching by exchanging course outlines, assignments and exams, and perhaps make a classroom visit.
- Ask students what they gained from a class or assignment by distributing a brief questionnaire that asks what ideas they have learnt that can be applied in their broader lives. Compare these responses with your own expectations and learning goals.
- Try one of the 'classroom assessment techniques' described by Cross and Angelo (1993), or develop one of your own that might measure success in encouraging lifelong learning. For example, at the end of the class allow five minutes to write down (and hand in anonymously) one or two things they learned about in the session that they intend to use in their lives beyond university. Next time

give the class a summary of the ideas submitted and perhaps have a brief discussion.

- If you have the chance, play the role of a student; for example, enrol in a distance course or sign up for an extension course that interests you; sit in on a class taught by a colleague at your own institution or another. Consider what changes might be desirable in the course from a student's point of view. If the course is in a different, but related, discipline, think about what ideas might be used in your own classes.
- Set an assignment on a topic you know little or nothing about and do the necessary background research yourself, sharing your findings with your students.
- Carry out research on your own teaching, as writers like Patricia Cross (1986) have suggested, stressing aspects that involve lifelong learning, for example by conducting a survey of former students to see how they have utilized ideas gained from your classes.
- Document your teaching efforts and accomplishments in a teaching dossier or portfolio (Shore *et al*, 1986), paying particular attention to activities related to lifelong learning, and present a summary of the dossier as part of the regular performance review. Criteria for academic advancement in most universities give high priority to teaching effectiveness, but review committees often lack convincing evidence on which to base a case.

Organizational changes affecting teaching

The suggestions given above all relate to aspects of instruction that are readily controlled by an individual teacher. But our framework for evaluation presented in Chapter 7 makes it clear that promotion of lifelong learning also requires changes in the organization of education. In many cases such changes lie beyond the authority of the individual faculty member – though most universities are organized on a collegial basis, and academic staff generally have considerable say on matters of internal policies and procedures. The following suggestions all concern ways in which organizational structures might be changed to help promote lifelong learning. Once again, they are presented in point form to suggest initiatives an individual teacher might take.

- Survey graduates to find out their perception of the education they have received and solicit suggestions for change in the light of their experience since leaving university.

- Survey employers to get their views on needed skills, knowledge, and values. Consider forming an advisory committee of employers relevant to your discipline which might act as a sounding board for proposed curriculum changes, academic standards, appropriate teaching experiences, etc.
- At the department or programme level, examine the curriculum carefully in the light of current developments in the field, the rapid expansion of knowledge, and need to provide students with tools for lifelong learning. Consider how much will be of relevance five years after graduation. Assess how much time is spent teaching content as opposed to more generic skills. Decide whether it is possible to reduce the 'seat time' required of students and substitute more independent study methods.
- Spend some time in class discussing with students aspects of university policies and procedures that affect them, such as grading practices, important curriculum changes, or admissions standards. Consider presenting this information to the policy-making committee concerned.
- Consider introducing a course that deals exclusively with the *process* of learning instead of the content of the discipline; for example, a course on effective problem-solving and decision-making.
- Lobby your institution or department to provide sabbaticals related to improving teaching skills and/or curriculum development relevant to promotion of lifelong learning. Although most sabbatical policies permit use of leaves for teaching-related activities, in practice there is much greater emphasis on leaves to undertake research.
- If your department or institution has awards for excellent teachers, press for criteria that include encouragement of lifelong learning (instead of emphasizing didactic teaching skills such as lecturing).
- If your institution has regular programme appraisals, press for attention to be paid to teaching quality as well as research output, and try to find indicators of the long-term impact of teaching programmes on the lives of students (such as the achievement of graduates).
- Work to include teaching and learning topics (eg on alternative teaching methods, relevance of the curriculum, etc) as part of your academic department's regular colloquium series.
- Ensure that teaching is a factor when hiring new staff. Make arrangements for applicants to do some teaching (of undergraduates, not just a research seminar for colleagues) and ask them about their teaching approach and philosophy. Require a teaching dossier as well as a traditional Curriculum Vitae.

Matching teaching strategies to lifelong learning criteria

Each of these suggestions can be evaluated in terms of the criteria for lifelong learning spelled out in Chapter 7, and summarized in Tables 7.1 and 7.2. Naturally, some ideas meet the criteria better than others. Many represent good educational practice, but are not uniquely characteristic of lifelong learning principles. Certainly, developing course goals is a widely recommended procedure in education. However, communicating such goals to students helps meet a number of the criteria listed in Table 7.1. For instance, the idea is consistent with having students plan their own learning, with active student learning, peer learning, and a stress on learning process versus course content. In the case of organizational criteria (Table 7.2), this suggestion supports the notion of course flexibility, self-instruction, and an emphasis on study skills. Similarly, arranging field trips in the local community might be said to encourage learning in informal settings, knowledge to tackle real-world problems (Table 7.1), use of non-professional instructors, and integration of general and vocational education (Table 7.2). It is not necessary here to go through all suggestions and relate each one to the full list of lifelong learning criteria. Readers can easily do this for themselves. We hope, however, that as individual teachers develop their own prescriptions, they will refer to our list of criteria as a convenient yardstick for measuring appropriateness. Of course, no single proposition can fulfil all, or even most, criteria. To achieve lifelong learning requires an eclectic mixture of strategies.

References

Aalbeck-Nielson, K, La pédagogie de la survivance. (Sur le but de l'éducation.) *Paideia*, 1973, *3*, 209–13

(AAMC), Association of American Medical Colleges *Physicians for the twenty-first century*. Washington, DC: Association of American Medical Colleges, 1984

(AAMC), *Educating medical students: Assessing change in medical education – the road to implementation*. Washington, DC: Association of American Medical Colleges, 1992

Abercrombie, M L J, Changing basic assumptions about teaching and learning. In D Boud (ed), *Developing student autonomy in learning*. London: Kogan Page, 1981

Agoston, G, La communauté en tant qu'éducateur. *Acta Universitatis Szegediensis de Attila József Nominatae Sectio Paedagogica et Psychologia*, 1975, *18*, 5–15

Albanese, M A and Mitchell, S, Problem-based learning: A review of literature on its outcomes and implementation issues. *Academic Medicine*, 1993, *68*, 52–81

Anderson, J R, *Rules of the mind*. Hillsdale, New Jersey: Erlbaum, 1993

Anderson, R S, Why talk about different ways to grade: The shift from traditional assessment to alternative assessment. In R S Anderson and B W Speck (eds), *Changing the way we grade student performance: Classroom assessment and the new learning paradigm*. San Francisco: Jossey-Bass, 1998

Anisef, P, Okihiro, N and James, C, *The pursuit of equality: Evaluating and monitoring accessibility to postsecondary education in Ontario*. Toronto: Ontario Ministry of Colleges and Universities, 1982

Annis, L F, The processes and effects of peer tutoring. *Human Learning*, 1983, *2*, 39–47

Astin, A W, *Four critical years: Effects of college on beliefs, attitudes and knowledge*. San Francisco: Jossey-Bass, 1977

Astin, A W, *What matters in college? Four critical years revisited*. San Francisco; Jossey-Bass, 1993

Aujaleu, E, Medicine of the future. *World Health*, April 1973, 23–29

Baldwin, R G, Technology's impact on faculty life and work. In K H Gillespie (ed), *The impact of technology on faculty development, life, and work.* San Francisco: Jossey-Bass, 1998

Barbuto, G, Motivation zur Teilnahme an einem Kursus an der Volkshochschule (Motivation for participating in an adult education course). Unpublished Master's thesis, University of Hamburg, 1993

Barr, R B and Tagg, J, From teaching to learning: A new paradigm for undergraduate education. *Change*, 1995, *27* (6), 13–25

Barton, A H, *Studying the effects of college education: A methodological examination of 'Changing values in college'.* New Haven, Connecticut: Hazen Foundation, 1959

Becher, T, The learning professions. *Studies in Higher Education*, 1996, *21*, 43–55

Becker, M S, Geer, B and Hughes, E C, *Making the grade: The academic side of college life.* New York: Wiley, 1968

Beecher, G, Chickering, A W, Hamlin, W G and Pitkin, R S, *An experiment in college curriculum organisation: Report of a six-year experiment (1959–1965).* Plainfield, Vermont: Goddard College, 1966

Beers, S E and Bloomingdale, J R, Epistemological and instructional assumptions of college teachers. Paper presented at the annual meeting of the American Educational Research Association, Montreal, April 1983

Berg, B and Ostergren, B, *Innovations and innovation processes in higher education.* Stockholm: National Board of Universities and Colleges, 1977

Bertrand, D and Knapper, C K, Contextual influences on students' approaches to learning in three academic departments. Unpublished honours thesis, University of Waterloo, 1991

Beuret, G and Webb, A, *Engineers: Servants or saviours?* Leicester: Leicester Polytechnic, 1982

Bligh, D A (ed), *Professionalism and flexibility in learning.* Guildford, Surrey: Society for Research into Higher Education, 1982

Bligh, D A, *What's the use of lectures?* (5th edn). Exeter: Intellect, 1998

Blumenstyk, G, Moving beyond textbook sales, Harcourt plans to open a for-profit university. *Chronicle of Higher Education*, 4 June 1999a, p A32

Blumenstyk, G, Distance learning at the Open University. *Chronicle of Higher Education*, 23 July 1999b, p A35

Blumenstyk, G and Magner, D K, As assessment draws new converts, backers gather to ask 'What works?' *Chronicle of Higher Education*, 11 July 1990, p A11

Boshier, R, Motivational orientations revisited: Life space motives and the Education-Participation-Scale. *Adult Education*, 1977, *27*, 89–115

Botkin, J W, Elmandjra, M and Malitza, M, *No limits to learning*. Oxford: Pergamon, 1979

Boud, D, *Implementing student self-assessment*. Kensington, New South Wales: Higher Education Research and Development Association of Australasia, 1986

Boud, D, *Enhancing learning through self assessment*. London: Kogan Page, 1995a

Boud, D, Assessment and learning: Contradictory or complementary? In P Knight (ed), *Assessment for learning in higher education*. London: Kogan Page, 1995b

Boud, D, Providing for lifelong learning through work-based study: Challenges for policy and practice. Paper presented at the International Conference on Lifelong Learning, Guildford, Surrey, 1997

Boud, D and Falchikov, N, Quantitative studies of student self-assessment in higher education: A critical analysis of findings. *Higher Education*, 1989, *18*, 529–50

Boud, D and Feletti, G (eds), *The challenge of problem-based learning*. London: Kogan Page, 1991

Boud, D, Dunn, J and Hegarty-Hazel, E, *Teaching in laboratories*. Guildford, Surrey: Society for Research into Higher Education and NFER-Nelson, 1986

Bouton, C and Garth, R Y, The learning group: What it is and why it may be better. *American Association for Higher Education Bulletin*, 1982, *35* (1), 7–9

Boyer, E L, *Scholarship reconsidered: Priorities of the professoriate*. Princeton, New Jersey: Carnegie Foundation for the Advancement of Teaching, 1990

Boyer, E L, Creating the new American college. *Chronicle of Higher Education*, *9* March 1994, p A48

Braun, H J, A school-based strategy for achieving work-readiness skills. In L B Resnick and J G Wirth (eds), *Linking school and work*. San Francisco: Jossey-Bass, 1996

Breathnach, A, University-industry cooperation in Canada. Unpublished manuscript, Organisation for Economic Co-operation and Development, Paris, 1983

Brennan, J and Little, B, *A review of work based learning in higher education*. Sheffield: Department for Education and Employment, 1996

Bringle, R G and Hatcher, J A, Implementing service learning higher education. *Journal of Higher Education*, 1996, *67*, 221–39

Broderick, R, How Honeywell teaches its managers to manage. *Training*, 1983, *20* (1), 18–22

Brooks, J G and Brooks, M G, *In search of understanding: The case for constructivist classrooms*. Alexandria, Virginia: Association for Supervision and Curriculum Development, 1993

Brown, J S, Collins, A and Duguid, P, Situated cognition and the culture of learning. *Educational Researcher*, 1989, *18* (1), 32–42

Bruenig, R H, Proposals for change: A study of proposals to establish development programs in five universities and one college of the California State University and Colleges. Unpublished PhD dissertation, Union Graduate School West, 1980

Brzustowski, T A B, Continuing education: Requirements of the modern industrial society. Paper presented at the Thirteenth Commonwealth Universities Congress, Birmingham, August, 1983

Bunting, C I, Looking back over a decade of innovation and alternatives. In *The test of time: Perspectives on innovation and educational improvement* (AASCU Studies, September 1982). Washington, DC: American Association of State Colleges and Universities, 1982

Cahn, S N, *Scholars who teach: The art of college teaching*. San Francisco: Jossey-Bass, 1978

Candy, P C, *Self-direction for lifelong learning: A comprehensive guide to theory and practice*. San Francisco: Jossey-Bass, 1991

Candy, P C and Crebert, R G, Ivory tower to concrete jungle. *Journal of Higher Education*, 1991, *62*, 570–92

Candy, P C, Crebert, R G and O'Leary, J O, *Developing lifelong learners through undergraduate education*. Canberra, Australia: National Board of Employment, Education and Training, 1994

Carnegie Foundation, *The fourth revolution: Instructional technology in higher education*. New York: McGraw-Hill, 1972

Cave, M, Hanney, S and Kogan, M, *The use of performance indicators in higher education: A critical analysis of developing practice* (2nd edn). London: Jessica Kingsley, 1991

Centra, J A, *Faculty development practices in U.S. colleges and universities*. Princeton, New Jersey: Educational Testing Service, 1976

Chickering, A W and Gamson, Z F, Seven principles for good practice in undergraduate education. *The Wingspread Journal*, 1987, *9* (2) (special insert)

Cohen, A M and Brawer, F B, *The two-year college instructor today*. New York: Praeger, 1977

Cohen, N H, *Mentoring adult learners: A guide for educators and trainers*. Malabar, Florida: Krieger, 1995

Cohen, P A, College grades and adult achievement: A meta-analysis of empirical research. Paper presented at the annual meeting of the American Educational Research Association, Montreal, April 1983

Coletta, N J, Formal, nonformal and informal education. In C Tuijnman (ed), *International Encyclopedia of Adult Education and Training* (2nd edn). Tarrytown, New York: Pergamon, 1996

Collier, K G, Peer-group learning in higher education: The development of higher order skills. *Studies in Higher Education*, 1980, *5*, 55–62

Collier, K G (ed), *The management of peer-group learning: Syndicate methods in higher education*. Guildford, Surrey: Society for Research into Higher Education, 1983

Coombs, P H, Critical world educational issues of the next two decades. *International Review of Education*, 1982, *28*, 143–57

Coombs, P H and Ahmed, M, *Attacking rural poverty: How nonformal education can help*. Baltimore, Maryland: Johns Hopkins University Press, 1974

Cottrell, P, *Professional accreditation of university teaching*. London: Association of University Teachers, 1996

Creed, T, PowerPoint, no! Cyberspace, yes. *National Teaching and Learning Forum*, 1997, *6* (4), 5–7

(CRHEFP) Committee of Review of Higher Education Financing and Policy, *Learning for life: Review of higher education financing and policy – policy discussion paper*. Canberra: Commonwealth of Australia Department of Employment, Education, Training and Youth Affairs, 1997

Cropley, A J, *Lifelong Education: A psychological analysis*. Oxford: Pergamon, 1977

Cropley, A J (ed), *Lifelong education: A stocktaking*. UIE Monograph, Number 8. Hamburg: UNESCO Institute for Education, 1979

Cropley, A J, Lifelong learning and systems of education: An overview. In A J Cropley (ed), *Towards a system of lifelong education*. Oxford: Pergamon, 1980

Cropley, A J, Lifelong learning: A rationale for teacher training. *Journal of Education for Teaching*, 1981, *7*, 57–69

Cropley, A J, Education. In M Runco and S Pritzker (eds), *Encyclopedia of creativity*. San Diego, California: Academic Press, 1999a

Cropley, A J, Creativity and cognition: Producing effective novelty, *Roeper Review*, 1999b, *21*, 253–60.

Cropley, A J and Dave, R H, *Lifelong education and the training of teachers*. Oxford: Pergamon, 1978

Cropley, A J and Dave, R H, Reforming initial and continuing education of teachers in the perspective of lifelong education. Unpublished manuscript, Hamburg: UNESCO Institute for Education, 1984

Cropley, A J and Kahl, T N, Distance education and distance learning: Some psychological considerations. *Distance Education*, 1983, *4*, 27–39

Cropley, A J and Kahl, T N, Face-to-face vs, distance learning: Psychological consequences and practical implications, *Distance Education*, 1986, *7*, 38–48

Cropley, A J and Knapper, C K, Lifelong learning and schools: Guidelines for practice. *Australian Administrator*, 1982, *3* (6), 1–4

Cropley, A J and Knapper, C K, Higher education and the promotion of lifelong learning, *Studies in Higher Education*, 1983, *8*, 15–21

Cropley, D H and Cropley, A J, Teaching engineering students to be creative: Program and outcomes. Paper presented at the Annual Meeting of the Australian Association for Engineering Education, Gladstone, Australia, 28 September 1998

Cross, K P, *Adults as learners*. San Francisco: Jossey-Bass, 1981

Cross, K P, A proposal to improve teaching or what 'taking teaching seriously' should mean. *American Association for Higher Education Bulletin*, 1986, *39* (1), 9–14

Cross, K P and Angelo, T A, *Classroom assessment techniques: A handbook for college teachers*. San Francisco: Jossey-Bass, 1993

Cuneo, C, *Some provocative considerations on the use of educational technologies*. Hamilton, Ontario: Network for the Evaluation of Education and Training Technologies, 1998

Daniel, J, Not-so distant competitors: Readers react. *American Association for Higher Education Bulletin*, 1998, *50* (9), 11

Darby, J, McIntyre, B, Gilham, A, Cantley, A and Beale, H, Lifelong learning from a connected Oxford. *Active Learning*, December 1998, 71–73

Dauber, H and Verne, E (eds), *Freiheit zum Lernen*. Hamburg: Rowohlt, 1976

Dave, R H, *Lifelong education and school curriculum*. UIE Monograph, Number 1. Hamburg: UNESCO Institute for Education, 1973

Dave, R H and Cropley, A J, *Lifelong education and the training of teachers*. Oxford: Pergamon, 1978

de Sanctis, F M , A victory by Italian workers: The '150 hours.' *Prospects: A Quarterly Review of Education*, 1977, *7*, 280–87

Dewey, J, *Experience and education*. New York: Collier, 1938

Dickson, D, French students schedule mass protests to coincide with debate on reform. *Chronicle of Higher Education*, 18 May 1983, pp. 25–26

Di Petta, T, Community on-line: New professional environments for higher education. In K H Gillespie (ed), *The impact of technology on faculty development, life, and work*. San Francisco: Jossey-Bass, 1998

Dohmen, G, *Weiterbildung in Deutschland*. (Continuing education in Germany.) Bonn: Federal Ministry for Education, Science, Research and Technology, 1997

Draves, B, *The free university: A model for lifelong learning*. Chicago: Association Press, 1981

Dubin, S S, The psychology of lifelong learning: New developments in the professions. *International Review of Applied Psychology*, 1974, *23*, 17–31

Duke, C, *Australian perspectives in lifelong education*. Melbourne: Australian Council for Educational Research, 1976

Earley, M, Mentkowski, M and Schafer, J, *Valuing at Alverno: The valuing process in liberal education*. Milwaukee, Wisconsin: Alverno College, 1980

Eble, K E, *Professors as teachers*. San Francisco: Jossey-Bass, 1972

Edgerton, R, The re-examination of faculty priorities. *Change*, 1993, *25* (4), 10–17

Eide, K, Work, leisure, education. Paper presented at the Seminar on Lifelong Learning and Recurrent Education, Haderslav, Denmark, May 1980

Elton, L, Assessment for learning. In D A Bligh (ed), *Professionalism and flexibility in learning*. Guildford, Surrey: Society for Research into Higher Education, 1982

Elton, L, Improving the cost-effectiveness of laboratory teaching. *Studies in Higher Education*, 1983, *8*, 79–85

Entwistle, N J, Improving teaching through research on student learning. In J J F Forest (ed), *University teaching: International perspectives*. New York: Garland, 1998

Environment Canada, *A framework for discussion of the environment: The Green Plan, a national challenge*. Ottawa: Environment Canada, 1990

Erikson, E H, *Childhood and society*. New York: Norton, 1963

European Commission European year of lifelong learning, *Magazine for Education, Training and Youth in Europe*, 1996, *5*, 8–10

Evans, R I, *Resistance to innovation in higher education*. San Francisco: Jossey-Bass, 1968

Evans, R I and Leppman, P K, *Resistance to innovation in higher education: A social psychological exploration focussed on television and the establishment*. San Francisco: Jossey-Bass, 1968

Exley, K and Dennick, R, *Innovations in teaching medical sciences*. Birmingham: Staff and Educational Development Association, 1996

Farago, J M, When they bought in, did we sell out? David Riesman on the student as consumer. *Journal of Higher Education*, 1982, *53*, 701–05

Farrington, G C, The new technologies and the future of residential undergraduate education. In R N Katz and Associates. *Dancing with the devil: Information technology and the new competition in higher education*. San Francisco: Jossey-Bass, 1999

Faure, E *et al*, *Learning to be: The world of education today and tomorrow*. Paris and London: UNESCO and Harrap, 1972

Ferrier, B, Marrin, M and Seidman, J, Student autonomy in learning medicine: Some participants' experiences. In D Boud (ed), *Developing student autonomy in learning* (2nd edn). London: Kogan Page, 1988

Fields, C M, New disputes erupt in 2 U.S. agencies over White House's civil-rights stance. *Chronicle of Higher Education*, 14 May 1983, 17–18

Finkel, D L and Arney, W R, *Educating for freedom: The paradox of pedagogy*. New Brunswick, New Jersey: Rutgers University Press, 1995

Finkel, D L and Monk, G S, *Contexts for learning: A teacher's guide to the design of intellectual experience*. Olympia, Washington: The Evergreen State College, 1978

Finkel, D L and Monk, G S, The design of intellectual experience. *Journal of Experiential Education*, 1979, *2* (3), 31–38

Frederiksen, J R and Collins, A, Designing an assessment system for the future workplace. In L B Resnick and J G Wirth (eds), *Linking school and work*. San Francisco: Jossey-Bass, 1996

Friedrich, R J and Michalak, S J, Why doesn't research improve teaching? Some answers from a small liberal arts college. *Journal of Higher Education*, 1983, *54*, 158–61

Gaff, J G, Overcoming faculty resistance. In J G Gaff (ed), *Institutional renewal through the improvement of teaching*. San Francisco: Jossey-Bass, 1978

Gaff, J G, *New life for the college curriculum*. San Francisco: Jossey-Bass, 1991

Gardner, H, *Multiple intelligences: The theory in practice*. New York: Basic Books, 1993

Geis, G L and Smith, R, If professors are adults. Paper presented at the annual meeting of the American Educational Research Association, Montreal, April 1983

Gelpi, E, Politics and lifelong education policies and practices. In A J Cropley (ed), *Towards a system of lifelong education*. Oxford: Pergamon, 1980

Giberson, M, Student overload. *University Affairs*, 1999, *40* (2), 14–16

Gibbs, G and Jacques, D, *Labs and practicals*. Oxford: Oxford Brookes University, Educational Methods Unit, 1990

Giles, D E and Eyler, J, A service learning research agenda for the next five years. In R A Rhoads and J P F Howard (eds), *Academic service learning: A pedagogy of action and reflection*. San Francisco: Jossey-Bass, 1998

Goad, L H, *Preparing teachers for lifelong education: The report of a multinational study of some developments in teacher education in the perspective of lifelong education*. Oxford: Pergamon, 1984

Goldschmid, M L, The learning cell: An instructional innovation. *Learning and Development*, 1971, *2* (5), 1–6

Goldschmid, M L, 'Parrainage': Students helping each other. In D Boud (ed), *Developing student autonomy in learning*. London: Kogan Page, 1981

Goodlad, S (ed), *Study service: An examination of community service as a method of study in higher education*. London: National Foundation for Educational Research/Nelson, 1982

Gose, B, University of Chicago president's plan to resign doesn't quiet debate over his agenda. *Chronicle of Higher Education*, 18 June 1999, p A43

Gow, L and Kember, D, Does higher education promote independent learning? *Higher Education*, 1990, *19*, 307–22

Grant, J, A Sandwich plan in England. In A S Knowles and Associates, *Handbook of cooperative education*. San Francisco: Jossey-Bass, 1971

Gray, P J, Campus profiles. *Assessment Update*, 1990, *2* (3), 4–5

Green, K C, When wishes come true: Colleges and the convergence of access, lifelong learning, and technology. *Change*, 1999, *31* (1), 10–15

Greenberg, E M (ed), *New partnerships: Higher education and the non-profit sector*. San Francisco: Jossey-Bass, 1982

Gustafson, K L, Can you really do instructional development on two cents a day? *Journal of Instructional Development*, 1977, *1*, 28–29

Gustafson, K L and Bratton, B, Instructional improvement centers in higher education: A status survey. Paper presented at the annual meeting of the American Educational Research Association, Montreal, April 1983

Hadwin, A F and Winne, P H, Study strategies have meager support: A review with recommendations for implementation. *Journal of Higher Education*, 1996, *67*, 692–715

Hartley, J, *Learning and studying: A research perspective*. London: Routledge, 1998

Hasan, A, Lifelong learning. In A C Tuijnman (ed), *International encyclopedia of adult education and training* (2nd edn). Tarrytown, New York: Pergamon, 1996

Hattie, J, Biggs, J and Purdie, N, Effects of learning skills interventions on studemt learning: A meta-analysis. *Review of Educational Research*, 1996, *66*, 99–136

Havighurst, R J and Taba, H, *Adolescent character and personality*. New York: Wiley, 1949

Hayes, R A and Travis, J H, *Employer experience with cooperative education: Analysis of costs and benefits*. Detroit: Detroit Institute of Technology Cooperative Education Research Center, 1974

Hazel, E and Baillie, C, *Improving teaching and learning in laboratories*. Jamison Centre, Australia: Higher Education Research and Development Society of Australasia, 1998

Health and Welfare Canada, *Achieving health for all: A framework for health promotion*. Ottawa: Health and Welfare Canada, 1986

Healy, P, SUNY trustees adopt mandatory core curriculum for baccalaureate students. *Chronicle of Higher Education*, 8 January 1999, p A48

Heath, D H, Academic predictors of adult maturity and competence. *Journal of Higher Education*, 1977, *48*, 613–52

Heerman, B, Enders, C C and Wine, E (eds), *Serving lifelong learners*. San Francisco: Jossey-Bass, 1980

Hefferlin, J B, *Dynamics of academic reform*. San Francisco: Jossey-Bass, 1969

Heller, J I, Reif, F and Hungate, H N, Theory-based instruction in scientific problem solving. Paper presented at the annual meeting of the American Educational Research Association, Montreal, April 1983

Henry, J, *Teaching through projects*. London: Kogan Page, 1994

Heron, J, Assessment revisited. In D Boud (ed), *Developing student autonomy in learning*. London: Kogan Page, 1981

Ho, A S P, A conceptual change staff development programme: Effects as perceived by the participants. *International Journal for Academic Development*, 1998, *3*, 24–38

Hoggart, R, Stephens, M, Taylor, J and Smethurst, R, Continuing education within universities and polytechnics. In D A Bligh (ed), *Professionalism and flexibility in learning*. Guildford, Surrey: Society for Research into Higher Education, 1982

Houle, C O, *The inquiring mind*. Madison: University of Wisconsin Press, 1961

Hounsell, D, Improving students' learning techniques. *University of Birmingham Teaching News*, March 1983, 4–5

Howard, A, College experiences and managerial performance. *Journal of Applied Psychology*, 1986, *71*, 530–52

Hubermann, M, Live and learn: A review of recent studies in lifelong education. *Higher Education*, 1979, *8*, 205–15

Hubert, G, Mixed mode study: Has it got a future? *Studies in Higher Education*, 1989, *14*, 219–29

Huczynski, A, *Encyclopedia of management development methods*. Aldershot: Gower, 1983

Hummel, C, *Education today for the world of tomorrow*. Paris: UNESCO, 1977

Illich, I and Verne, E, Le piège de l'école à vie. *Le Monde de l'Education*, 1975, *1*, 11–14

Jacks, M L, *Total education: A plea for synthesis*. London: Paul, Trench, Trubner, 1946

Jackson, K (ed), *Redesigning curricula: Models of service learning syllabi*. Providence, Rhode Island: Campus Compact, 1994

Jacob, P E, *Changing values in college: An exploratory study of the impact of college teaching*. New York: Harper and Brothers, 1957

Jacoby, B, Service-learning in today's higher education. In B. Jacoby and Associates, *Service-learning in higher education: Concepts and practices*. San Francisco: Jossey-Bass, 1996

Jalling, H and Carlsson, M, *An attempt to raise the status of undergraduate teaching*. Stockholm: Council for Studies of Higher Education, 1995

Johnes, J and Taylor, J, *Performance indicators in higher education: U.K. indicators*. Buckingham: Open University Press, 1990

Johnson Foundation, *An American imperative: Higher expectations for higher education*. Milwaukee, Wisconsin: Johnson Foundation, 1993

Kabel, R L, Ideas for managing large classes. *Engineering Education*, 1983, *74* (2), 80–3

Karpen, U, Implementing lifelong education and the law. In A J Cropley (ed), *Towards a system of lifelong education*. Oxford: Pergamon, 1980

Katz, R N and Associates, *Dancing with the devil: Information technology and the new competition in higher education*. San Francisco: Jossey-Bass, 1999

Kegan, R, *In over our heads*. Cambridge, Massachusetts: Harvard University Press, 1994

Kember, D, A reconceptualisation of the research into university academics' conceptions of teaching. *Learning and Instruction*, 1997, 7, 255–75

Kember, D and Gow, L, Orientations to teaching and their effect on the quality of student learning. *Journal of Higher Education*, 1994, *65*, 58–74

Kirby, J R, Knapper, C K and Carty, A E, *Approaches to learning at work: A report to the Bank of Montreal*. Kingston, Ontario: Queen's University, Faculty of Education, 1997

Kirsch, I S and Jungeblut, A, *Literacy: Profiles of America's young adults*. Princeton, New Jersey: Educational Testing Service, 1986

Kjersdam, F and Enemark, S, *The Aalborg experiment: Project innovation in university education*. Aalborg, Denmark: Aalborg University Press, 1994

Kloss, G, A suitable case for treatment. *Times Higher Education Supplement*, December 12, 1982, 10

Knapper, C K, *Evaluating instructional technology*. London: Croom Helm, 1980

Knapper, C K, *Teaching effectiveness at the University of Alberta*. Edmonton: University of Alberta, 1988a

Knapper, C K, Lifelong learning and distance education. *American Journal of Distance Education*, 1988b, *1*, 63–72

Knapper, C K, Technology and lifelong learning. In D Boud (ed), *Developing student autonomy in learning* (2nd edn). London: Kogan Page, 1988c

Knapper, C K, Lifelong learning and university teaching. In I Moses (ed), *Higher education in the late twentieth century: A Festschrift for Ernest Roe*. Kensington, New South Wales: Higher Education Research and Development Society of Australasia, 1990

Knapper, C K, Approaches to study and lifelong learning: Some Canadian initiatives. In G Gibbs (ed), *Improving student learning through assessment and evaluation*. Oxford: Oxford Centre for Staff Development, 1995

Knapper, C K, Rewards for teaching. In P Cranton (ed), *Teaching improvement from an international perspective*. San Francisco: Jossey-Bass, 1997

Knapper, C K, Is academic development a profession? *International Journal for Academic Development*, 1998, *3*, 93–96

Knapper, C K and Rogers, P, *Increasing the emphasis on teaching in Ontario universities*. Toronto: Ontario Council on University Affairs, 1994

Knapper, C K, Cropley, A J and Moore, R J, A clinical/quantitative analysis of public opinions about seat belts, *International Review of Applied Psychology*, 1977, *9*, 43–49

Knight, P (ed), *Assessment for learning in higher education*. London: Kogan Page, 1995

Knights, S and McDonald, R, Adult learners in higher education: Some study problems and solutions from Australian experience. *British Journal of Educational Technology*, 1982, *13*, 237–46

Knoll, J H (ed), *Motivation for adult education*. Munich: K.G. Saur, 1985

Knowles, M S, *The modern practice of adult education: Andragogy versus pedagogy*. New York: Association Press, 1970

Knowles, M S, Non-traditional study: Issues and relations. *Adult Leadership*, 1975, *23*, 232–35

Knox, A B, Higher education and lifelong learning. *Journal of Research and Development in Education*, 1974, *7*, 13–23

Kolb, D A and Fry, R, Towards an applied theory of experiential learning. In C L Cooper (ed), *Theories of group processes*. New York: Wiley, 1975

Konrad, A G, Faculty development practices in Canadian universities. *Canadian Journal of Higher Education*, 1983, *13* (2), 13–25

Kozma, R B, Belle, L W and Williams, G W, *Instructional techniques in higher education*. Englewood Cliffs, New Jersey: Educational Technology, 1978

Kuh, G D, *Indices of quality in the undergraduate experience*. AAHE-ERIC Higher Education Research Report, Number 4. Washington, D C: American Association for Higher Education, 1981

Kulich, J, Lifelong education and the universities: A Canadian perspective. *International Journal of Lifelong Education*, 1982, *1*, 123–42

Kurland, N D, Alternative financing arrangements for lifelong education. In A J Cropley (ed), *Towards a system of lifelong education*. Oxford: Pergamon, 1980

Larson, C O, Dansereau, D F and Goetz, E, Cooperative learning: The role of individual differences. Paper presented at the annual meeting of the American Educational Research Association, Montreal, April 1983

Lawson, K, Lifelong education: Concept or policy? *International Journal of Lifelong Education*, 1982, *1*, 97–108

Lazar, A M, Who is studying in groups and why? Peer collaboration outside the classroom. *College Teaching*, 1995, *43*, 61–65

Leavitt, M O, A learning enterprise for the cybercentury: The Western Governors University. In D G Oblinger and S C Rush (eds), *The learning revolution: The challenge of information technology in the academy*. Bolton, Massachusetts: Anker, 1997

Lengrand, P, *An introduction to lifelong education*. Paris: UNESCO, 1970

Lengrand, P, *Areas of learning basic to lifelong education*. Oxford: Pergamon, 1986

Leverhulme Programme of Study into the Future of Higher Education, *Excellence in diversity: Towards a new strategy for higher education*. Guildford, Surrey: Society for Research into Higher Education, 1983

Levine, A, Service on campus. *Change*, 1994, *26* (4) 4–5

Lindquist, J, *Strategies for change*. Berkeley, California: Pacific Soundings Press, 1978

Linsky, A S and Straus, M A, Student evaluations, research productivity, and eminence of college faculty. *Journal of Higher Education*, 1975, *46*, 89–102

Little, T C, The institutional context for experiential learning. In T C Little (ed), *Making sponsored experiential learning standard practice*. San Francisco: Jossey-Bass, 1983

Lockwood, T, What should the baccalaureate degree mean? *Change*, 1982, *14* (8), 38–44

Long, H B, Lifelong learning: Pressure for acceptance. *Journal of Research and Development in Education*, 1974, *7*, 2–12

Loring, R K, The continuing education universe – USA. Paper presented at the Salzburg Seminar on Continuing Education, 6–26 August 1978

Lynch, J, *Policy and practice in lifelong education*. Driffield, East Yorkshire: Nafferton Books, 1982

Mackeracher, D, *Making sense of adult learning*. Toronto: Culture Concepts, 1996

Marchese, T, Not-so-distant competitors: How new providers are remaking the postsecondary marketplace. *American Association for Higher Education Bulletin*, 1998, *50* (9), 3–7

Marriott, S, *A backstairs to a degree: Demands for an open university in late Victorian England*. Leeds: Leeds Studies in Adult and Continuing Education, 1982

Marshall, J, Putting things right by degrees. *Times Higher Education Supplement*, 24 October 1982, 10

Marshall, L A and Rowland, F, *A guide to learning independently* (3rd edn). New York: Longman, 1998

Martin, E, Conceptions of workplace university education. *Higher Education Research and Development,* 1998, *17*, 191–205

Marton, F, Review of 'Student Learning in Higher Education'. *Journal of Higher Education*, 1983, *54*, 325–31

Marton, F and Saljo, R, On qualitative differences in learning: I – Outcome and process. *British Journal of Educational Psychology*, 1976a, *46*, 4–11

Marton, F and Saljo, R, On qualitative differences in learning: II – Outcome as a function of the learner's conception of the task. *British Journal of Educational Psychology*, 1976b, *46*, 115–27

Maslen, G, Part-timers' myth dispelled. *Times Higher Education Supplement*, 24 December 1982, 7

Maslow, A H, *Motivation and personality*. New York: Harper and Row, 1954

Massy, W F, and Wilger, A K, It's time to redefine quality. Paper presented at the fourth AAHE conference on faculty roles and rewards, Atlanta, January 1996

Masuda, Y, *The information society as post-industrial society*. Washington, DC: World Future Society, 1981

Matthews, D, Transforming higher education: Implications for state higher education finance policy. *Educom Review*, 1998, *33* (5), 48–57

Mayo, M, *Imagining tomorrow*. Leicester: National Institute of Adult Continuing Education, 1997

McCabe, R H, *Academic-economic planning systems*. Miami: Miami-Dade Community College, 1978

McClusky, H Y, The coming of age of lifelong learning. *Journal of Research and Development in Education*, 1974, *7*, 97–106

McConnell, J V, On becoming a student – again. Presidential address to Division Two of the American Psychological Association, Montreal, September 1980

McDonald, R and Knights, S, Returning to study: The mature-aged student. *Programmed Learning and Educational Technology*, 1979, *16*, 101–05

Mendel-Reyes, M, Pedagogy for citizenship: Service learning and democratic education. In R A Rhoads and J P F Howard (eds), *Academic service learning: A pedagogy of action and reflection*. San Francisco: Jossey-Bass, 1998

Menges, R J and Mathis, B C, *Key resources on teaching, learning, curriculum, and faculty development: A guide to higher education literature.* San Francisco: Jossey-Bass, 1988

Mentkowski, M and Strait, M J, *A longitudinal study of student change in cognitive development and generic abilities in an outcome-centered liberal arts curriculum.* Milwaukee, Wisconsin: Alverno College, Office of Research and Evaluation, 1983

Mezirow, J and Associates, *Fostering critical reflection in adulthood.* San Francisco: Jossey-Bass, 1990

Miller, C M L and Parlett, M, *Up to the mark: A study of the examination game.* London: Society for Research into Higher Education, 1974

Millis, B J and Cottell, P G, *Cooperative learning for higher education faculty.* Phoenix, Arizona: Oryx Press, 1998

Milton, O, *Will that be on the final?* Springfield, Illinois: Charles C. Thomas, 1982

Morgan, A, Theoretical aspects of project-based learning in higher education. *British Journal of Educational Technology*, 1983, *1*, 68–78

Morgan, A, Taylor, E and Gibbs, G, Variations in students' approaches to studying. *British Journal of Educational Technology*, 1982, *13*, 107–13

Morton, K, *Models of service and civic education.* Occasional paper of the Project on Integrating Service and Academic Study. Boston: Campus Compact, 1993

National Commission on Excellence in Education, *A nation at risk: The imperative for educational reform.* Washington, DC: National Commission on Excellence in Education, 1983

National Research Council, *From analysis to action: Report of a convocation.* Washington, DC: National Academy Press, 1996

(NCIHE) National Committee of Inquiry into Higher Education *Higher education and the learning society.* London: NCIHE, 1997

Neice, D C and Murray, T S, Literary proficiency and adults' readiness to learn. In P Belanger and A C Tuijnman (eds), *New patterns of adult learning: A six-country comparative study.* Oxford: Pergamon, 1997

Newman, J H, *The idea of a university.* (Originally published 1852.) Westminster, Maryland: Christian Classics, 1973

Newman, J H, Rapprochement among undergraduate psychology, science, mathematics, engineering, and technology education. *American Psychologist*, 1998, *53*, 1032–43

Noble, D, Digital diploma mills: The automation of higher education (Part one). *OCUFA Forum*, Spring 1998, pp 12–16

Nordvall, R C, *The process of change in higher education institutions.* AAHE-ERIC Higher Education Research Report, Number 7. Washington, DC: American Association for Higher Education, 1982

(NTIA) National Telecommunications and Information Administration, *Falling through the digital divide: Defining the digital divide. A report on the telecommunications and information technology gap in America*. Washington, DC: United States Department of Commerce, National Telecommunications and Information Administration, 1999

Nuttgens, P, *What should we teach and how should we teach it? Aims and purpose of higher education*. Aldershot: Wildwood House, 1988

Oblinger, D G and Verville, A-L, *What business wants from higher education*. Phoenix, Arizona: Oryx Press, 1998

OECD, *The OECD jobs study: Evidence and explanations*. Paris: Organisation for Economic Cooperation and Development, 1994

OECD, *Education at a glance: OECD indicators*. Paris: Organisation for Economic Cooperation and Development, Centre for Educational Research and Evaluation, 1996

Ostar, A W, Part-time students: The new majority for the 1980s. *Chronicle of Higher Education*, 7 October 1981, 56

Parjanen, M (ed), *Values and policies in adult higher education*. Tampere, Finland: University of Tampere Institute for Extension Studies, 1993

Pascarella, E T and Terenzini, P T, *How college affects students*. San Francisco: Jossey-Bass, 1991

Pask, G, Styles and strategies of learning. *British Journal of Educational Psychology*, 1976, *46*, 128–48

Perry, W G, *Forms of intellectual and ethical development in the college years: A scheme*. New York: Holt, Rinehart and Winston, 1970

Pflüger, A, Lifelong education and adult education: Reflections on four current problem areas. In A J Cropley (ed), *Lifelong education: A stocktaking*. UIE Monograph, Number 8. Hamburg: UNESCO Institute for Education, 1979

Pickering, M, Are lab courses a waste of time? *Chronicle of Higher Education*, 19 February 1980, 80

Pillay, H, Cognitive skills required in contemporary workplaces. *Studies in Continuing Education*, 1998, *20*, 71–81

Pineau, G, Organization and lifelong education. In A J Cropley (ed), *Towards a system of lifelong education*. Oxford: Pergamon, 1980

Pothof, F A M, *Educational systems as related to the functioning of university graduates in their first job: A comparison between project oriented and subject oriented education*. Twente, The Netherlands: Universiteit Twente, Onderwijskundig Centrum, 1995

Powar, K B, Globalisation of distance learning system: Implications for developing countries. *Staff and Educational Development International*, 1998, *2*, 203–07

Privateer, P M, Academic technology and the future of higher education: Strategic paths taken and not taken. *Journal of Higher Education*, 1999, *70*, 60–79

Pucheu, R, La formation permanente: Idée neuve? Idée fausse? *Esprit*, 1974, *10*, 321–36

Ramsden, P, How academic departments influence student learning. *Higher Education Research and Development Society of Australasia News*, 1982, *4* (3), 3–5

Ramsden, P and Entwistle, N J, Effects of academic departments on students' approaches to studying. *British Journal of Educational Psychology*, 1981, *51*, 368–83

Ramsden, P, Margetson, D, Martin, E and Clarke, S, *Recognising and rewarding good teaching in Australian higher education*. Canberra, Australia: Committee for the Advancement of University Teaching, 1995

Rao, V R and Khan, Z, Satellite-based interactive learning system: A case. *Staff and Educational Development International*, 1998, *2*, 27–34

Rappleye, W C, *Medical education: Final report of the Commission on Medical Education*. New York: Association of American Medical Colleges, 1932

Reardon, K M, Participatory action research as service learning. In R A Rhoads and J P F Howard (eds), *Academic service learning: A pedagogy of action and reflection*. San Francisco: Jossey-Bass, 1998

Resnick, L B, Mathematics and science learning: A new conception. *Science*, 1983, *220*, 477–78

Resnick, L B, *Education and learning to think*. Washington, DC: National Academy Press, 1987

Resnick, L B and Wirth, J G, The changing workplace: New challenges for education policy and practice. In L B Resnick and J G Wirth (eds), *Linking school and work*. San Francisco: Jossey Bass, 1996

Rhoads, R A and Howard, J P F (eds), *Academic service learning: A pedagogy of action and reflection*. San Francisco: Jossey-Bass, 1998

Richardson, J T E, Mature students in higher education: II. An investigation of approaches to studying and academic performance. *Studies in Higher Education*, 1995, *20*, 5–18

Ricks, F, Principles for structuring cooperative education programs. *Journal of Cooperative Education*, 1996, *21*, 8–22

Rüegg, W, Le role de l'université dans l'éducation permanente. *CRE-Information*, 1974, *25*, 3–20

Rust, C and Wallace, J (eds), *Helping students to learn from each other: Supplemental instruction*. Birmingham: Staff and Educational Development Association, 1995

Samson, C E, Graue, M E, Weinstein, T and Walberg, H J, Academic and occupational performance: A qualitative synthesis. Paper presented at the annual meeting of the American Educational Research Association, Montreal, April 1983

Sarason, S B, Carroll, C, Maton, K, Cohen, S and Lorentz, E, *Human services and resource networks: Rationale, possibilities and public policy.* San Francisco: Jossey-Bass, 1977

Sassoon, J, Studying outside the red brick wall. *Times Higher Education Supplement,* 17 September 1982, 10

Sawhill, J C, Lifelong learning: Scandal of the next decade? *Change,* 1978/79, *10* (11), 7, 80

(SCANS) Secretary of Labor's Commission on Achieving Necessary Skills, *What work requires of schools: A SCANS report for America 2000.* Washington, DC: United States Department of Labor, 1991

Schein, E H, *Professional education.* New York: McGraw-Hill, 1972

Schiefelbein, E, Planning implications of lifelong education. In A J Cropley (ed), *Towards a system of lifelong education.* Oxford: Pergamon, 1980

Schneider, A, At Chicago meeting, defenders of traditional curriculum assume embattled air. *Chronicle of Higher Education,* 30 April 1999, p A15

Scully, M G, Bachelor's degree a worthless credential, conference concludes. *Chronicle of Higher Education,* 24 November 1982, p 8

(SEDA) Staff and Educational Development Association, *The accreditation of teachers in higher education.* Birmingham: Staff and Educational Development Association, 1994

Selingo, J, University of Phoenix picks New Jersey for its first foray in eastern U.S. *Chronicle of Higher Education,* 23 October 1998, pp A28–A30

Semlak, W D, Comadena, M E, Escott, M D and Stockman, C L, The systems matrix model of adult learning. In *Proceedings of the Project for the Study of Adult Learning.* Carbondale, Illinois: Illinois State University, 1991

Senge, P M, *The fifth discipline: The art and practice of the learning organization.* New York: Doubleday, 1990

Shor, I, *Critical teaching in everyday life.* Boston: South End Press, 1980

Shore, B M, Foster, S F, Knapper, C K, Nadeau, G G, Neill, N and Sim, V, *The teaching dossier: A guide to its preparation and use* (Revised edition). Ottawa: Canadian Association of University Teachers, 1986

Sikes, W W, Schlesinger, L E and Seashore, C N, *Renewing higher education from within.* San Francisco: Jossey-Bass, 1974

Skager, R and Dave, R H, *Curriculum evaluation for lifelong education.* Oxford: Pergamon, 1977

Slavin, R E, Meta-nonsense: Misuse of meta-analysis in educational research. Paper presented at the annual meeting of the American Educational Research Association, Montreal, April 1983

Slowey, M (ed), *Implementing change from within colleges and universities: 10 personal accounts.* London: Kogan Page, 1995

Smith, S L, *Report of the Commission of Inquiry on Canadian Higher Education.* Ottawa: Association of Universities and Colleges of Canada, 1991

Smith, W A S and Stroud, M A, Distance education and new communications technologies. In C K Knapper (ed), *Expanding learning through new communications technologies.* San Francisco: Jossey-Bass, 1982

Snyder, B R, *The hidden curriculum.* New York: Knopf, 1971

Solomon, P R, Kavanaugh, R D, Goethals, G R and Crider, A, Overcoming fragmentation in the undergraduate psychology curriculum. *Teaching of Psychology*, 1982, *9*, 201–05

Somers, C N and Bridges, J A, *Post-graduate success: The relationship between experiential learning programmes and liberal studies – An exploratory model.* Michigan Consortium for the Evaluation of Nontraditional Education, 1982

Steiner, C J, Educating for innovation and management: The engineering educator's dilemma. *Institute of Electric and Electronic Engineers Transactions of Education*, 1998, *41*, 1–7

Stevens, A, Grannies are on the march to a better life. *The Observer*, 25 September 1983, 5

Stiles, L J and Robinson, B, Change in education. In B Zaltman (ed), *Processes and phenomena of social change.* New York: Wiley, 1973

Stock, A K, Developing lifelong education: Post-school perspectives. In A J Cropley (ed), *Lifelong education: A stocktaking.* UIE Monograph, Number 8. Hamburg: UNESCO Institute for Education, 1979

Stonier, T, Changes in western society: Educational implications. In T Schuller and J Megarry (eds), *Recurrent education and lifelong learning.* London: Kogan Page, 1979

Suchodolski, B, Education between being and having. *Prospects: A Quarterly Review of Education*, 1976, *2*, 142–54

Talbott, S, Who's killing higher education? *Educom Review*, 1999, *34* (2), 26–33

Tannenbaum, R S, Education or training: Reflections of a life in computing. *Educom Review*, 1999, *34* (1), 10–15

Task Force on Resource Allocation, *Undergraduate teaching, research and consulting/community service: What are the functional interactions? A literature survey.* Toronto: Ontario Council on University Affairs, 1994

Taylor, P G, Institutional change in uncertain times: Lone ranging is not enough. *Studies in Higher Education*, 1998, *23*, 269–79

Terenzini, P T, Pascarella, E T and Lorang, W G, An assessment of the academic and social influences on freshman year educational outcomes. *Review of Higher Education*, 1982, *5*, 86–109

Thompson, P, Itzin, C and Abendstern, M, *I don't feel old: The experience of later life*. Oxford: Oxford University Press, 1990

Thornton, C, Back to school, Web style. *PC World*, July 1999, 39–40

Tough, A, *The adult's learning projects*. Toronto: Ontario Institute for Studies in Education, 1971

Trigwell, K and Reid, A, Work-based learning and the students' perspective. *Higher education Research and Development*, 1998, *17*, 141–54

Trotter, B, The teacher and the goals of the university. In C K Knapper, G L Geis, C E Pascal and B M Shore (eds), *If teaching is important... The evaluation of instruction in higher education*. Toronto: Clarke, Irwin, 1977

Trueman, M and Hartley, J, A comparison between the time management skills and academic performance of mature and traditional-entry students. *Higher Education*, 1996, *32*, 199–215

Tuijnman, A C, Kirsch, I S and Wagner, D A (eds), *Adult basic skills: Advances in measurement and policy*. Creskill, New York: Hampton Press, 1997

Turchenko, V, Continuity as the cornerstone of the new paradigm of education. Paper presented at an International Meeting of Experts on the Implementation of the Principles of Lifelong Education, Hamburg, May 1983

Tweddell, E, The role of universities in Australia in 2010. Paper presented as part of a series on the role of universities, University of South Australia, 7 October 1998

Ügeöz, P, Schlechte Zeiten für Bildung: Globalisierung, Deregulierung und Privatisierung im Ländervergleich Türkei und Bundesrepublik Deutschland [Hard times for education: A comparison of globalization, deregulation and privatization in Turkey and the Federal Republic of Germany]. *International Review of Education*, 1998, *44*, 507–29

Unesco, Final report of the International Meeting of Experts on the Implementation of the Principles of Lifelong Education. Paris: UNESCO, 1983

van der Kamp, M and Scheeren, J, New trajectories of learning. In P Belanger and A C Tuijnman (eds), *New patterns of adult learning*. Oxford: Pergamon, 1997

van Horn, C E, *Enhancing the connection between higher education and the workplace: A survey of employers*. Denver, Colorado: State Higher Education Executive Officers and the Education Commission of the States, 1995 von Bernem, T, Motivational problems of lifelong learning. In J Eccleston and F Schmidt (eds), *School and lifelong learning*. Neuss: Landesinstitut für Curriculumentwicklung, Lehrerfortbildung und Weiterbildung, 1981

Wales, C E and Stager, R A, *Guided design*. Morgantown, West Virginia: West Virginia University, 1977

Wales, C E, Nardi, A H and Stager, R A, Emphasizing critical thinking and problem solving. In L Curry and J Wergin (eds), *Educating professionals: Responding to new expectations for competence and accountability*. San Francisco: Jossey-Bass, 1993

Walker, W G, Leadership for lifelong education: The role of educational administration. In A J Cropley (ed), *Towards a system of lifelong education*. Oxford: Pergamon, 1980

Wallis, C, Med school, heal thyself: New studies prescribe better ways of training doctors. *Time*, 23 May 1983, 40–43

Walvoord, B E and Anderson, V J, *Effective grading: A tool for learning and assessment*. San Francisco: Jossey-Bass, 1998

Warr, P and Allan, C, Learning strategies and occupational training. In C L Cooper and I T Robertson (eds), *International Review of Industrial and Organizational Psychology, Volume 13*. Chichester: Wiley, 1998

Watkins, D, Student perceptions of factors influencing tertiary learning. *Higher Education Research and Development*, 1984, *3*, 33–50

Watkins, K E and Marsick, V J, *Sculpting the learning organization*. San Francisco: Jossey-Bass, 1993

Weimer, M, *Improving college teaching: Strategies for developing instructional effectiveness*. San Francisco: Jossey-Bass, 1990

Weinstein, C E and Hume, L M, *Study strategies for lifelong learning*. Washington, DC: American Psychological Association, 1998

Wiens, B J, *Higher education's commitment to inservice education*. ERIC Document ED 141 528, 1977

Wilkerson, L and Gijselaers, W H (eds), *Bringing problem-based learning to higher education*. San Francisco: Jossey-Bass, 1996

Williams, G, *Towards lifelong education: A new role for higher education institutions*. Paris: UNESCO, 1977

Wilson, E K, The entering student: Attributes and agents of change. In T M Newcomb and E K Wilson (eds), *College peer groups*. Chicago: Aldine, 1966

Wilson, J W and Lyons, E H, *Work-study college programs: Appraisal and report of the study of cooperative education*. New York: Harper and Brothers, 1961

Wilson, T C, Pedagogical justice and student evaluation of teaching forms: A critical perspective. Paper presented at the annual meeting of the American Educational Research Association, Washington, DC, April 1987

Wisker, G and Brown, S, *Enabling student learning: Systems and strategies*. London: Kogan Page, 1996

Wolfe, A, How a for-profit university can be invaluable to the traditional liberal arts. *Chronicle of Higher Education*, 4 December 1998, pp B4–B5

Woods, D R, *Problem-based learning: How to gain the most from PBL*. Hamilton, Ontario: McMaster University Bookstore, 1994

Woodward, C A and Neufeld, V, *Medical education since 1960: Marching to a different drummer*. East Lansing, Michigan: Kellogg Center for Continuing Education, 1978

Young, J R, Universities create on-line education 'portal'. *Chronicle of Higher Education*, 25 June 1999, p A35

Zmeyov, S I, Andragogy: Origins, developments and trends. *International Review of Education*, 1998, 44, 103–08

Index